BANKING *In The*
GREAT NORTHERN TERRITORY

For the Silver Bay Library

Richard Slack

BANKING In The GREAT NORTHERN TERRITORY

An Illustrated History

GEORGE RICHARD SLADE

Foreword by David Lilly

Afton Historical Society Press

Afton Press is grateful to the following generous donors who have made possible the publication of

BANKING In The
GREAT NORTHERN TERRITORY
An Illustrated History

Pete and Margie Ankeny

Bruce and Martha Atwater

Alexandra Bjorklund

Jim and Carmen Campbell

Judy Dayton

Peter and Scotty Gillette

Nancy Ottis Harris

John and Lucy Hartwell

Ben and Pat Jaffray

David and Perrin Lilly

Whitney and Betty MacMillan

George and Dusty Mairs

Harry McNeely

Joe and Diana Murphy

Dick and Nancy Nicholson

Anne Rogers

Mary Vaughan

Ted and Nancy Weyerhaeuser

Mike and Penny Winton

Angus and Margaret Wurtele

A friend of the author

and

U.S. Bank

Wells Fargo, N.A.

Front cover: The First National Bank at Jackson and Fourth Streets in St. Paul, ca. 1905, Minnesota Historical Society; James J. Hill, 1916, James J. Hill Reference Library.

Page 2: First National Bank at Fifth and Marquette in Minneapolis, ca. 1915.

Page 4: St. Paul's skyline includes First National Bank of St. Paul (right) and Wells Fargo (third from left) in this photograph taken from the High Bridge over the Mississippi River by Steve Dahlman.

Edited by Michele Hodgson
Designed by Mary Susan Oleson
Production assistance by Beth Williams
Printed by Pettit Network, Inc., Afton, Minnesota

Library of Congress Cataloging-in-Publication Data

Slade, George Richard.
Banking in the Great Northern Territory / by George Richard Slade.
    p. cm.
Includes bibliographical references and index.
  ISBN 1-890434-66-3 (hardcover : alk. paper)
1. Banks and banking—Minnesota—History. I. Title.

HG2611.M6S53 2005
332.1'09776--dc22

2004028155

Printed in China

Afton Press receives major support
for its publishing program
from the Sarah Stevens MacMillan Foundation
and the W. Duncan MacMillan family.

W. Duncan MacMillan

President

Patricia Condon Johnston

Publisher

AFTON HISTORICAL SOCIETY PRESS

P.O. Box 100, Afton, MN 55001
800-436-8443
aftonpress@aftonpress.com
www.aftonpress.com

CONTENTS

The First National Bank of St. Paul (in the background) towers over Minnesota Street in downtown St. Paul in this 1967 painting by artist Francis R. Meisch.

FOREWORD

WHILE *Banking in the Great Northern Territory* tells the tale of Northwest Bancorporation and First Bank Stock Corporation, it is, more specifically, a history of the persons and circumstances that created those two Twin Cities bank holding companies in early 1929. It is also the history of events that unfolded over the seventy years following their creation—events that turned the American banking industry upside down and rebuilt it.

Dick Slade is uniquely qualified to tell this intriguing story. As a rising star in Twin Cities banking during five of those seven decades, Dick had a front-row seat to the drama as regional banks disappeared in a massive series of mergers. As the great-grandson of railroad baron James J. Hill—who orchestrated the reorganization of the First National Bank of St. Paul, a cornerstone of the First Bank Stock entity and thus U.S. Bancorporation—Dick has had more than a passing interest in the history of Twin Cities banking.

As it happens, Dick's family history and mine are entwined, at least when it comes to banking. His great-uncle—James J. Hill's son, Louis Hill—owned the First National Bank of St. Paul when it merged with that city's Merchants National Bank, where my father, Richard Lilly, was president. Later, my father served as vice president of the newly formed First Bank Stock Corporation. The foundation of my relationship with Dick, however, has been more personal than business in nature. He and I served together on the boards of directors of two prominent St. Paul nonprofit organizations: the Wilder Foundation and the Ordway Theater. As members of the "Old Goats," we also skied down many an Aspen slope together, although I admit I spent most of my time chasing my younger, faster friend.

Like many young people who got their start in banking in the 1950s, Dick was fresh out of college (Yale University) when he joined Northwestern National Bank of Minneapolis. He was hired in June 1955 as a trainee in the trust department at a salary of $275 a month. Six months after he learned basic accounting, he transferred to the trust investment department, where he served first as a security analyst and then as a portfolio manager. Senior analysts became experts on the trends and challenges of the specialized industries they oversaw (and the companies within those industries). Dick's area of expertise was technology stocks, including those in the emerging electronics and

9

Skiing with the "Old Goats" (Snowmass, Colorado, 2000) made friends of author Dick Slade (right circle) and David Lilly (left). Their banking ties are familial.

computer industries. Soon he took on the role of "planner" for the trust department, which entailed turning such divisions into businesses with market opportunity and profit potential. In 1968 Dick became manager of Northwestern Bank's semi-moribund bond department. Under his careful watch, as inflation-driven interest rates rose and banks became short-term sources of cash, the department developed a money desk for such cash management needs—and in the process created BancNorthwest, a prosperous joint venture of the five largest members of the Banco family of banks.

Title-wise, Dick had risen on the ladder from assistant trust officer to trust officer and assistant secretary, to assistant vice president, to vice president and later to senior vice president of the bond division.

In 1973, after his novel analysis of Northwestern's balance sheet and cash sources helped the bank set funding priorities for its borrowing clientele (primarily, to explore use of Euro dollars, short-term loans against securities, and discrete use of the Federal Reserve discount window to fund the loan portfolio), Dick became president of Northwestern National Bank of St. Paul. Although he had planned to attend the Advanced Management Program at the Harvard University School of Business in 1974, he deferred participation to learn how a full-menu bank ran. At that time, Northwestern/St. Paul still managed its own check-processing systems, assumed its own operating and administrative responsibilities, and possessed its own board of directors, whose main responsibility (beyond regular monitoring of the business) was to determine the fitness of its proposed senior officers. The bank also invested heavily in its community, supporting the St. Paul mayor's office (particularly George Latimer's) and such entities as the Port Authority, the Chamber of Commerce, the United Way, Junior Achievement, the St. Paul Foundation, the Wilder Foundation, the Boy Scouts, the Arts and Science Council, the Minnesota Club, and the St. Paul Athletic Club. During that time, Dick collaborated with Phil Nason, CEO of the First National Bank of St. Paul, to develop St. Paul's Seventh Place and the Radisson Hotel.

Following the 1980 death of his mentor Richard Vaughan, president of Banco, Dick was at sea. Since Vaughan had encouraged Dick's attendance at Harvard's management program, Dick delegated his duties and headed east for the thirteen-week session. When he returned, filled with ideas for moving the corporation ahead, the main office was still in transition and Dick's future was uncertain. He resigned the following spring, and his hiatus from the industry lasted a decade. During that time he served eight years as president of the Minneapolis College of Art and Design and, in 1990, became acting director of the Corcoran School of Art in Washington, D.C.

In 1991 Dick joined First Trust—the historic market leader in St. Paul and the corporate manager for Twin Cities trust business through First National of Minneapolis—as senior vice president and manager of foundation and endowment accounts. For the next five years, he held various management positions, including several in trust administration. He retired from First Trust (which had become U.S. Bancorp/First Trust) in 1996. For the next year he served (appropriately enough, given the familial connection) as acting president of the James J. Hill Reference Library—the second time he had filled that role while a search was held for a permanent head.

Dick's knowledge of Twin Cities banking and the twin holding companies born in 1929 is broad and unconventional: broad in that the story is not peculiar to Minnesota or the Ninth Federal Reserve District, and unconventional in that he earned his credentials from the trust side of the industry. *Banking in the Great Northern Territory* addresses national changes in banking regulation and in the procedures that had a lasting impact on this country's regional banks. Given his nontraditional rise within the industry, Dick himself is a product of the dynamic changes that challenged banking in more recent times— changes that prompted so-called "real" bankers to embrace (or at least accept) trust officers like Dick and other "outsiders" as worthy leaders in banking. His firsthand experience with those changes during the last half of the twentieth century makes Dick Slade's *Banking in the Great Northern Territory* an essential work among Twin Cities history books.

David Lilly
St. Paul, Minnesota
October 2004

ACKNOWLEDGMENTS

WHEN I JOINED the trust department of Northwestern National Bank of Minneapolis as a trainee in June 1955, I really didn't know much about the city beyond the fact that I could find Charlie's Café Exceptionale. I also didn't know much about banking, at least as it related to trusts. Thankfully, my boss, Ruth Hong, was a tough manager who had some accounting tricks that allowed her to check her trainees' work in an instant and send us back to the drawing board until we had gotten it done right—right by accounting criteria, right by her banking/ client criteria. Northwestern was a great place to start a career in banking, thanks to tutelage of her caliber.

I was fortunate to have worked for banks belonging to both Minnesota bank holding companies whose stories are told in this book. My job assignments within Northwest Bancorporation and First Bank Stock Corporation were divided in time and space and character, and although I invested many more years at Wells Fargo (successor to Norwest Corporation and Northwest Bancorporation), I cannot describe—nor do I try to describe—one as better or worse than the other throughout this abbreviated history. I've admired and respected the leaders of both banking

systems as managers and competitors. I've been impressed by those persons in the trenches who accommodated the changes and growth of their respective employers and yet maintained as much personal contact with their clientele as they could in an age of telephone automation and the ATM.

While a purist might challenge my credentials as a "real" banker, as I was mostly on the trust side, I've known enough real bankers to recognize them when I see them and to describe them in a historical sense. My definition of a "real" banker includes a strong commitment to communities served by a bank, reflected in various forms of reinvestment in those communities. Phil Nason, CEO of First National Bank of St. Paul when I was president of Northwestern National of St. Paul, was very much this sort of banker. A few others are still extant, although the bean counters and techies increasingly outnumber them. Jim Campbell, retired president of Wells Fargo/Minnesota, is a real banker. (He's also the son of a small-town banker. How small? Legend has it that the bank's restroom was housed in a building across the street.) Jon Campbell, Jim's younger brother and successor front man for Wells Fargo/Minnesota, shows promise, particularly as he leads the committees through which Minnesota's business community addresses regional social issues. (Although Jon got his start as a commercial banker at Northwestern National Bank of St. Paul when I was its president, it is *not* true that I taught him everything he knows.)

I decided to write *Banking in the Great Northern Territory* to tell the stories about bankers and banking that were bottled up in my memory. There were other, more compelling reasons, of course. First, I was interested in the close relationship between two competing regional bank holding companies. My work in the bond business had shown me that this was a pattern in American cities—two lead banks jockeying for the number-one position—and a recurring pattern in which one bank would move ahead, get complacent, and in a decade or so be surpassed by its reinvigorated competitor. Second, I felt that the bad-guy reputation that banks often get was undeserved; in fact, state and federal regulations tilted the playing field not in favor of banks, but toward their competition. Third, with strong community leaders like Ed Decker, C. T. Jaffray, John Moorhead, and Phil Nason being replaced in banks (as such leaders have vanished from most other public businesses) not only by MBAs, CIOs, and CFOs but also by technology itself, I believed their considerable legacy should not vanish without a nod.

Last, I was intrigued by the side story of

the First National Bank of St. Paul—where it came from, how it was distinctly different from any other bank in the territory, and why this difference ultimately required the dismantling of a proud, and perhaps arrogant, organization. I should mention that my great-grandfather, James J. Hill, owned First National Bank of St. Paul, and I have always looked up to him as a self-made entrepreneur who was a champion of the land from Minnesota to the West—the Great Northern Territory.

A great many people helped me with this book, and representatives of both holding companies cooperated generously. Rob Sayre and Wally Norlander at U.S. Bancorp dug among archives and personal files to find invaluable corporate details and unpublished stories. Gary Stern and Art Rolnick at the Ninth Federal Reserve Bank bought me lunch, opened their library, and gave me encouragement. Jim Campbell and Larry Haig at Wells Fargo/Minnesota were more than helpful, reflecting their corporation's deep concern for its history and traditions, evident in its publications and lobby displays. Andy Anderson, the Wells Fargo corporate historian in San Francisco, reinforced the notion that this was a worthwhile project. The Minneapolis Public Library was a convenient and reliable resource for back issues of Minneapolis newspapers, files on banking, and general reference materials. As custodian of the James J. and Louis W. Hill papers, the James J. Hill Reference Library in St. Paul produced interesting (and, I believe, hitherto unpublished) information on the background of First Bank Stock Corporation. The Hill Library's unparalleled collection of corporate annual reports also permitted me to research thirty-plus years of local banking history.

A caveat about those annual reports, however: While they're valid primary-source documents for historical research, they're also continuing classics of spin, of making the absolute best out of any blip on a company's radar. As such, the annual report is a notoriously bad forecaster of the future, being both timid and overly optimistic. Except for the intervention of "generally accepted accounting procedures," there are no requirements for consistency among competitors' annual reports. The facts provided are both the minimum required by the Securities Exchange Commission, the New York Stock Exchange, and the company auditors, as well as the maximum editorializing by public relations staff to reinforce and promote the corporate interest. Any

discussion of corporate shortcomings or failures is ignored and the results of any financial impact is mentioned only in a report's footnotes, which often make for the best reading. Nietzsche or another pragmatist (or relativist) might argue that history is immaterial. For a modern American corporation, that is a near truth.

There is no sufficient way to thank my wife, Ella Slade, and Carol Pine for their efforts in reading and critiquing the manuscript and in tolerating the author's foibles. D. H. Ankeny Jr., Bruce Atwater, Ken Dayton, David Lilly, Peter Gillette, Ed Spencer, Mike Winton, and many others offered important details and small anecdotes, provided encouragement, and vastly improved the product. Publisher Patricia Johnston, director of operations Chuck Johnston, production assistant Beth Williams, and designer Mary Susan Oleson, all of Afton Historical Society Press, made it happen after Michele Hodgson worked her editor's wiles on the text. Thanks.

G. R. S.

INTRODUCTION

ALTHOUGH BANKING as a trade and as an integral thread in the commercial weave of civilized life goes back millennia, the history of banking in Minnesota goes back a mere 150 years, to the founding of Parker Paine and Company in the territorial capital of St. Paul in 1853. As in the rest of the world, banking in Minnesota was first and foremost a local enterprise, with financial institutions started by, and serving, the emerging businesses of nascent communities. The resources of those early banks—namely, the intelligence and capital of their founders and directors—were intended to serve the business needs of those very founders and directors and their associates. Such intentions have, of course, been subsequently sanitized under conflict-of-interest regulations, while the increasing numbers of national and international customers have necessarily broadened the markets served by larger banking institutions, with only nominal interest remaining for the "local" consumer or small-business operator.

But back in 1929, just months before the stock market crashed, the stability of the regional banking scene was the raison d'être for two bank holding companies in Minneapolis and St. Paul: Northwest Bancorporation and First Bank Stock Corporation. The twin enterprises carpentered together comparable portfolios of banks in the Upper Midwest for parallel purposes: first, to protect good banks in the region from predatory purchase by non-area bankers, and second, to provide a stronghold of capital and management that would keep these critical banks solvent during difficult times. (No bank owned by either holding company failed during the Depression while many of their regional competitors fell by the wayside.) These dual progeny were created by the officers and directors of three strong, competitive regional banks: Northwest Bancorporation by managers of Northwestern National Bank of Minneapolis, and First Bank Stock Corporation by officers of the First National Bank of Minneapolis and the First National Bank of St. Paul.

Banking in the Great Northern Territory tells the story of these twin enterprises— formed in the same act of passion, born but historic moments apart, and equally molded by the maelstrom of the Depression and World War II. Much of the story picks up where C. Sterling Popple, a security analyst with IDS (Investors Diversified Services) in Minneapolis, left off. In 1944 Popple published "Two Bank

Holding Companies in the Upper Midwest"—a work cited extensively in this narrative—as his doctoral thesis at Harvard University. *Banking in the Great Northern Territory* continues the tale through the end of the twentieth century.

For almost seventy years these two Minnesota holding companies dominated the banking scene in the Ninth Federal Reserve District. Northwest Bancorporation (also known as "Banco") and First Bank Stock Corporation ("First Bank Stock") were structurally competitive in market after market, providing sound financial support to their affiliate banks and businesses throughout the region. (In the 1980s, First Bank Stock even bragged to the New York Society of Security Analysts that "one of the great strengths of the First Bank System was that their banks competed with each other.") Substantial commercial customers doing business in Minnesota could get three comparable proposals for their banking needs: from First National Bank and Northwestern National Bank in Minneapolis and from First National Bank in St. Paul. Of course, moderate genetic differences between the twins emerged over time. On the one hand, Banco was slightly broader geographically and included the largest banks in several states. Yet it was less metropolitan than First Bank Stock, whose assets were more concentrated, two-thirds held by the First National Banks of Minneapolis and St. Paul, but with the balance spread among more and smaller banks than Banco. Despite their

differences, competition remained gentlemanly, symptomatic of that phenomenon known as "Minnesota Nice."

By 1997 and 1998, the two holding companies—by then known as U.S. Bancorp (after some years as First Bank System) and Wells Fargo (formerly doing business as Norwest Corporation)—both took the giant steps that marked their emancipation from the regionalism of their birth and brought about the final dissolution of the twin effect. But as the larger of the two grew into national and international presences, and as size and geographic growth became inevitable for both, the regional approach of each bank system began to fall short of their clients' needs. Finer strategies began to emerge that were clearly different. Such distinctions were analyzed in stories of the time, such as that reported by Aldo Svaldi in the *Denver Business Journal* on December 20, 1999:

> Colorado has held a ringside seat as U.S. Bank and Norwest Bank boxed toe to toe for most of the decade over the right way to bank.
>
> The battle was one between high tech and high touch, between cutting costs and growing revenues, between pleasing shareholders and winning customer loyalty.
>
> With the bell ringing on the '90s, U.S. Bank and those that followed a similar strategy are on the mat.
>
> Norwest, taking a path long unpopular with Wall Street, can finally claim victory.

Victory in this arena, however, is never absolute, and the battles are far from over. The two bank holding companies have continued their competition in national and international markets into the twenty-first century, with assets and liabilities measured in tens of billions, not buckets. ("Score cards" showing the companies' comparative growth for each decade of operation through the twentieth century are included following key chapters. Balance sheets, earning statistics, and market data for each company appear in two appendices.) Competition in the future will not be limited to Wells Fargo and U.S. Bancorp, but will include all of the other large national and international players in the worldwide game of banking.

As far as historians of the banking world are concerned, both of the twins' biographies are little more than provincial footnotes in the story of larger banking ventures. The existence of Northwest/ Norwest, for example, has been subsumed by Wells Fargo's 150-year participation in the nation's financial world, despite the critical role the Minnesota corporation played in the modern-day survival of Wells. And although a comprehensive history of both Wells Fargo and U.S. Bancorp would certainly include discussions of vast components of banking in California and Oregon respectively—details not addressed in this particular discourse— telling the history of the original "Minnesota twins" requires a broader view. It necessarily includes changes that affected banks throughout the United States and propelled the evolution of mega holding companies. Indeed, the life and transformation of Minnesota's twin holding companies during the twentieth century is a story that echoed around the country as historic financial institutions struggled with technology, inconsistent regulation, and burgeoning nonbank competition that stressed, stretched, and reformed the entire national system.

Above all, the story of the "Minnesota Twins"-of Banking in the Great Northern Territory is the story of individuals with vision and energy and a peculiar persistence. Some were bankers of an old and vanished school, while others were entrepreneurs in step with the times. Officed a block apart in Minneapolis, the twin holding companies shared directors from community corporations and competed on friendly terms until they were forced to change by rules of marketing, internationalism, and nonbank competition. While a few dynamic early players remained by the end of the twentieth century, they were no longer visible in the grand lobbies of their banks, shaking hands and smoking cigars. Managers who had long rubbed shoulders at the Minneapolis Club, at a circle of country clubs, and at Twin Cities social events did so no longer. Not only were most of the characters gone by the beginning of the new millennium, so were most of the lobbies. Yet the enterprises that evolved from the original twins are built on solid and similar foundations. That is the key to their strength, and their reason to continue to fare well.

A smart young lady saves for a rainy day at the First National Bank of St. Paul in 1913.

Twins in the Making

To 1930

SETTING the STAGE

ON ANY GIVEN DAY, customers of those banks that made up the holding companies once known as Northwest Bancorporation and First Bank Stock Corporation conduct more than two million financial transactions. Few are perceived as *banking* transactions, however, mostly because they're not conducted in a *bank*. More and more customers manage their money matters by mail, phone, Internet, fax, ATM, and credit card than through tellers in a bank lobby. While doing so, they are likely to be thinking of something other than banking, like paying the rent, buying a gift, taking a trip—accomplishing or acquiring some item on their to-do list via a financial intermediary called a megabank.

Some observers of the banking scene struggle to understand the transformation of this essential industry over the last fifty years. Grand lobbies have been replaced with unassuming ATMs, letters of credit with debit cards, discount windows with "instant cash." A greater measure of industry change is that three-quarters of the sixty largest commercial banks in 1949 became indistinguishable components of the nation's giant holding companies by 1999. Bank of America, A. P. Giannini's flagship in California, was the world's largest bank at midcentury, with deposits

of $5.8 billion. That bank alone carried 10 percent of total deposits of the sixty largest.

EARLY AMERICAN BANKING

The growth of American banking in the twentieth century far exceeded the modest ideas the nation's founders had about the industry. Most thought of a bank as a community amenity whose services were limited to currency exchange and small loans. Broader-minded individuals like Alexander Hamilton promoted a central institution that was essential to economic growth and the management of government funds. In 1791, Congress approved a twenty-year charter for the Bank of the United States. Although well run, the bank lost favor by not working with state banks, and its charter lapsed in 1811. When fiscal chaos caused by the War of 1812 proved that a central bank was needed to deal with foreign bankers and governments, the bank was rechartered in 1816. Populist Andrew Jackson soon saw to its demise. After losing the 1824 election, whose results he felt were decided by partisans in the House of Representatives, Jackson made a comeback in 1828 and 1832 and turned against the "establishment" and its banking ideas. He ordered the transfer of all government funds from the Bank of the United States, which barely survived until its charter expired in 1836. The fissure was a major contributor to the roller-coaster fortunes in the banking system that ended only when the Federal Reserve was established in 1913.

The central system was expected to facilitate transfers of funds between smaller banks, stabilize the public currency, and manage transactions overseas. Mortgages and business loans were to be handled by community banks. Since deposits typically came from a bank's community, it was logical for the community to expect that most of those monies would be reinvested in their credit needs. By the 1930s, the country boasted a sizable network of strong, independently owned regional banks. A few holding companies did exist—Bank of America, Marine Midland, and "Minnesota twins" Northwest Bancorporation and First Bank Stock Corporation—but even these groups were generally identified by the names of their biggest banks. First Bank Stock Corporation, for example, had the First National Banks of Minneapolis and St. Paul as its lead banks, while Northwest Bancorporation had the Northwestern National Bank of Minneapolis, plus Iowa–Des Moines National Bank, First National Bank of Sioux Falls (South Dakota), and U.S. National Bank of Omaha (Nebraska). Yet the second half of the twentieth century saw the virtual disappearance of these once dominant city banks as the rules of the banking game changed repeatedly and as the needs of banking customers became broader and more sophisticated. The dynamics of change were not always pretty in their effects on banks and thrifts

(savings and loan) institutions, and some resolutions to the challenges of the decades were neither happy nor proud.

One could always blame it on the New York City banks. During colonial times, New York established itself as the country's principal commercial center, in part because of its substantial harbor and its

Once-dominant city banks have disappeared, thanks to big New York banks like Chase, itself now just another component of a larger banking behemoth.

TABLE I
Sixty Largest U.S. Banks—December 31, 1949

Rank	Name	State	Deposits - 1949 (000,000)	Name/Status - 1999
1	Bank of America	CA	$5,775.1	**Bank of America Corporation**
2	National City Bank	NY	4,669.3	Component of Citicorp
3	Chase National Bank, New York	NY	4,384.6	Component of Chase Manhattan
4	Continental Illinois National Bank	IL	2,348.2	Component of BankAmerica
5	Guaranty Trust Company	NY	2,299.9	Component of J. P. Morgan & Co.
6	Manufacturers Trust Company	NY	2,281.7	Component of Chase Manhattan
7	First National Bank, Chicago	IL	2,278.6	Component of BancOne
8	Security First National Bank	CA	1,602.9	Component of BankAmerica
9	Chemical Bank & Trust	NY	1,449.7	Component of Chase Manhattan
10	Central Hanover Bank & Trust	NY	1,448.1	Component of Chase Manhattan
11	Bankers Trust Company	NY	1,431.5	Owned by Deutsche Bank
12	First National Bank, Boston	MA	1,376.7	Merging into Fleet Financial
13	National Bank of Detroit	MI	1,293.8	Component of BancOne
14	Mellon National Bank Trust	PA	1,217.8	**Mellon Bank Corporation**
15	Bank of the Manhattan Company	NY	1,058.4	Component of Chase Manhattan
16	Cleveland Trust Company	OH	1,052.4	Component of Key Corporation
17	Irving Trust Company	NY	937.4	Component of Bank of New York
18	American Trust Company	CA	766.8	Component of Wells Fargo
19	Corn Exchange Bank	NY	687.3	Component of Chase Manhattan
20	Philadelphia National Bank	PA	653.4	Component of First Union
21	Northern Trust Company	IL	627.3	**Northern Trust Company**
22	New York Trust Company	NY	600.6	Component of Chase Manhattan
23	Seattle-First National Bank	WA	599.4	Component of BankAmerica
24	First National Bank/New York	NY	589.6	Component of CityCorp
25	J. P. Morgan & Company	NY	587.0	**J. P. Morgan & Company**
26	Pennsylvania Company	PA	577.1	Component of First Union
27	Harris Trust & Savings	IL	576.6	Owned by Bankmont Financial
28	Anglo California Nattional Bank	CA	551.7	Component of Wells Fargo
29	Detroit Bank	MI	542.8	Component of Comerica, Inc.
30	First Wisconsin National Bank	WI	527.2	**Firstar**
31	United States National Bank	OR	505.3	Component of U.S. Bancorp
32	Public National Bank & Trust	NY	492.7	Component of Bankers Trust
33	National City Bank	OH	476.4	**National City Corporation**
34	First National Bank, Portland	OR	471.3	Component of Wells Fargo
35	Manufacturers National Bank	MI	463.2	Component of Comerica
36	Wells Fargo Bank & Union Trust	CA	440.4	**Wells Fargo**
37	California Bank	CA	434.9	Component of Wells Fargo
38	First National Bank, St. Louis	MO	397.2	Component of First Union
39	Bank of New York, Fifth Avenue	NY	394.4	**Bank of New York**
40	Peoples First National Bank	PA	389.9	**PNC Bank**
41	Commerce Trust Company	MO	380.7	**Commerce Bankshares**
42	Central National Bank	OH	374.3	Component of Key Corporation
43	National Shawmut Bank	MA	373.6	Component of Fleet Financial
44	Fidelity Union Trust Company	NJ	364.1	**Fidelity Union Bancorporation**
45	Marine Midland Trust Co.	NY	354.6	Owned by HSBC America
46	Mercantile/Commercial Bank	MO	354.1	Component of Firstar
47	Northwestern National Bank	MN	345.7	Component of Wells Fargo
48	National Bank of Commerce	WA	340.6	Component of BankAmerica
49	First National Bank, Minneapolis	MN	339.9	Component of U.S. Bancorp
50	Republic National Bank	TX	333.3	Liquidated
51	City National Bank & Trust	IL	332.6	
52	First National Bank, Dallas	TX	331.1	First International Bank Shares
53	Whitney National Bank	LA	330.0	**Whitney National Bank**
54	Citizens National Bank, Trust	CA	329.9	Component of Wells Fargo
55	Marine Trust Company	NY	316.5	Owned by HSBC America
56	Crocker-First National Bank	CA	312.5	Component of Wells Fargo
57	Bank of California	CA	309.2	BanCalTriState
58	First National Bank, St. Paul	MN	298.8	Component of U.S. Bancorp
59	Riggs National Bank	DC	298.3	**Riggs National Corporation**
60	Indiana National Bank	IN	<u>297.8</u>	Component of BancOne
			$55,976.2	

relatively central location among the industrial northern states. The Wall Street coterie of banking and trust institutions—literal ancestors of today's giants—were founded by Dutch and English financiers and became the default heirs of the vanished First and Second Banks of the United States. Many of these institutions had been designated as banking houses by and for European trading companies and continued to serve a specialized clientele. These banks had linkages with English and Continental bankers and the businessmen whom American merchants needed to know in exporting their wares. As minuscule banks proliferated along the country's western frontiers, they would try to establish a relationship with one or more of the New York institutions—for capital, for advice, and for referrals, often in both directions.

By the latter nineteenth century, New York banks were dominant players in U.S. banking: politically potent, aggressive—and categorically smug. (So smug, in fact, that when the Federal Reserve System was legislated in 1913, New York banks proposed that there should be only one Federal Reserve Bank, not twelve, and that this entity should be located in Lower Manhattan.) Historically, New York banks have controlled export/import financing and the underwriting and maintenance of markets for the U.S. government and its agency bonds, bills, and notes. They have served, in cooperation with the Federal Reserve System, as the principal vehicles through which the U.S.

Treasury attempted to manage the nation's money supply. (Conversely, the slightest troubles of New York banks could bring queasiness—nay, a panic—to the whole country.) From their position at the top of correspondent bank linkages that tied the national system together, they could easily lure larger commercial banking customers of regional institutions into a Big Apple relationship. Even the consumer-based Bank of America in California, which for most of the twentieth century was the largest U.S. bank measured by deposits, was just another rich parcel of prospect pastures for New York correspondent bankers, who were often pirates in Ivy League clothing.

For reference, look at the roster of America's sixty largest banks in 1949 (Table I, at left). The group was unusually healthy at that time, having survived World War II with burgeoning deposits and having both the appetite and capacity to fund the postwar recovery, a vast economic expansion that has more or less continued. The group also consisted almost entirely of freestanding units, banks with charters dating back to the 1863 establishment of "national banks" and earlier. The 1949 list was just large enough to include all three of Minnesota's nationally recognized institutions: First National Bank and Northwestern National Bank of Minneapolis, and First National Bank of St. Paul. Some members on the list had a system of branches, determined by individual state legislation. Virtually no interstate constituency existed.

First National Bank of St. Paul had few competitors in the city's skyline (and virtually none in the city's banking) in 1952. This is the view that cheered F. Scott Fitzgerald in writing of his hometown.

Northwestern National Bank of Minneapolis decks its halls for Christmas in 1953.

The right-hand column of Table I reflects the status of the 1949 banks fifty years later, after the revolutions that swept the industry for the balance of the twentieth century. Three-quarters of these proud, independent symbols of regional history, of meeting the needs of their several constituencies, had vanished. They had become components of huge bank holding companies, depersonalized, institutionalized, and broadened geographically. Some that appear to have survived untouched in fact had undergone massive surgery and reconstruction. Bank of America, for example, in its newly minted corporate persona as BankAmerica Corporation, found itself taking up residence in North Carolina. The two Minnesota holding companies, in different scenarios, also had changed. In terms of corporate structure, Norwest Corporation (formerly Northwest Bancorporation) was the surviving legal entity in 1998 after its merger with Wells Fargo, its Delaware charter still in place.[1] As part of the merger, however, the organization changed its name to Wells Fargo and moved corporate headquarters to San Francisco. The matter of legal domicile is now one for trivia buffs. The circumstances of U.S. Bancorp are somewhat similar. First Bank System acquired the U.S. National Bank of Oregon in August 1997 and changed its name from FBS to that of the Oregon institution—generic, national in coverage, noncontroversial. In February 2001, Firstar—a growing holding company headquartered in Milwaukee, with components in St. Louis

In 1946, the lobby of First National Bank of Minneapolis epitomized friendly banking.

and Cincinnati—acquired USB and changed its name to U.S. Bancorp. Perhaps as an acknowledgment of First Bank Stock's seventy-year presence in the Minnesota market, the board of the enlarged USB moved its headquarters to Minneapolis.

The determined construction of what is today known as J. P. Morgan Chase and Company to the number-two spot among U.S. bank holding companies has now accumulated 20 percent of the top sixty banks of 1949 in a matrix crossing the United States—dominated, however, by Chase Bank's persistent accumulation of historic New York City banks. CitiBank, number three among U.S. holding companies in 2004, has maintained its position through aggressive marketing, not

TABLE II

15 Largest U.S. Bank Holding Companies
(with acquisitions from 60 largest banks in 1949)

Rank Corporation 6/30/04 (billions)	Acquisitions	Assets
1 Bank of America	Bank of America, Continental Illinois, Security First National, First National Bank of Boston, Seattle-First National, National Shawmut, National Bank of Commerce	$920.6
2 J. P. Morgan Chase Bank	Chase National Bank, Guaranty Trust, Manufacturers Trust, First National Bank of Chicago, Chemical Bank, Central Hanover Bank, National Bank of Detroit, Bank of Manhattan, Corn Exchange Bank, New York Trust, J. P. Morgan & Co., Indiana National Bank	900.4
3 CitiBank/CitiGroup	National City Bank, First National, New York	648.2
4 Wachovia Bank	Philadelphia National Bank, Pennsylvania Co., First National Bank, St. Louis	368.9
5 Wells Fargo Bank	American Trust, Anglo California, First National of Portland, Wells Fargo, California Bank, Northwestern National Bank, Citizens National Bank/Trust, Crocker-First National Bank	364.9
6 U.S. Bank	First Wisconsin, U.S. National, Mercantile/Commercial Bank, First National Bank of Minneapolis, First National Bank of St. Paul	189.7
7 Suntrust Bank		125.9
8 HSBC/America	Marine Midland Trust, Marine Trust	110.3
9 Bank of New York	Bank of New York, Irving Trust	94.5
10 State Street Bank & Trust		90.9
11 Branch Banking & Trust		74.9
12 KeyBank/KeyCorp	Cleveland Trust, Central National Bank	74.8
13 PNC Bank	Peoples First National Bank	67.5
14 LaSalle Bank/Ambro		62.8
15 Fifth Third Bank		60.5

Source: Federal Reserve System, National Information Center

acquisition, in its home city and around the world, although its breakthrough merger with Travelers Insurance in 1998 made it the leading financial services entity among U.S. bankers. The Wells Fargo portfolio, historically dominated by California banks, added Minnesota and Oregon through larger acquisitions and gained a virtually nationwide presence through smaller continuing transactions.

The roster of the fifteen largest U.S. bank holding companies as of June 30, 2004 (Table II, left), itemizes for each the principal acquisitions of or mergers with banks on the list of 1949's sixty largest. The corporate names of these enterprises are largely generic, bland but marketable. J. P. Morgan Chase hints both of a New York City background but also the need for a playbill to identify the actors. One interesting by-product of the numerous accessions and compressions is the rapid falloff in size of these financial conglomerates: two just under $1 trillion, three in the mid-$100 billion group, and three over $100 billion. The smallest in the group of fifteen are survivors of premerger days. One interesting anomaly is Branch Banking and Trust, eleventh on the list. This entity is not named by its merger activity, but rather after its founder. Yet when the definition of size is changed to "financial services" institutions rather than "commercial banks," all of these compilations become moot. The latest list of the twenty-five largest organizations providing financial services identifies General Electric as the largest player in the world. CitiGroup

ranks fifth, with AIG sixth and Berkshire Hathaway as eighth. Five European organizations are ranked in the middle, and toward the bottom of this list are Bank of America and J. P. Morgan Chase, rated twentieth and twenty-fourth respectively.

In the mid-twentieth century, regional banks, with occasional help from a New York correspondent, provided all the banking services their regional clients might need or want. Those needs changed with the subsequent explosion of information technologies and transportation systems that led to dynamic growth by regional businesses into national and international arenas. Decisions as to plant locations and corporate strategies became computer-based and took into consideration the availability of labor, the cost of construction and maintenance of plants, and the cost of raw materials and transportation. Neither last nor least among these considerations was the availability of flexible, effective, and adequate financial services. When these needs first arose, the hometown banker's hands were often tied by lack of communications or an effective correspondent banking relationship, frustrating his desire to keep up with his regular customer. New suppliers of financial services, as well as other regional and/or more national banks, eagerly courted the expanding local business.

Three major forces worked and re-worked the banking industry throughout those years: technology, marketing, and regulation. Technology encompassed communication and electronic book-keeping, while marketing emphasized corporate products and names that could be sold on television in national, not just regional, markets. Regulation at first limited the scope of banking activity. Later, by reempowering the bank holding company and arrogating restrictive state legislation, regulation opened the floodgates to interstate banking and the unrestricted establishment of branch offices. In 1999, the largest banking organizations were more than 100 times larger than the same entities in 1949, reflecting the effects of inflation to some degree, but more precisely the outcome of a rational consolidation of the industry. The matter of size suggests that $250 billion in assets may not be big enough for an entity to stand alone in the first decade of the twenty-first century, and that the economies of scale in transaction management will surely drive the creation of banking/financial organizations of more than $1 trillion. Conversely, the wider the gap between globally and locally oriented banks, the more opportunity will exist for the small, customer-directed entrepreneur.

A coincidental victim of these dynamic changes has been the U.S. Federal Reserve and its reporting system. When interstate banking was limited and the relatively few mergers that occurred were within state lines, the reporting function of the Federal Reserve had some value in terms of matching a given regional economy with its regional banking system. Although the Fed reports on banks and

holding companies alike, national banking behemoths have blurred the lines of such reporting to virtual meaninglessness. The *nonbank* assets owned by most contemporary financial conglomerates mean that the sum of bank ownership is less than the total assets of the holding companies. The Federal Reserve System's roster of the Top 100 Largest Banks by Total Assets as of 12/31/1998[2] began with NationsBank, the largest at $317.1 billion. At the holding-company level, NationsBank—as part of BankAmerica—did not exist. CitiBank at $300.9 billion was second, with Chase Manhattan third (at $296.7 billion) and Bank of America fourth (at $257.5 billion). The Federal Reserve's year-end 1998 ranking of the Top 100 Bank Holding Companies[3] began with CitiGroup in first place with assets of $668.6 billion, BankAmerica (including NationsBank and Bank of America) ranked second at $617.7 billion, with Chase Manhattan Corporation a distant third at $365.9 billion. The largest *bank* in Minnesota in 1998—ranked thirteenth nationally—was U.S. Bank/Minneapolis, at $69.7 billion and representing all of the banking units the First Bank System had consolidated after Minnesota's permissive 1989 legislation. That included the First National Banks of Minneapolis and St. Paul, and also the assets acquired in 1997 of U.S. National Bank in Portland, Oregon. Wells Fargo (located in California), including its First Interstate acquisition, was in eighth place nationally with $87.3 billion, while Norwest Bank/Minnesota ranked twenty-sixth with $31.3 billion in assets. Even further down the rankings were (at number 75) Norwest Bank of Colorado and Wells Fargo Bank (Texas) at number 91. The Minnesota holding companies, whose balance sheets consolidated each of those state banks with substantial other assets, were ranked seventh (Wells Fargo) and fourteenth (U.S. Bancorp).

The Federal Reserve tends to site the assets/deposits of such institutions in the states as reported. The local Fed continuously examines bank operations and management at the local level, coordinated across state lines by the Federal Reserve Bank in the district housing the holding bank headquarters. On June 27, 1997, a special notice issued by the Fed recognized the distortions inherent in the reporting of all banking assets and balances based on the location of headquarters or a lead bank when the balances were actually sited in several states and more than one Federal Reserve District. The reasonable reaction was to stop reporting such district-specific figures. Using the leverage inherent in bank supervision, the Federal Reserve Banks have not only made it clear to the boards of supervised holding companies that the directors are responsible for all banks in the enterprise under their purview, but also have defined the measures and expectations that examiners will apply to analyses of this expected oversight.

SOMETIMES THE STORY of an individual is illustrative of the whole narrative:

the tale of Walter Briggs is a case in point. Briggs found a job at Northwestern National Bank in Minneapolis shortly after his graduation from college in the late 1920s. That was his first and only stop in what proved to be a five-decade career ending with his retirement as a vice president in trust administration. Early in his career, Briggs was "given an opportunity" by management to buy a few shares of Northwest Bancorporation, the newly founded bank holding company that had become the owner of Northwestern National. The offer was most attractive, and the bank advanced the money to make the purchase at a nominal interest rate. Edward Decker, president of the bank, was taking a big chunk for himself.

After the stock market crashed in 1929, Banco shares were soon trading for 10 percent of the price Briggs had paid. By 1956, soon after I came to work at Northwestern, Briggs's stock was still under water and would be until 1958. The happy ending is that Walter Briggs, a frugal man who lived with his sister and, with her, built a modest collection of fine furniture and high-quality art prints, left a significant bequest to the Minneapolis Institute of Arts, a place where the two siblings had spent many happy hours. Not surprisingly, that bequest was substantially composed of earnings from his original Northwest Bancorporation shares.

The story of that stock is one of the threads of this history.

MONEY and BANKING 101

AS BROADLY DEFINED, money became a part of the human inventory in the earliest times. The sacrifice to primitive gods of a rabbit, a sheep, or even a vestal virgin represented the exchange of one thing of perceived value for something else: rain, good crops, a fertile marriage. Gradually, a scale of difference in values entered the equation. A rabbit might be worth the sacrifice for rain, but five rabbits or a small goat might be more appropriate in a plea for a full season of good weather. A vestal virgin might be the equivalent of ten sheep or 100 rabbits and would never be sacrificed frivolously.

Over millennia, equivalency structures became more sophisticated as "made" products entered the value scale and became part of barter transactions. A coat, a pair of shoes, or a length of cloth could be exchanged for each other or for different equivalents of value.[4] As part of their transactions, the Aztecs threw in cocoa beans—the equivalent of pocket change to balance the scales in an exchange of goods—or perhaps a cotton cloak, which was valued at sixty to 300 beans.[5] Early Norwegians used butter, dried cod fillets, and salt in exchanging goods. (Although the word root of "salary" means "money paid," its semantic derivation is "salt.") On the small Pacific island of Yap, family wealth in ancient times was represented by large sculpted rocks that were imported from great distances in canoes and placed around the owner's home for admiring neighbors to count— more being better.

Coins gradually made their appearance, and as early as 640 B.C.E. in Mesopotamia, standardized weights of precious metals were given a specific value.[6] Then as now, a coin's assigned value protected the interest of its holder. Early coins of silver and gold were marked with symbols of their exchange value—a rabbit, an ox, two fish—and until recently, pocket change in Ireland was stamped with domestic symbols of equivalency. Early on, coins were also marked on one side with the visage of the omnipotent ruler who, in effect, stood as both guarantor of the specie's value and a threat to potential counterfeiters.

Virtually all currency in circulation carries a promise to pay the bearer something from the issuing authority's treasury, but the specie itself has only nominal intrinsic worth. The *value* of money lies in its convertibility into other assets, whether a jar of peanut butter, a Maserrati, or common stocks. To complete a transaction, the vendor of the commodity must accept the value of the currency offered. Each vendor expects that the promise to pay is real and that a third party will accept the money at the same parity the vendor did. This works well in the United States, less well in Malaysia, and scarcely at all in Afghanistan. In fact, the banking system that has evolved in western civilization works only in a privately based capitalist economy in which financial decisions are made by choice: that is, with the freedom to accept or reject goods for goods, goods for specie, and specie for specie.

Renaissance townspeople were challenging the dominance of the church in everyday life when Flemish artist Quentin Metsys painted *The Money Lender and His Wife* in 1514. The banker's wife pretends piety by leafing through a religious book while stealing a glance at her husband's gold.

The Russian banking system's failure to thrive is particularly illustrative. In "The Cash Don't Work," an essay on Russians and money, *The Economist* cites James Buchan, author of a history of money titled *Frozen Desire,* to show that the link between money and freedom is basic to liberal economics: "Adam Smith spoke of money as the 'obvious and simple system of natural liberty.'" The essay emphasizes that, because Russia operated a closed economic system since the 1920s, it lacked a fundamental understanding of the purpose and function of a free economy. In the heyday of Joseph Stalin and the Five Year Plan, the distribution of rubles within the country constituted a token economy. Currency was used to buy a controlled variety of goods, and the value of Russian money was not supported outside of the country's borders. Thus, Russia could print all the currency it needed without the inflation that such a strategy produces in a free economy. What is being demonstrated under the more open system under Vladimir Putin, said the *Economist,* is that the token currency could not survive in a free market. Further, a working banking system in the country still does not fully exist. The average Russian has centuries of history to tell him to save his money under his mattress rather than entrust it to a public institution. From this mindset, it's easy to understand why in Russia there's no public shame in not repaying a loan, and why fraud is barely a crime. As the *Economist* put it, "When nobody (including the central bank) knows what banking entails, anybody can be a banker."[7]

EARLY ROLES OF BANKERS

Banking is an old profession, perhaps the second oldest. The earliest bankers served as safekeepers of monies earned by anyone with exchangeable services or goods to offer, prostitutes included. If those services or goods were worth a hat or a rabbit, a banker would safeguard the representative coins in an account until the owner wished to exchange them for a real hat or rabbit.

Despite their usefulness, bankers could be judged harshly. In *The Frogs,* Aristophanes spoke of such individuals in derogatory terms, saying, "Oftentimes have we reflected on a similar abuse in the choice of men for office, and of coins for common use . . . [they] are rejected and abandoned . . . for a vile, adulterate issue, drossy, counterfeit and base, which the traffic of the city passes current in their place." Bankers of biblical times suffered the same fate, according to the Gospel. The predominance of religious orders in business affairs, as well as a presumption of integrity among priests, meant that much banking activity occurred in the precincts of several faiths. But when moneychangers took advantage of that "halo effect," they were driven from the temple.

Banking institutions have always served three primary functions: storing clients' assets safely, determining the exchange value of out-of-region monies, and lending and/or investing funds held in deposit. An individual or institution engaged in banking might offer all or only one of these services. From the beginning, banks and bankers also have been subject to public scrutiny, legislation, and regulation. Public interest is close to the surface and clearly at risk; legislative bodies have always felt comfortable in defending their constituents against potential abuse by bankers. In 400 B.C.E., for example, the Roman senate decreed that interest rates would be capped at 8⅓ percent and that banks could be held liable fourfold for misplaced deposits. On the other side of the coin, debtors ran the risk of being committed into slavery for nonpayment of loans.[8] A wonderful social oxymoron in the western world persists to this day that can put bankrupt persons into jail until they pay their debts.

BANKING DURING THE CRUSADES

Banking was formalized on a large scale during the Crusades, when wealthy men in Europe left their homes and estates for years, even decades, to participate in pilgrimages. The Knights Templar, in addition to being fierce warriors against the infidels, were also fiduciary opportunists. They offered Crusaders their special services of safekeeping valuables and delivery of funds, even to the field of battle. Not only would the debts of the soldier be paid, the balance of his property would be secured, perhaps even enhanced by a bit of interest. Security was considerably more important to the Crusader than possible earnings, and there were no problems with that expectation so long as the banker/agent didn't make speculative

investments with his customer's funds or mix them up with those of another.

The Knights Templar proved to be better bankers than warriors, eventually managing a worldwide banking empire that survived for almost two centuries. They accumulated so much treasure that Philip IV of France one day determined that he needed their resources for his royal purposes. Around A.D. 1300, Philip leaned hard on Pope Clement V to take control of the Templar funds. Threats of war and excommunication were loudly exchanged, but in the end the Templars closed their banking business.[9]

The three early functions of banking evolved into three subprofessions, each serving a distinct social class. Money lenders, usually pawnbrokers or usurers, dealt with lower levels of society. Deposit bankers and moneychangers were engaged with merchants and the middle class, while merchant bankers did business at the highest levels:

The latter were the new elite of the profession, unprecedented in antiquity and in the early Middle Ages. Wealthy commercial and industrial entrepreneurs, uncrowned governors of their city-states, lenders to monarchs, relatives of popes, they were in no way embarrassed by canonical strictures.

At the opposite level of the profession, the pawnbrokers were degraded successors of the early medieval usurers. Indispensable but malodorous, they were

Cosimo dé Medici raised his family's banking house to the peak of its power in fifteenth-century Florence.

deliberate public sinners, likened to prostitutes, and hence tolerated on earth but earmarked for hell unless they repented and made full restitution of their accursed gains.

At the middle level, the money changers and deposit bankers, splintered away from the moneyers, formed the core of the (banking) profession.[10]

Usury as such was universally deemed to be a dire sin. No theologian could endorse a practice that allowed a person to earn money while asleep; this was not "by the sweat of one's brow," as honest men behave. The Third Lateran Council (A.D. 1140) endorsed excommunication for professed usurers, as well as refusal of burial rights in blessed grounds and refusal of their offerings to the Church. The Council of Vienne in 1311 extended excommunication to those who "author-ized usury or protected usurers; legislators authorizing a minimum usury rate; . . . and confessors offering absolution to unrepentant usurers."[11] The Church did offer an escape clause from the pains of hell, but only if the pope were to permit an individual's burial in blessed ground, if the usurer might have a good wife who would intercede for him, or if the usurer would truly repent.

After the Templars folded their banking tents, the state of money management and the legitimacy of coinage was in chaos. Greek and Roman coins were still in circulation, often abused by "sweaters," who roasted coins to extract small particles of silver or gold to be melted down and converted to salable coinage, and "clippers," who snipped or filed coin edges for the same purpose. One function of moneychangers was to weigh coins accurately to determine how much value they might have lost to these processes or (more subtly) to dilution by royal prerogative, which might devaluate the metal/alloy mix of coins. As merchants and traders traveled their part of the known world, it became increasingly important to determine a fair exchange rate for coins neither locally issued nor commonly used.

BANKING IN RENAISSANCE ITALY
Between the fourteenth and seventeenth centuries, private banking houses opened in numerous Italian cities to deal with issues of coinage. Italian bankers found that there were socially tolerable profits to be made by the ethical exchange

process involving the hundreds of coin varieties in circulation in the Mediterranean and European worlds. Banks in Genoa and Florence also issued new coins that they hoped would establish parity and carry a stable value. Genoese bankers introduced the "genoin" coin in 1252, just months before the Florentines minted their new "florin." Both coins established a reputation for stability, but the genoin disappeared around 1300 after a series of military and political disasters crushed the Genoan banking community, including the Leccacorvo family of bankers. The florin, on the

other hand, survived and served as an exchange medium for several hundred years, as did the ducat, issued in Venice from 1284 to 1797.

Successful Italian bankers in Lucca around 1250 established a lending relationship with British royalty and funded, among other things, construction of the great series of coastal castles in western Wales. The early loans were repaid by a lien on the royal customs; however, later borrowings by Edward III to finance the Hundred Years' War went delinquent. The Peruzzi and Bardi family banks in

Lorenzo dé Medici, grandson of Cosimo, allowed the family banking house to slide while he won the accolade "Il Magnifico" for his patronage of the arts. Botticelli painted him in this proud stance as a figure (at the far left) in his *Adoration of the Magi.*

Florence fell victim to Edward's nonperformance and brought to a close the practice of unsecured lending to monarchs who believed that their "divine rights" transcended ordinary repossession or foreclosure.[12] (Charles I taught bankers in Great Britain the same severe lesson. For many years, British bankers believed that their cash would be safe in the Tower of London, and indeed it was—from ordinary thieves. But when in 1640 Charles found himself short on pocket change, he

The banking family of Mayer Rothschild had its home and began its rise to financial power in the Frankfurt ghetto, depicted by Anton Burger in *The Judengasse*.

bank also served as a depository, but made no loans for almost 200 years.

Ultimately, these conservative Dutch bankers found the opportunity for perceived profits too tempting, and made a series of speculative investments in the explorations of the Dutch East India Company. Thus, the bank found itself increasingly leveraged as it became mired in advances to the East India group. The weakened Amsterdam bank failed in 1819, falling victim (along with many of its clients) to the tulip-market crash. So long as they minded their principal businesses, bankers could maintain reasonable, if unspectacular, profitability. As venture capitalists, however, they were neither more nor less successful than some of their twentieth-century successors.[14]

Jakob Fugger was the greatest money man of sixteenth-century Europe. "Many are hostile to me," he said. "They say I am rich. I am rich, by God's grace, without injury to any man."

helped himself to 160,000 of the bankers' English pounds. Henceforth, British bankers used goldsmiths' vaults.)

Other Italian families were more successful and gradually extended their experienced banking services into Northern Europe. They helped found Ludwig Meuting's bank in Antwerp (1479), Jakob Fugger's bank in Germany (1487), and the municipal bank in Basel (1504).[13] In 1609, the city of Amsterdam, then as now a burgeoning trade center, established a banking office to weigh and evaluate coins and thereby establish exchange rates for the 341 varieties of silver coins and the 505 varieties of gold coins then in European circulation. The Amsterdam

More sophisticated banking organizations developed in Europe in the seventeenth and eighteenth centuries as the Hanseatic and other trading leagues required cross-border financial services, including convertibility of currencies, letters of credit, and international exchange of cash and indentures. Families such as the Rothschilds became identified with banking functions, and different branches of such families opened offices in trading centers of several countries. The blood relationships of merchant banking families created at least a perception of trust and reliability. Letters of credit were essential facilitators to international trade. Bankers were also pressed into service with the kings and queens of Europe as war and other

Frontier banks in Minnesota—such as the Bank of Brainerd in 1881—were often storefront affairs run by grocers and barkeeps.

international royal excursions required budgeting and massive levies of capital.

BANKING IN THE NEW WORLD

Banking practices followed colonists to North America, with financial services provided by those settlers with a head for money management rather than agriculture or politics. In Boston, New York, and Philadelphia, banks were cloned in the image of their ancestors and served as correspondents of related institutions in London, Paris, and The Hague. Farther out in the colonies, banks were as pioneer as the people they served.

Depositors and borrowers in nineteenth-century America would most likely have been small businesses, stores, and workshops rather than individuals. The founders

of frontier banks were businesspersons in and of their community, generally starting a financial institution with their own imported capital. Grocers and saloonkeepers would cash paychecks as part of a purchase transaction. Individuals able to set money aside were likely to use a savings association, where interest rates were modest and security was high. While the net effect was much the same, bank failures had a more immediate impact on local businesses than the citizenry.

A frontier population of fur traders, market hunters, and winners and losers in the establishment of law and order was not the stuff of stable banking customers. Most pioneers used little cash and were likely to live in a barter economy, exchanging services for products or vice versa. A bank was an institution that could exist only in a settled community, with a clientele of some permanence and earning power and—even better— collateral. Bankers sought the rancher or farmer with deeded land and a homestead, the merchant with a store and inventory, and the schoolteacher and other salaried professionals. In turn, these good citizens needed a secure depository and an occasional source of loans.

As now, banks then were intended to be short-term lenders, providing working capital for a farming season, for a merchant's slow months, for those times between predictable flows of other capital. In a large, established city, the mix of banking business is such that most finan-

cial institutions are not at risk to a single industry or one dry summer. The diversity of their loan portfolios provides a measure of internal insurance. On or near the frontier, however, banks and the communities they served were at far greater risk to the vagaries of weather, the fertility of the surrounding land, and the prices of commodities.

Whatever the long-range future for a region might have been, frontier periods were times of great short-term banking risk. This risk could have an impact on depositors and bank owners alike, with simultaneous and complete loss: if the banker could not collect his loans, he could not pay off his depositors. In the early nineteenth century, the First and

The First National Bank of Lake Crystal, Minnesota, ca. 1907.

Pope County State Bank,
Glenwood, Minn.

Literal pillars of strength were added to early bank facades to convey financial stability. Built in 1875, the Pope County State Bank of Glenwood, Minnesota, boasted a Classical Revival façade.

Second Banks of the United States did provide a limited stability. These national organizations recognized and redeemed some of the better currencies issued by local banks across the country, and accepted limited kinds of collateral for discount borrowing by those regional banks. The U.S. Congress allowed the charter of the Second Bank of the United States to expire in 1838, leaving no national standards in place at the time Minnesota's banking industry was born.

word "national" in the name was limited to those banks that received a charter from the government under terms of the National Banking Act of 1863. National charters were numbered sequentially in communities; the First National Bank would thus be older than the Second National, and so forth. (Mel Brooks's Last National Bank is apocryphal.) To keep its charter, a national bank was subject to uniform accounting requirements and periodic examinations of its books and cash vaults.

BANKING ON APPEARANCE

A country banker took all available steps to provide real and implied strength for his institution. On the practical side, a bank's name was more than symbolic. Use of the

A bank's physical design also conveyed stability. Size alone was a significant characteristic, often emphasized by an overstated façade enhanced by literal pillars of strength, which added character

A row of orderly teller cages helped impart a big-city feel in territorial banks.

and sophistication. Inside the building, the most visible signs of secure banking were the president's desk (and, as the bank's primary representative, the president himself), plus one or more uniformed guards and the door to the cash vault. With its clockwork latching mechanism and stainless-steel locking bars, the vault door instilled confidence that deposits placed in that institution would be safe. A large lobby with a tidy row of tellers' cages was impressive in a frontier community, remindful of bigger city organizations. These days, as one drives through small, sometimes withering prairie towns, it's an idle game to scan the high lintels of one-time bank buildings for the date of construction and the vanished bank name. Because the buildings were usually well constructed, they have survived multiple reincarnations, providing a good environment for restaurants in particular, with the old and ornate vault often serving as wine storage.

Typically, a country bank would try to establish and maintain a correspondent relationship with a large, recognized, accessible (relatively) big-city bank. Initially, the relationship was conducted by mailed letters (hence the term), later by bank wire and Telex, currently by cable optics. Among other roles, the primary correspondent would be a source of cash for emergency withdrawals, a buyer of loans to generate liquidity, and a secured lender to the smaller bank; it could also be a source of advice and/or

new business. On the human level, the corresponding officers who knew each other well were entertained in each other's communities, and throughout a career could become fast friends.

RUNS, PANICS, CRISES

Correspondent arrangements were individual and, of course, subject to the larger bank's liquidity. Troubles of the smaller country banks could affect the liquidity of their city correspondents and, in the case of a national financial crisis, vice versa. As it turned out, some national banking crises began with small banks and ran upstream. Others, however, began with a credit or cash crunch in New York or London and gradually infected the smaller institutions.

Dime novels are filled with tales of burglars burrowing through the bottom or back of a bank's vault and stripping its contents. No mere robbery, however, could be more catastrophic than the run on a bank, whose only purpose is to reassure depositors, substantial or modest, that they are able to withdraw some or all of their funds at any time. A run might be, and often was, caused by a rumor of weakness in the local bank. Nervous clients might imagine that the bank had sent too much vault cash to Chicago or that the chief cashier had slipped out of town with bags of depositors' money. Others might fret that the bank president was using their funds to finance too nice a home or too fancy a car.

A crowd of depositors makes a run on the Farmers and Mechanics Savings Bank of Minneapolis during the panic of 1893. The bank survived.

The run was often literal, a footrace to the bank to withdraw a savings account. If a fellow *could* make such a withdrawal, he might stash the money under his mattress overnight, and, if all seemed under control, redeposit it the next morning. Should a substantial number of depositors become concerned enough to withdraw their funds, a bank might exhaust its supply of vault cash and stop paying out, probably closing the bank for the rest of the day. The next few hours would test

the bank's survival power. If it had good relations with its correspondent bank and that entity was located within a few hundred miles, currency and gold might be shipped in by train overnight, allowing the target bank to open as usual the next morning. If the bank had no correspondent friends, it might never reopen, leaving the owner to begin liquidating assets to pay back as much of the depositors' money as possible. Until such liquidation, depositors were out of luck.

A run was usually a local phenomenon, lasting one or two days. While a banking panic had similar psychological roots, it manifested itself in more than one bank, might cover a region or even the country, and, depending on initial and subsequent events, could last for years. It was possible for a small, regional run on banks to escalate into significant pressure on larger, money-center banks, but the modern protection afforded by the Federal Deposit Insurance Corporation and other agencies—virtually no-limit insurance for all depositors—has made the run a phenomenon of yesteryear. Yet even during the Great Depression, depositors weren't comfortable with the concept of deposit insurance, particularly since the insured limit at that time was just $2,500. Rumors still started, even about the strongest banks, and may well have been caused by malice. Such rumors plagued the First National Bank of St. Paul in the early 1930s to such an extent that the FBI was asked to investigate. The bureau sniffed about and concluded that any such rumors should be attributed to "Communists and anarchists."

The Panic of 1836–1837—paralleling the decline and fall of the Second Bank of the United States' charter—had no particular impact on the Northern Plains, except to temporarily slow the burgeoning demand for beaver pelts from South Dakota's Black Hills (for the prototypical banker's hat). In the 1830s, there was no banking business in the Northern Plains.

ENLIGHTENED SELF-INTEREST

On the settled frontier, at the outer perimeters of urban civilization, banks were generally formed by a community's leading citizens and businessmen who could subscribe the capital necessary to meet the requirements of state (or territorial) banking statutes. As a community grew, competing groups of business owners might start a second or third bank.

By modern standards, incorporators of nineteenth-century banks were dangerously in conflict of interest. It was assumed they would conduct all of their financial transactions through "their" bank and would expect preferential treatment in terms of interest rates and repayment schedules. They would expect to serve as directors of their bank and thus know a great deal more about the financial affairs of the community than their competitors, increasing their opportunities for personal investment in their town.

This is in sharp contrast to modern regulations, which ensure that bank directors will not only borrow at terms at least as rigorous as those offered to other good customers, but they will also disclose, in regular public reports, all dimensions of their banking activity. This often has had the interesting effect of forcing (or at least encouraging) bank directors to do business with their competition. Any officer or director taking personal advantage of confidential bank information these days is likely to be prosecuted and jailed.

The First National Bank of Alexandria, Minnesota, ca. 1876.

Despite opportunities for self-dealing, frontier banks and their boards of directors were as often the victims of hard times as they were the villains. The dilemma and challenge of early nineteenth-century banking is well described by Theodore A. Andersen in *Banking in Wisconsin:*

The charters (of new banks founded in the Wisconsin territory in 1836) were patterned after that which the Bank of Wisconsin had received from the Michigan Territory. No provision was made for the pledge of specific assets as collateral for bank notes, and the materials with which the notes were printed were placed under the control of the respective bank officials. No system of examination was established to insure that banks were living up to their charters. Thus the director of a bank began operations with only his conscience to guide him.

The territorial banks were badly mismanaged, but they would probably have failed even if they had not violated their charters. The early settlers needed longterm credit, and the banks were prepared to extend only short-term credit. The notes issued by the banks had to be redeemable in gold to be acceptable, yet the community needed notes in excess of the gold reserves. Thus in financing the early development of Wisconsin, the banks faced an impossible situation.[15]

Such were the conditions of frontier banking when it entered the Territory of Minnesota in 1853, with the creation of several small private banks in the territorial capital of St. Paul.

FRONTIER BANKING in MINNESOTA

JONATHAN RABAN'S *Bad Land* focuses on the challenges of early-twentieth-century settlers in eastern Montana, yet it also reveals the ambitions of frontier bankers, as well as some of the perils:

> It was the season of the smiling bank manager. The Wollastons had an account at the new Mildred Bank, run by a shock-haired young Missourian named Hayden Bright, who raced around the countryside in an open Ford tourer, accompanied by his jack-rabbit chasing brindled English bulldog, and pressed loans on his clients.
>
> All the homesteaders were undercapitalized and it was the banker's pleasant duty to lend them the means to buy the stock, the seed, the machinery needed to bring them into certain profit. Percy (Wollaston) remembered Hayden Bright warmly, for his friendliness, his memory for children's names, his bullet-speed driving, and his crazy dog. Once, during a small agricultural crisis, Hayden—as even young Percy knew him—passed a new cheque book across his desk, saying, "Take this and don't come back until you've got some hogs. And when you write out the cheque, don't act timid. Write 'er out as though you had all the money in the world." . . .
>
> The bank lending rate was 5½ per cent,

> $55 p.a. on $1,000. Or say, an acre and a half of next year's wheat, set against a brand-new gas-engined tractor, which could double, or triple, one's workable acreage. It was cheap money, and it was logical, inevitable, un-turn-downable money. There was almost no loan so large that it would not pay for itself handsomely within a farming year.
>
> Hayden Bright and the other local bank managers saw themselves as cashing in on the homesteaders' success, and in their turn they too borrowed up to the hilt, to get as big a share of this sure-fire farm business as they possibly could.
>
> The homesteader had his milch cow; the banker had a milch cow in the shape of the homesteader; and so the line of credit stretched back eastwards, to investors in Boston and New York who'd read the brochures, and wanted a slice of the brilliant future of the West.[16]

The myopia of prosperity in Montana in the 1910s was trained on an evanescent combination of sufficient rain and high grain prices that drove banks to lend and homesteaders to borrow. When both of these blessings failed, and homesteaders were unable to repay what they borrowed, they packed up and moved farther west, leaving land, houses, outbuildings, even new tractors as collectable collateral for the bank loans. Sadly, the combined value of the assets—in a prairie sea of failed farmers—was not enough to save the banks. They too failed. The seismic consequences were felt across the region and into eastern financial markets. Even as early as the 1830s in Wisconsin, mistakes made in the name of progress were too frequently compounded by malfeasance that went along with stupidity and led to numerous bank failures. The Wisconsin legislature thought it had solved the problem by banning "banking" until 1853.

BANKING COMES TO MINNESOTA

By 1853, Minnesota's territorial capital of St. Paul was some years ahead of

Minneapolis, its twin city across the Mississippi River, both in relative prosperity and stability. The small community at the head of commercial navigation on the Upper Mississippi was the largest town in the state and the center of emerging regional businesses. Parker Paine and Company, one of the city's few banking houses, opened in September of that year, established with $40,000 of capital. Within a decade, Parker Paine and Company—only modestly successful—became the only survivor of note among St. Paul's initial financial institutions. In surviving, it also became the ancestor of the First National Bank of St. Paul, and thus a parent to the First Bank Stock Corporation.

In 1853, Parker Paine and Company was one of a handful of banks in St. Paul. It became the First National Bank of St. Paul and, ultimately, a parent to First Bank Stock Corporation in 1929.

A century later, at the 1953 dinner in celebration of the First National of St. Paul's centennial, Julian Baird, chair of the bank's board, described Parker Paine and Company as "dealing in Eastern exchange, depreciated state notes, land scrip, and real estate"—a host of functions common to the time.[17] Baird noted that the bank charged 3 percent per month in interest on borrowing and paid 1 percent per month to depositors. The venture struggled through a couple of years, too small to be much more than viable. But in 1859, when brothers Horace and James E. Thompson moved to St. Paul from Americus, Georgia, and joined Mr. Paine's bank, they added capital—enough so that the bank was reinvigorated and renamed Thompson-Paine and Company. When Paine retired in 1860, the business became Thompson Brothers for a short time, and, in 1862, was renamed Bank of Minnesota. After Congress passed the National Banking Act of 1863, the brothers were granted National Charter 203 and called the institution the First National Bank of St. Paul. James Thompson served as its president until his death in 1870. He was succeeded by his brother Horace, who enjoyed some

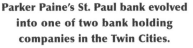

Parker Paine's St. Paul bank evolved into one of two bank holding companies in the Twin Cities.

unexpected notoriety in 1876 while hunting near Madelia, Minnesota. There he surprised members of the Jesse James gang, fleeing from their now famous bank robbery in nearby Northfield, and managed to detain them until the posse arrived.

James C. Burbank, a founder of St. Paul Fire and Marine, along with three brothers named Harrison—Thomas A., William M., and Hugh G.—added $100,000 to First National's capital accounts, making the bank overcapitalized, especially for its time.[18] The Harrisons, who had been successful in Minneapolis logging and sawmilling, later became part of the group that founded Security National Bank in Minneapolis, an institution that would merge into the First National Bank of Minneapolis in 1915. Tom Harrison served a decade as vice president of the St. Paul bank.

NATIONAL BANKING CRISES
A moderate national banking crisis arose in 1857 but caused no major upheaval in the Central Northwest; any lingering aftershocks were absorbed during the Civil War. Yet banking's hard times increased after the war, with different crises troubling the money-center banks

First National Bank, Northfield, Minn., Where the James & Younger Bros. Made Their Last Raid on Sept. 7, 1876.

Jesse James robbed the First National Bank of Northfield, Minnesota, in 1876. As members of his gang fled through Madelia, they were detained by Horace Thompson, president of the First National Bank of St. Paul, who happened to be hunting in the area.

and ultimately triggering Congress into passing the Federal Reserve Bank legislation of 1913.

To understand that sequence of increasingly serious eruptions, consider the history of U.S. banking as pragmatically outlined in the chapter titles of the *History of Crises under the National Banking System:* "The Crisis of 1873," "The Panic of May 1884," "Financial Stringency in 1890," and "The Crisis of 1893."[19] The following brief summaries of the chapters show some causes and effects of those economic phenomena.

The banking crisis of 1873 was somewhat unusual, at least from a banking perspec-

tive, because it began in the East, where city banks were under stress and country banks were not. It was a crisis fueled by an avalanche of more or less noxious railroad bonds. Transcontinental rail systems, which were highly desired by Congress to reinforce national unity after the Civil War, were generally built along rights-of-way as fast as promoters could sell bonds. First- and second-mortgage bonds were backed by the railroads and, when attainable, so was the acreage the government had granted to the railroads to spur their construction.

The proximate cause of the 1873 banking crisis was the September 8 failure of the New York Warehouse and Security

In 1869, the new First National Bank of Minneapolis was located on Washington Avenue, just west of Northwestern National Bank.

Company (a subsidiary of Jay Cooke and Company, a major U.S. banking organization), precipitated by a lack of cash proceeds from its holdings of the Missouri, Kansas, and Texas Railroad. On September 13, the "important banking house" of Kenyon, Cox, and Company also failed because of its endorsement of $1.5 million in bonds of the Canada Southern Railroad. But these two incidents were small potatoes compared with the September 18 closing of Jay Cooke and Company, itself a major player in the early financing of the Northern Pacific Railway.[20] The Cooke failure had a domino effect on several other brokerage firms,

starting with Fisk and Hatch of New York City, which closed September 19. The Fourth National Bank in New York City was the subject of a run, which it met with the only surefire technique it could: by remaining open after its usual hours and meeting every demand for payment.

The National Bank of the Commonwealth in Detroit was the only bank of its kind to fold in the crisis of 1873, the victim of an overextended loan of $1.75 million to the Lake Shore and Michigan Southern Railroad, further compounded by a defalcation by the bank's secretary of some $500,000. Thus, the overt effects of that crisis were the failure of one national bank, the closure of a handful of brokerage offices, and the suspension of New York Stock Exchange trading for ten days. Secondary effects were more widespread, since the New York banks had substantially drawn down their cash reserves to meet heavy customer demand and to make supportive advances to their correspondent banks. Large cash withdrawals by manufacturers wanting to meet payrolls were subsequently held up and some workers furloughed. Routine payments for retail goods also were stalled, which slowed sales. The earlier success of Jay Cooke, as the Mike Milken of his day, in selling marginal railroad securities affected numerous banks, which did not necessarily fail but were substantially restrained in meeting the financial needs of their communities. The Northern Pacific survived through recapitalization, further borrowings against its massive land grants, and a change in management. Thus, although the banking crisis of 1873 may not have been a major disaster, the nation's economy continued to feel its ripple effect.

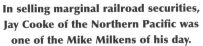

In selling marginal railroad securities, Jay Cooke of the Northern Pacific was one of the Mike Milkens of his day.

The panic of May 1884 had even less of an impact on the banking world outside of New York, but once again reflected the culmination of increasingly casual behavior by several financial organizations— casual in the sense of internal administration, supervision, and regulation. General business had been slowing, with manufacturers' prices declining, and a nervous stock market was affecting brokers.

On May 8, the failure of Grant and Ward, a New York brokerage, was announced. The president of Marine National Bank was a partner in Grant and Ward, and his bank's successive failure was the result of loans to that broker. The following week it was revealed that the president of the Second National Bank in New York had stolen $3 million from his bank, and that the city's Metropolitan National Bank had closed.

The stock market spent several days sorting good news from bad, and finally settled. Help from the New York City Bank clearinghouse made it possible for Metropolitan National Bank to reopen after a couple of days; the Second National also withstood the spate of withdrawals caused by news of the theft. Although commentators noted that changes should be made in the payment system to avert such damage in the future—essentially changes to establish schedules and deadlines for interbank transactions—none occurred.

The financial stringency of 1890 hit at a time when no national banking system yet existed and New York was still the United States' de facto banking center. With a New York correspondent bank serving as clearinghouse and discount banker, the country banker would develop a depend-

ency on his city cousin. A measure of this dependence is an 1890 statistic noting that Chicago banks were drawing some $222 million on New York correspondents while the same New York banks drew only $82,000 on their Chicago peers.

Sales of European securities in the New York market in 1890 pulled unusually large amounts from the gold reserves of the city's banks. By November, London banks were under pressure to meet their advances, and the Bank of England raised its discount rate to 6 percent. European stock markets were troubled, and events at several well-known brokerages, such as Villard and Baring Brothers and Company, reflected these concerns. Baring was one of a handful of European bankers that had raised the massive capital to build U.S. railroads, including James J. Hill's Great Northern Railroad. (Baring's troubles in 1890 anticipated by a century its fatal fiasco with an unsupervised futures trader in Hong Kong who caused his firm to lose hundreds of millions of pounds, and thus forced the historic firm's dissolution.)

Back in New York, no banks failed as a result of the "stringency" of 1890, but there was a continued attenuation of resources, an increased stretching of cash and reserves to meet the demands of foreign exchange and trade, correspondent loan discounts, and local clientele. Again observers noted the need for some sort of structure that could provide flexibility and a security-blanket response to shelter an embarrassed country bank. But the

A. Moorman and Company built the Commercial State Bank of Two Harbors, Minnesota, four years prior to the panic of 1893.

After a 1908 fire, the First National Bank of Chisholm, Minnesota, reopened in temporary quarters.

ability of banks to survive past crises without major disaster led to further legislative procrastination. The year 1893 would prove to be a different story.

By the time the crisis of 1893 hit, the U.S. farm economy had been deteriorating for years as burgeoning demand for foodstuffs had encouraged massive imports of foreign grain and kept prices for U.S. farm products in a declining trend. Fewer shipments meant less business for long-haul railroads, so that two major components of the economy were now in trouble. In February 1893, the Philadelphia and Reading Railroad failed. A lack of *any* good news caused the stock market to collapse May 4.

Analysts and economists were concerned about unusual demand for gold in payments by New York banks. Because silver was not monetized, it was not well received as substitute backing for currency.

Lack of liquidity in the banking system was exacerbated by normal seasonal loan activity, and by July New York City banks were in a deficit reserve status. Across the country, banks limited loans and attempted to build liquidity. Such reining in initiated a sense of nervous urgency among bank clients across the country. In late July, a wave of regional bank failures swept across the country, while the Erie Railroad went into receivership. Thirty-three

A parade in downtown St. Paul celebrated the 1893 completion of James J. Hill's Great Northern Railroad. This float, sponsored by the Ryan Drug Company, won first prize.

national banks suspended between mid-July and the end of August. By the end of July, larger-city banks began to limit cash withdrawals and to issue clearinghouse loan certificates in lieu of money. But money was essential to purchase raw materials and to pay the workforce, and the shortage of cash had an immediate impact on the nation's business:

The month of August (1893) will long remain memorable as one of the most remarkable in our industrial history. Never before has there been such a sudden and striking cessation of industrial activity.[21]

By September, national evidence of a general recession was becoming clear, which

effectively transcended the banking crisis. Sixty-five national banks failed, and the shortage of cash and currency in the banking system drove a slowdown in business that lasted five years. In Minneapolis, five small state banks failed and were liquidated, but the larger banks survived. In the general difficulties of the time, however, it appeared that the First National Bank of Minneapolis was having problems. The bank didn't close, but the board found the management of the bank wanting and determined to address the problem.

In St. Paul, James J. Hill noted with great satisfaction the completion of his Great Northern Railroad's westward expansion to Seattle in September. His use of the Marias Pass through the Montana Rockies made the Great Northern the most efficient rail line to the West Coast. In recognition of the mood of financial gloom, however, there was no national celebration.

TOWARD A NEW CENTURY

The closing years of the nineteenth century saw the country gradually shrug off the effects of the crisis of 1893. Business began a new round of expansion and banks were ready to meet corporate needs for loans. Once again, the consensus among bankers, politicians, and businessmen was that something concrete *must* be done about creating an entity that would support a stressed national banking system. The series of financial crises that had marked the last four decades of the nineteenth century created the very real prospect that the country's entire economic infrastructure could be at risk during periods of banking distress—and that such periods of distress were to be expected as part of the domestic business cycle. Yet another two decades would pass before Congress would create the Federal Reserve System.

Meanwhile, the larger banks in Minnesota survived the financial crises of the late nineteenth century, and the managers of those banks had learned some lessons about the risks of correspondent banking and about potential shortages of liquidity. They also began to consider what might be done on a regional basis to protect themselves and the banks out in their territory.

It was rare in 1905 to associate women with banks. An exception was the Wabasso, Minnesota, bank.

TWIN CITIES BANKING REFINED

BY 1900, THE BANKING scene in Minneapolis and St. Paul had been winnowed to a handful of doughty survivors:

> When the padlocks were all counted, the leading survivors in Minneapolis were the Northwestern National, the First National, the Security, the Minnesota Loan and Trust Company, the Minneapolis Trust Company, the Hennepin County Savings Bank, and the Farmers and Mechanics Savings Bank. In St. Paul, they were the First National, the Merchants National, the Capital National Bank, the Capital Trust and Savings Bank, and the National German-American Bank.[22]

The frontier banker/manager/entrepreneur who had founded these and other, now vanished Twin Cities banks was gone—retired, bankrupt, dead. Running the surviving institutions at the beginning of the twentieth century were trained, professional bankers—annealed, if you will, by the stress and pain of the 1893 bank panic and its seismic aftershocks. Opportunity aplenty awaited them and the Twin Cities' young banking system.

MAJOR BANKS IN MINNEAPOLIS

A vigorous downtown business district in the booming city of Minneapolis reflected the dynamic times of the new century. A new bridge—the first to span the Mississippi River—linked the west bank and its water-powered flour mills with old St. Anthony, the lumber milling center on the east bank. The St. Paul and Pacific Railroad, which had originally connected the St. Paul waterfront with St. Anthony, was now part of James J. Hill's Great Northern Railroad and crossed the Stone Arch Bridge on its way to the West Coast.

Two major banks existed at that time in Minneapolis: the First National and Northwestern National. First National was the older, its parentage dating back to the 1857 organization of Sidle, Wolford, and Company. After Peter Wolford left town in 1864, the company was reorganized in January 1865 as the First National Bank of Minneapolis under National Charter 710. Henry Sidle became president in 1888 upon the death of his brother Jacob, with whom he had chartered the bank. Despite its troubles in the wake of the financial crisis of 1893, the First National Bank had endured. But Henry Sidle was seen as arbitrary in his decision-making and unwilling to delegate authority, so in 1894 the bank's board replaced him with a troika: John Martin, a long-time director, as president; Frank

Moody Prince as cashier (chief operating officer); and Clive Talbot Jaffray (always known as C. T.) as Prince's assistant, with promotion to cashier in January 1895 when Prince was named vice president. In 1913, First National established an affiliated relationship with the Minneapolis Trust Company. In 1915, after it merged with the good-sized Security National Bank, the First National had deposits of approximately $66 million—almost twice the size of Northwestern National, its next competitor, which averaged deposits of $36 million.

Northwestern National, the other major banking institution in Minneapolis, was a relative newcomer among Twin Cities banks. It was founded in 1872 under National Charter 2006 after several Minneapolis businessmen decided that Sidle, Wolford, and Company was an unsatisfactory place to do business; they believed there should be room in Minneapolis for a new bank. Northwestern was capitalized with representation by the Morrison, Welles, Heffelfinger, Pillsbury, Lowry, Gale, and Loring families, many of whose members served on the board throughout its history. The bank later became one of the city's largest, particularly when the crisis of 1907 prompted the Swedish American National Bank and the National Bank of Commerce to merge into

M-92—Streamliner Crossing Mississippi River over Stone Arch Bridge, Minneapolis, Minn.

The Minneapolis Union Railway, a subsidiary of James J. Hill's railroad ventures, completed the Stone Arch Bridge in 1884 as a necessary first step toward the Pacific Northwest.

Northwestern in 1908. A year later, Northwestern arranged a formal affiliation with the Minnesota Loan and Trust Company.

Joining Northwestern National Bank in 1887 as a messenger was Edward Williams Decker, a recent high-school graduate who became the young bank's seventeenth employee. A few days later, C. T. Jaffray applied for the same position and was likewise hired. Their mentor and supervisor was James B. Forgan, who had left the Bank of Nova Scotia to become cashier of Northwestern and who had immediately directed a thorough upgrading of the bank's internal administration

and bookkeeping. When Forgan resigned from Northwestern in 1891 to join the First National Bank of Chicago, Decker and Jaffray stayed in Minneapolis, although Jaffray moved to the city's First National Bank in 1895 to be assistant to Frank Moody Prince, the chief operating officer. In January 1912, Decker, then forty-three, would be elected president of Northwestern National. In due time, both he and Jaffray would become president of their respective bank holding companies.

Although Decker and Jaffray were lifelong friends, they were also competitors for fifty years. Decades after their financial

The North Western National Bank at First Avenue South and Washington Avenue in Minneapolis, ca. 1875. "North Western" would become "Northwestern" in 1880. Note the coffin maker's office.

careers were past, and years after their deaths the two bankers remained a presence in downtown Minneapolis: two peregrine falcons nesting atop the city's Multifoods Tower were nicknamed after them. As one wag observed, "Decker and Jaffray are still looking for pigeons."[23]

OTHER MILL CITY BANKS

By 1920, the seven Minneapolis banks identified in 1900 as survivors of the 1893 crisis were reduced by mergers and affiliations to four: Northwestern, First National, Hennepin County Savings Bank, and Farmers and Mechanics Savings Bank. Hennepin County Savings would be merged in late 1922 into the Minneapolis Trust Company, itself a First National affiliate. Farmers and Mechanics would maintain its independence for another sixty years.

Under its charter as a savings bank, Farmers and Mechanics prospered and suffered under somewhat different regulations and supervision than commercial banks. The narrow focus of savings banks on long-term mortgages and time savings made them vulnerable to the wild gyrations of interest rates that were to occur in the 1970s and 1980s. Negative earnings caused by using short-term, high-cost funds to finance a long-term, low-rate mortgage portfolio brought Farmers and Mechanics to the brink of insolvency. Regulators who took over the bank essentially forced the sale of the institution's assets and liabilities to the Marquette Bank Group of Minneapolis—ultimately to become a part of U.S.

Bancorp—at substantial discounts to their real value. The Kingman family, which had served F & M as responsible custodians and managers for decades, fell victim to a system and a sequence of events over which they had little or no control. They were personally desolate, even though—happily—their depositors had always been fully protected. (As a mutual savings bank, the institution was actually owned by its depositors.)

MAJOR BANKS IN ST. PAUL

Across the Mississippi, downtown St. Paul was enjoying a building boom that was relocating most of the city's banks into new facilities. This burst of activity disguised a reality about St. Paul that would become more evident during the remaining decades of the twentieth century—namely, that it lacked a business generator that would create the expanding economic base critical to a modern metropolis. As the result of legislative high jinks, St. Paul had the state capital with its broad employment base; the city was likewise home to five liberal arts colleges, providing an intellectual stimulus. As the head of navigation on the Mississippi, St. Paul boasted the remnants of fifty years of being an entrepôt, with a collection of regional warehouse systems and transfer facilities (from ox carts to railroads) between the water and land. The town was wealthy, but as Mary Lethert Wingerd pointed out in her thesis *Claiming the City,* the wealth came from out-of-town activity (railroads and timber), not from local manufacturing. Minnesota Mining

The Farmers and Mechanics Saving Bank, located at 115 South Fourth Street in Minneapolis, boasted a Classical-style façade.

(3M) had not yet migrated south from Duluth and, in any case, had not yet become much of a generator of jobs and capital. St. Paul would become the proud parent of Fortune 500 companies, but they would develop a tendency to merge into a national company, and sell out or shut down.

The dominant bank in the capital city at the turn of the century was the First National Bank of St. Paul, formerly Parker Paine and Company. Back in 1880, Henry P. Upham had succeeded Horace Thompson as president. Well regarded for his conservative management style—an approach that was not only wiser but essential to survival—Upham steered the small bank through several regional and national financial crises until 1907. The cost of conservatism was that out-state bankers and potential clients were not particularly welcome customers. Upham's retirement resulted in the election of Everett Bailey as the new leader.

Thanks to the presence of James J. Hill on the First National's board of directors, the bank had most of the local railroad banking business. Hill was a ubiquitous presence in the Twin Cities from the 1880s, when his "great adventure" of acquiring and driving the Great Northern Railroad to the Pacific began to flourish, until his death in 1917. Not only was he a corporate and personal client of First National, as well as a director, he also held a small percentage of its shares.

When Hill stepped down as chair of the Great Northern's board in 1912 and retired from its day-to-day operations, he turned to the banking industry as an extended part of his grand dream of building the territory. Hill wished to enrich the economic and agricultural capacity of the regions served by his railroad by establishing long-term two-way traffic. His dream evinced itself in many

ways, including efforts at his North Oaks farm in suburban St. Paul to develop cattle and grain products that might thrive on the vast prairie. To Hill's mind, banking services were a critical part of an effective business system, so he designed space for banking offices into his newly constructed railroad headquarters in St. Paul. One day he made a personal offer to Everett Bailey of the First National Bank of St. Paul to buy its outstanding shares. To his surprise, Hill was turned down. The bank was not for sale, said President Bailey, and even if it were, it would be too expensive for Hill.[24]

Down the street Hill went to the Second National Bank of St. Paul to call on another old friend, William B. Dean, the acting president. The Second National was smaller

Downtown St. Paul was a hotbed of banking activity in the early twentieth century. John M. Doherty painted this view of the city—*St. Paul, Sixth and Jackson Streets*—in 1926.

Henry Pratt Upham (ca. 1875) was the long-time manager and early president of First National Bank of St. Paul.

James J. Hill would not take no for an answer when he made a bid to buy the outstanding shares of the First National Bank of St. Paul.

than the First, but well regarded. Like the First National, the Second also traced its roots to 1853, when it was founded under the name of Mackubin and Edgerton. It was chartered as the Second National Bank in 1859 and designated in 1868 a U.S. depository, a measure of size and quality of management. Dean allowed as how the bank could be for sale; thus Hill bought all of the stock of the Second National in October 1912 for $1.24 million.

Hill went back to Everett Bailey at the First National Bank to announce what he had done and how he probably would have to transfer all of his railroad and personal business from the First to the Second National. The board and principal shareholders quickly grasped the logic of Hill's plan and agreed to sell him the First for $3.35 million. The two banks were consolidated on January 1, 1913, into the First National Bank of St. Paul, with Hill as the sole shareholder, excepting the directors' qualifying shares.[25] Hill also purchased the Northwestern Trust Company, which oversaw many of his family's affairs as well as those of other First National clients. Northwestern Trust eventually would become an affiliate of the First National with a state charter and a new name: the First Trust Company.

OTHER CAPITAL CITY BANKS
Eventually, the First National Bank of St. Paul would merge with descendants of the frontier bank of Meyer and Willius, opened in March 1856 by German immigrants Ferdinand Willius and Henry Meyer.

Under the cautious management of brothers Ferdinand and Gustav Willius, the bank evolved into a national charter as the National German-American Bank. When effects of the crisis of 1893 forced the German-American to suspend operations, a committee of directors was formed to reorganize and reopen the bank as soon as possible. Members of this group were, notably, Frederick Weyerhaeuser, Albert H. Lindeke, and John A. Humbird. Weyerhaeuser continued as a member of the bank's board of directors and was elected a vice president. After its resuscitation, the National German-American Bank resumed its role as an effective but quiet

The First National Bank of St. Paul offices at Jackson and Fourth Streets, ca. 1905.

James J. Hill's summer farm, North Oaks, north of St. Paul, was a gathering place for his large brood, but also an outdoor laboratory where he bred cattle and developed crops that would thrive on the western prairies served by his Great Northern Railroad.

contributor to the St. Paul banking scene. A large portion of its loan portfolio was stabilized and characterized by one officer as being "mostly HOGs" (honest old Germans).[26] Although the bank survived the crisis of 1907, by 1912 its directors felt that its future lay in a merger with Merchants National Bank of St. Paul.

Merchants National Bank, a relative newcomer in St. Paul banking circles, was founded in 1872 by and for St. Paul merchants. By the turn of the century, Merchants National was the second- largest bank in the city. Long-time directors included such well-known St. Paulites as Amherst Wilder, Charles Bigelow, Craw-

ford Livingston, and Frank B. Kellogg. Although Merchants National had weathered the major banking crisis of 1893, it became clear by 1897 that the bank was struggling and the board acted swiftly to install new management, recruiting Kenneth Clark from the smaller Capital National Bank of St. Paul to become president. Clark promptly brought in George Prince, whose brother Frank was then the senior banking officer of the First National Bank of Minneapolis, to serve as cashier. Clark and George Prince reorganized and revitalized Merchants National, and with their protégé, Richard (Dick) Lilly, soon regained for Merchants its reputation as the most aggressive of St. Paul's larger banks.

An offer was on the table as Merchants reacted to the consolidation of the First and Second National Banks of St. Paul, which had created a bank more than twice its size. Thus, Merchants was open to the 1912 National German-American Bank merger proposal. The consolidation added several notable directors to its board, including Frederick Weyerhaeuser, Roger B. Shepard, Albert H. Lindeke, Carl Schuneman, Thomas Irvine, and Frank Schlick. In early merger discussions, it was suggested that the new institution be named the Merchants German-American National Bank, recognizing that the German-American bank was, in fact, slightly the larger of the two new partners.

Weyerhaeuser stated flatly that "we are all Americans now," and the shorter name was adopted.[27] George Prince was elected chair and CEO of the new bank; in 1918 Dick Lilly, at the age of thirty-three, was elected president. Weyerhaeuser continued as a board member and vice president until the 1929 merger of Merchants and the First National of St. Paul, becoming an advisory vice president and director of that institution. He resigned the vice presidency in 1933, but continued on First National's board until 1945.

Lesser known among St. Paul's banks were the two somewhat related Capital banks, products of the late nineteenth

In 1912, Everett H. Bailey, president of the First National Bank of St. Paul, capitulated to James J. Hill's wish to buy the bank after Hill bought the Second National, a smaller competitor.

To ensure the future of the bank he founded, Ferdinand Willius of St. Paul's National German-American Bank chose to merge it in 1912 with Merchants National, also of St. Paul.

century and survivors of earlier banking crises. Capital Trust and Savings Bank collapsed in May 1924 in what would prove to be the city's worst-ever bank failure. Its sister organization, Capital National Bank, was teetering dangerously as well. Loath to have a second failed bank in its midst, the St. Paul financial community pressed for a speedy resolution of the crisis. Capital National was saved by an immediate and fortuitous merger into Merchants National Bank. The initial proposal to rescue Capital National was a fifty-fifty venture between Merchants National and First National of St. Paul, but management of the First dithered about the matter, so Merchants acted preemptorily and singly.[28]

The five larger St. Paul banks that had survived the early decades of Minnesota

banking and the national bank crises had become two strong competitors. By the mid-1920s, therefore, the cast of banks and bankers in both Twin Cities—First National and Northwestern National of Minneapolis and First National and Merchants National of St. Paul—was well defined. A few years remained to develop the rationale for Minnesota's twin bank holding companies in 1929. The chain of events leading to their birth took a critical turn with the banking crisis of 1907, leading to the introduction in 1913 of a player that would have a significant presence in the banking industry in years to come: the Federal Reserve System.

THE BANKING CRISIS OF 1907

After the United States had endured banking crises in the 1870s and 1880s, and memories of the 1893 crisis had faded, the urgent feeling that something needed to be done to support the nation's banking system passed. Loan demand had steadily expanded for almost a decade, and rebuilding after the 1906 San Francisco earthquake gave an unanticipated boost to an already crowded municipal bond market and booming stock market.

The U.S. Treasury, meanwhile, was complicating business for the six largest New York City banks by arbitrarily depositing and withdrawing funds in an effort to manage liquidity and thus the economy. These banks—the City, Bank of Commerce, the First, the Park, Chase, and the Hanover— held some 60 percent of the resources of all New York City national banks, up from 30 percent in 1873. Due to their size and location, the six banks were not only increasingly depended upon by other banks countrywide for credit and reserve accommodations, they also bore the major impact of foreign-exchange fluctuation.[29]

Reserves of the six banks were doubly squeezed during early 1907 by actions of the Bank of England that limited British sales of gold. Unable to pay U.S. banking claims with gold, British banks were forced to redeem finance bills, which American banks had been using

By 1900, Merchants National Bank of St. Paul had moved to its own building at Fifth and Jackson. Edward P. Bassford designed the Richardsonian Romanesque structure.

to fund the unpredictable transactions of the U.S. Treasury and a high but normal domestic loan demand. The liquidity problem moved quickly into the stock market, where prices showed a downward volatility not seen again for twenty years. Raw-material prices collapsed, reflecting disappearing patterns of demand, and the bond market was in a state of denial. In the fall of 1907, a cluster of small and midsized banks and brokers failed following the collapse of a scheme to corner the copper market.

An environment of nervousness led to runs on several of the larger New York City trust companies as well. While these were only quasi-bank entities, their cash function heavily affected the six principal banks. The evident lack of liquidity among this

In 1924, Capital National Bank of St. Paul (360 Robert Street) was acquired by Merchants National. The space was then used by National Exchange Bank, which also failed. A few St. Paul businessmen rescued it and renamed it Empire National Bank, which was acquired by Northwest Bancorporation in 1930. Renamed the Northwestern Bank of St. Paul, it moved across the street into new digs in 1970.

group led one after another to suspend payments or cash withdrawals, offering IOUs in lieu of cash. J. Pierpont Morgan personally led the organization of a $25 million credit pool to help several of the stressed banks meet short-term needs.[30] New York's troubles spread across the country, however, and suspension of cash payments became endemic. Governors of several states declared "bank holidays" to permit their banking institutions to draw a few collected breaths—and collected deposits. With the exception of the National Bank of Commerce in Kansas City, no major bank failures occurred in reaction to the crisis of 1907, but it was widely recognized that the industry's response mechanisms were even less effective than in earlier crises. The U.S. Treasury and the six large New York banks had not only been slow to recognize the emergency, but also reluctant to act expeditiously to deal with it. As O. M. W. Sprague concluded in his 1910 study of banking crises:

> Somewhere in the banking system of a country there should be a reserve of lending power, and it should be found in its central money market. . . . Provision for such reserve power may doubtless be made in a number of different ways. This investigation will have served its purpose if . . . it brings home to the reader the need not only of this reserve power, but also the willingness to use it in future emergencies.[31]

The stage was set to introduce this "reserve of lending power." While it seemed clear that "something" needed to be done, there was no consensus as to what or how. The primary debate was a continuation of one that began when the Constitution was first written: should such a proposed agency be in the private or public sector? The private banking sector thought that a private concordat would work, while the political argument persisted that only Congress had the wisdom and strength to manage the country's banking system.

THE FEDERAL RESERVE SYSTEM

In July 1912, the Republicans—holders of a Congressional majority and the White House—drafted legislation that would have created a private sector entity of reserve lending power. The three-way split of the 1912 election, however, fractured the Republican Party and thus the legislation. President William Howard Taft, the incumbent and Republican nominee, received only 23 percent of the popular vote, while Theodore Roosevelt, the former Republican president running as a Progressive, collected 27 percent. Woodrow Wilson, the Democratic nominee, won the election with a 42 percent plurality, helping his party to capture both the House and the Senate. Almost immediately, Senator Robert L. Owen of Oklahoma and Congressman Carter Glass of Virginia assumed the role of draftsmen for a monetary reserve system that would be a combination of public and private appointments. Two decades later, Franklin D. Roosevelt described Glass as an "unreconstructed rebel."[32] The phrase described a man of southern roots, strong opinions, and dogged energy who came from a newspaper background and served in the House and Senate between 1902 and 1944. Glass became chair of the House Banking and Currency Committee upon Wilson's election, and immediately accepted the political hot potato as his own.

Back in St. Paul, James J. Hill weighed in with perspectives from the private sector. Speaking to the annual convention of the American Bankers Association, he opined:

> Our monetary system is the wonder of intelligent men abroad and the despair of intelligent men at home. A definite proposal to change it has been before the Congress and the country for months past. . . . This (American Bankers) Association should not hesitate to express its opinion and offer its advice. . . .
>
> One serious defect is that the bill will not and cannot do what on its face it proposes to do. It professes to aim at a comprehensive reform of currency and banking by establishing a logical and permanent system. We have never had that since this government was founded. We shall not have it if this bill should become law. . . .
>
> There are practical working weaknesses even more serious. First among these is the projected political control of the currency and banking of the country. The establishment of a federal reserve board, vesting control of our banking, credit and note issues in men chosen necessarily with some reference to political considerations, and at least partially subservient to party demands, is a proposition that

sets reason and all our experience at defiance. . . .

> The details . . . contain other minor features just as doubtful or objectionable. The managers of a nation's finances are to be paid $10,000 a year, when bankers in charge of financial institutions relatively small command $50,000 or more. The position is not made attractive by life tenure, like that of a justice of the Supreme Court. What sort of ability can be purchased, for a term limited to eight years, for a salary at best not over one-fifth as much per annum as less onerous services would command in private life? Necessarily the political possibilities must become the chief inducement to serve.[33]

Hill concluded that members of the American Bankers Association might be able to help constructively amend the proposed legislation and that, if the new system could not be changed, members of the ABA could consider escaping the anticipated Federal Reserve net by converting to state charters.

Actually, Glass was Jeffersonian in his thinking and preferred a decentralized model. He was also determined that the reserve system should be privately (that is, not Congressionally) controlled. Wilson proposed that the governors of the Fed be appointed by the president and confirmed by Congress, a compromise Glass accepted. Congressman Charles A. Lindbergh Sr. of Little Falls, Minnesota, of the House Banking and

Congressman Carter Glass (second from left) coauthored the Federal Reserve Act of 1913 and served as Woodrow Wilson's secretary of the treasury. In 1932 Glass reunited with past cabinet members. From left: A. Mitchell Palmer, former attorney general; Glass; William Gibbs McAdoo, former secretary of the treasury and Wilson's son-in-law; and Senator John S. Cohen of Georgia.

Currency Committee, was strongly opposed to the bill. Nonetheless, it was signed into law in December 1913, and provided, among other things, that:

- a Federal Reserve System would be headquartered in Washington, D.C., with up to twelve regional banks;

- all national banks would be required to be members and eligible state banks would be invited to join;

- the board could establish minimum capital requirements and set reserve levels for different categories of liabilities;

- the regional reserve banks could accept loans and other assets from members as discount collateral;

- the regional reserve banks would issue Federal Reserve notes as legal tender; and that

- the Office of the Comptroller of the Currency would be required to examine each member bank twice a year.

The law provided that there could be *up to* twelve regional banks. The New York financial district thought that *one* bank—on Wall Street—would be perfect. That location

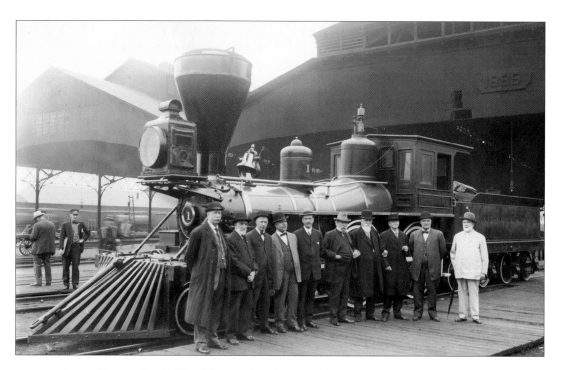

James J. Hill, "the Empire Builder" (far right), celebrates his seventy-fourth birthday in 1912. That same year, Hill stepped down as chair of the Great Northern Railroad and took up banking. The boundaries of the new Ninth Federal Reserve District fell between Hill's northern lines.

would be conveniently absorbed into the New York private banking giants' ongoing dominance of the nation's financial affairs. Grudgingly, big-city bankers allowed that one or two additional banks might be acceptable in, say, Chicago and/or San Francisco. Treasury Secretary William Gibbs McAdoo and Agriculture Secretary David Franklin Houston, however, listened to the populist overtones of the legislation and determined to locate all twelve banks in present and potential financial centers across the nation. The action would prevent New York banks from further dominating the national dialogue on the industry, and encourage communication about banking around the country between central policymakers.

One criterion used in determining the sites of the district reserve banks was access to transportation (read *railroads*), with the intent that the network be designed so that no member bank would be farther than an overnight train trip from the nearest reserve city.[34] A sense of congruency made it logical that the Ninth Federal Reserve District would prove to be the territories served by James J. Hill's "northern lines," both east and west of the Twin Cities.[35] The size of this district was such that a branch office of the Fed was established in Helena, Montana. (Other states in the district were the Dakotas and Minnesota, plus parts of Wisconsin.) St. Paul was strongly proposed as the Ninth District's Federal Reserve city, but it lacked a strong enough advocate. Minneapolis was already perceived as the more dynamic of Minnesota's Twin Cities, and the logic of a strong banking center located in a more diverse business community resulted in the Mill City being designated. Establishment of the Ninth District essentially defined the service areas of the Twin Cities banks and their primary country correspondents. This

In 1922, architect Cass Gilbert designed this Beaux Arts–style building at Fifth and Marquette in Minneapolis to house the new Ninth District's Federal Reserve Bank.

would surface again as the holding companies were put together (and explains the title of this book).

Once the Federal Reserve System was in place, it promptly went to work on its clearinghouse function. One of its first priorities was to achieve universal acceptance at par (face value) of checks issued by member banks. Back then, customers depositing out-of-town checks in their local bank not only were denied use of those funds until they were "collected," they also could be slapped with a variable discount charge on the funds. The collection process involved sending a packet of out-of-town checks to one or more big-city correspondent banks that might have accounts for several of the check writers. The remaining checks would be forwarded by mail to the designated banks around the country. The collection process might take a week or more, although the timing for funds availability was generally three to five days. The discount from par for out-of-town checks could be thought of as a service fee rather than a levy, and it was a meaningful percentage of a small bank's earnings.

The practice of discount as a source of earnings prevailed for sixty-six years until 1979, when the New Orleans Federal Reserve Bank was finally able to advise one of its rural Louisiana members that it was about to become the last "non-par" bank in the country. Rather than accept that doubtful recognition, the Louisiana bank quietly dropped its charge system.

Today, electronic funds transfer has effectively eliminated the collection delay, just as the ATM has facilitated virtually immediate availability of funds for individuals and businesses locally, nationally, and internationally. The business traveler and the tourist in particular are beneficiaries of ATM technology, which has rendered obsolete such long-time (and profitable) fiscal institutional favorites as letters of credit and traveler's checks. As the ATM system has matured, the service fee for "out of town" clients has reappeared.

There was no way to test the capabilities of the Federal Reserve System in dealing with national financial crises until one arose. The concerns of Hill and his peers about the system's potential effectiveness were widely held in the private banking community. But as Carter Glass observed, the old order was gone:

> The Federal Reserve Act revolutionized this wretched system by providing a reserve bank currency based on sound, liquid commercial paper, responsive at all times and to the fullest extent to every reasonable demand of legitimate business. . . . At the same time, it wrecked the old system of reserve deposits which was a breeder of panics.[36]

As neither a fully public nor fully private organization, the U.S. Federal Reserve was both undefined and questioned with regard to its stature and authority. Secretary of the Treasury William McAdoo went to President Wilson, who was also

By 1920, 3,551 banks existed in the Ninth Federal Reserve District, including Winona National Savings Bank. George W. Maher designed the Egyptian Revival–Prairie School building in 1914.

his father-in-law, and inquired about the relative rank of the system among Washington institutions. "I can do nothing about it," Wilson said. "I am not a social arbitrator." "I know that, Mr. President," responded McAdoo, "but they want you to decide." "Decide what?" asked Wilson. "Decide their rank," said McAdoo, "in the scale of social precedence." "Well," said Wilson brightly, "they might come right after the fire department."[37]

HARDSHIPS IN THE UPPER MIDWEST

As a Republican president, Theodore Roosevelt had shaken the traditional standards of his party by advocating strong federal intervention in matters historically thought to be private sector. Popularism

in the banking world argued for easy access and limited supervision, with the thought that small banks would make it simpler for the farmer to find loans or for small businesses to find backing. With wisdom honed by decades of booms and busts in the banking system, and facing a Federal Reserve System of uncertain will and undefined capacity, the bankers of the earlier twentieth century were worried men: worried about the whole system, not only their individual institutions. Branch banking was one of the totemic points of the public/private debate. The populists wanted numbers of small and accessible banks. The more pragmatic bankers argued that this was high risk and that a branch system could provide

Bank Failures in the Ninth Federal Reserve District			
Year	**Failed Banks**	**Year**	**Failed Banks**
1920	35	1925	168
1921	73	1926	283
1922	64	1927	142
1923	279	1928	94
1924	295	1929	84

accessibility without as much risk. At any rate, the argument went back and forth.

In 1920, on the basis of banks per unit of population, the Ninth Federal Reserve District was the most "overbanked" section of the country.[38] In 1920, there were 3,551 banks in Minnesota, North Dakota, South Dakota, and Montana. This proliferation was encouraged by optimism, lax banking laws, and the nominal amount of capital needed to organize a bank. One banker noted that "it actually cost less to start a bank than it did to buy a good farm."[39] Many small rural banks were perennially stretched in providing agricultural credit that could, predictably, become long-term debt. At the same time, they were at the mercy of their city correspondents to make sufficient liquidity available on a continuing basis.

In "Two Bank Groups in the Central Northwest," C. Sterling Popple quotes from a correspondence between a small country banker and Paul J. Leeman, long-time correspondent banker at the First National Bank of Minneapolis. The letters detail the characteristic stickiness of agricultural loans, reliance on weather and prices, and the annually recurring inability

to repay the First National. The correspondence continued from 1917, when the cashier at the small bank was replaced, to the end of 1923, when the small bank failed.[40] What at first seemed to be attractive short-term lending opportunities in the country were too often permanently underwritten by the rural bank, to its ultimate detriment. When farm and crop production were high, for instance, prices would collapse. When prices were good, the weather would turn disastrous.

Historically speaking, the general impression has been that the great wave of banking failures in the United States occurred between 1930 and 1935, during the Great Depression. But the failures actually began and accelerated during the Roaring Twenties. Bank failures in the Ninth Federal Reserve District grew steadily throughout the decade (see chart above).

Total failures in the Ninth District by decade's end, adjusted for a few banks that were recapitalized and reopened, was 1,198—approximately one for every three banks in 1920. Although the Federal Reserve System was well aware of the difficulties facing the industry in the Ninth District and the nation in general, it was neither inclined nor empowered to alleviate the mounting stresses. The Fed did send bankers a series of "letters of concern," cautioning them about speculative lending practices, but the regional bankers believed that their agriculturally based lending was essential, not speculative—at least as long as principal and interest payments were paid when they were due.

Yet the Ninth District Reserve Bank itself (and several of its peers) had unexpectedly developed serious operating problems. The challenge was the disappearance of the Reserve Bank's earning assets. Congress had created the Federal Reserve System with the notion that each of its banks would fund itself through interest income from the discount window: that is, the money that banks would pay to borrow from the Fed against qualified collateral. In 1920, the Minneapolis Fed averaged better than $80 million of daily discounts (loans against "good" collateral) outstanding and earned $5.3 million from that portfolio. As the decade moved along, however, a gradual slowdown in commercial banking activity meant that regional banks had far less need for discount loans. By the end of January 1922, it appeared that the Minneapolis institution, as well as other reserve banks, might not earn enough to cover expenses. In response, the Federal Reserve Banks bought portfolios of Treasury bonds, which generated the necessary income but unwittingly eased

During World War I, women were conspicuously placed in the main floor lobby of the First National Bank of Minneapolis to sell Liberty Loan bonds, which helped finance the fight.

money in local communities and thus further reduced the system's reliance on the Fed's discount window. Inadvertently, the Open Market Committee—a strategic operating function of the Fed—had discovered that it could affect monetary policy. (This committee, which ultimately found it had considerable ability to affect security markets, was originally baptized the Committee on Centralized Execution of Purchases and Sales of Government Securities by Federal Reserve Banks. It was felicitously renamed the Open Market Committee, and operates to this day with occasional great success.)[41]

The Ninth Federal Reserve's problems affected all Twin Cities banks as well as larger banks across the district. The larger banks proposed several strategies that would address the potential failure of small banking facilities in Minneapolis and St. Paul. A long-tenured U.S. Comptroller of the Currency had held that national banks could not establish branches, and thus promulgated struggling and often inefficient smaller banking units. In 1921, however, a new comptroller ruled that national banks *could* operate branch offices within their home cities. Moving quickly, Minneapolis's First National Bank and Northwestern National Bank each opened five branches during 1922.[42] The two banks concluded that such actions would stabilize the local banking scene and that they wouldn't need to expand further in the Minneapolis market. Fine-tuning of their strategy resulted in readjustments of charters, with selected branches

new and old being converted to independent but wholly owned banks and with others continuing as offices. The McFadden Act, when passed by Congress in 1927, did allow limited branch banking within state boundaries, subject to individual state regulations, but prohibited interstate branching. Nearing the end of the 1920s, Minneapolis's First National and Northwestern National Banks had brought a degree of stability to their immediate market area, but both were highly concerned about the potential for further trouble among their country correspondents.

Banks in St. Paul had not been caught up in branch office concerns, nor were they as broadly committed to the universe of country bankers. One difficulty—the failure of the smallish National Exchange Bank in 1926—had been resolved as a joint venture between St. Paul's First National Bank and Merchants National Bank. Together the two institutions restored solvency to the smaller bank, which reopened on the Monday after its closure the preceding Friday under a new name: the Empire National Bank of St. Paul. Primary investors in the recapitalized bank included Louis W. Hill and brewer Jacob Bremer, who had built his own regional banking group. David Shepard, a vice president of the First National Bank of St. Paul, became the Empire's first president. These good Samaritan investments were handsomely repaid in 1930 when the Empire would become a small window in the St. Paul market for a new enterprise known as Northwest Bancorporation.

SECURITY BANK AND TRUST CO., OWATONNA, MINN.—2

Chicago architect Louis Sullivan designed the National Farmers Bank in Owatonna, Minnesota, in 1907. By 1925, it had changed its name to Security Bank and Trust Company.

The ornate interior of Sullivan's National Farmers Bank featured semicircular windows, terra cotta frescoes, and cast-iron ornamentation.

5

BIRTH of the HOLDING COMPANIES

BY 1927, IT'S PROBABLE that at least preliminary thoughts had entered the minds of senior managers of Northwestern National Bank of Minneapolis about the desirability of creating a regional bank holding company. It's possible, however, that the officers of their principal competitors in either of the Twin Cities had no such ideas. The First National Bank of Minneapolis was busy both with its local offices and branches and with its extensive network of regional correspondent banks. The First National Bank of St. Paul was looking over its shoulder at Merchants National Bank, whose aggressive staff was gradually but surely narrowing the gap in size that separated the two entities. But an unexpected offer from New York interests to buy shares in the First National Bank of St. Paul—and thus take ownership of the bank out of Minnesota—made the notion of regional holding companies a more likely reality for the Twin Cities' largest banks.

A FAMILY AFFAIR

Louis W. Hill, chair of the First National Bank of St. Paul after his father, James J. Hill, died in 1917, was surprised to receive a report in November 1927 via the St. Paul brokerage firm of Kalman & Company that Blair & Company of New York was looking to buy blocks of the bank's stock. The sizable Wall Street brokerage had been commissioned to compile a portfolio of strong regional bank stocks for "an Eastern Estate wishing to diversify their portfolio of bank stocks."[43] Blair & Company was looking for holdings of 1,000 or 2,000 shares. First National's directors sent a letter to their relatively few shareholders, asking for a first refusal against any prospective offer.

Louis W. Hill was shocked to learn he was not controlling owner of the First National Bank of St. Paul after the death of his father, James J. Hill.

80

The new First National Bank of St. Paul tower was completed in 1931, a notable feat in the midst of the Great Depression.

Louis W. Hill was the majority shareholder of the First—or so he thought. When his father died without leaving a will, Louis and his mother and siblings (two brothers, six sisters, all married) inherited James J. Hill's considerable assets, including control of the Great Northern Railroad and the First National Bank of St. Paul. One-third of his estate passed to his wife and two-thirds equally to his children. Although Louis, the second son, was chair of the bank board, a majority of the 30,000 outstanding shares of stock were owned by the six Hill sisters, most of whom lived on the East Coast.

The Hill sisters had no great friendship for "L.W.," whom they believed had treated their financial interests with less than brotherly concern. They had been particularly upset when he convinced their mother that their father's North Oaks farm was an unprofitable investment and that he might take it off her hands. She gave him several hundred thousand dollars to defray the costs of that substantial piece of real estate. Several of the sisters subsequently sued their brother, claiming undue influence, but lost. The Hill sisters were further concerned by the lack of growth and nominal return on the bank investment. Thus, it's not surprising they were susceptible to what appeared to be a reasonable offer to buy their stock. Blair & Company's offer to them was for as many as 18,000 shares (60 percent of the total) at $285 per share, or roughly $600,000 for each daughter's interest. Ruth Hill's husband, Anson Beard, was the primary contact with Blair and

served as spokesperson for the East Coast sisters. Beard was a man of short temper, and he had little patience with Louis. He enthusiastically urged acceptance of the Blair offer, but when no progress appeared, he sent his brother-in-law a telegram that reflected both his exasperation and his interest in closing the deal before the end of 1927:

> I SUGGEST THAT YOU AND OSCAR KAHLMAN (sic) PARTICIPATE IN BLAIR SYNDICATE NO DESIRE TO ELIMINATE EITHER OF YOU WILL ASK BLAIR IF YOU WISH AND AM SURE THEY WILL WELCOME YOUR PARTICIPATION CONTRACT READY TO EXECUTE . . . MINIMUM TEN THOUSAND SHARES ANY AMOUNT ABOVE TEN THOUSAND NO STRINGS TO OFFER TOO LATE TO CONSIDER ANY OTHER OFFER WHY DON'T YOU AND KAHLMAN STOP PROCRASTINATING AND PLAY BALL WITH REAL PEOPLE BLAIR CONNECTION WILL BE BENEFICIAL TO BANK AND YOUR CITY.[44]

Louis Hill and Everett Bailey, the bank's former president and current chair of its Executive Committee, took counsel with financier C. O. ("Oscar") Kalman, Hill's long-time confidant. Hill had tallied the share totals and realized, to his surprise, that his siblings' added holdings were sufficient to take control of the bank, despite the stock he owned.[45] Hill and Kalman then took two expeditious steps: First, Hill persuaded his older sister Mary and his younger brother Walter to give him a

After an acrimonious dialogue, the Hill sisters sold their controlling shares in the First National Bank of St. Paul to a syndicate of Blair & Company and to their brother Louis. Seated from left: Rachel, mother Mary T. Hill, and Mary. Standing from left: Clara, Gertrude, Charlotte, and Ruth.

short-term option for their shares, making it impossible for Blair & Company to win control of the bank. Second, Hill and Kalman proposed that Blair assume a 50 percent interest in underwriting the sale of the stocks. Seeing that control of the First was out of reach without messy legal action, Blair agreed to participate. Besides, the new plan would mean a quicker and surer profit, albeit probably less than the control option might have produced.

As loyalists to their brother, Mary and Walter Hill ultimately received $300 per share for their holdings. Blair's share of the purchased stock was reoffered in New York, Chicago, and the Twin Cities at $350 per share. And Louis Hill gained personal control over the bank.

THE CASE FOR HOLDING COMPANIES

The Blair offer was a jolt to the Twin Cities business community. Here was an eastern opportunist making a bold and nearly sufficient offer to buy one of the area's four largest banks. It was common knowledge that A. P. Giannini and his Bank of Italy also were interested in expanding his

California base of banks, and had already made modest purchases of shares in the First National Bank of Minneapolis. Marine Midland, an established bank holding company in upstate New York, had stated its intentions to expand as well. Not only were one or more of the larger Twin Cities banks at risk of being acquired, but so were any of the larger banks in nearby states with whom they did friendly business. Suddenly, the Twin Cities' larger banks had both reason and motivation for creating holding companies: first, Northwest Bancorporation and, on its heels, the First Bank Stock Investment Company.

That motivation was fueled by a classic combination of enlightened self-interest and fear. Enlightened self-interest was the prospect of creating an owned satellite network of banks throughout the service territory, a network that could transcend the challenges of working with poorly financed, weakly managed regional correspondents. The fear factor was more complex. There was fear of state and federal government regulation and/or other interference that might make future joint actions difficult or impossible. There was fear that the Federal Reserve System, as yet untested, might fail in any sustained effort to buoy the banking industry in times of national need. And there was fear that eastern or western interests might want to control the local banks that were so advantageous to regional bank managers. While bankers of that generation maintained their primary fiduciary

duty to depositors, and then to shareholders, a secondary motivation—of making money as individuals—was emerging. Making a profit was not seen as evil; indeed, at times moderate greed on the part of bank owners expedited creation of the holding companies.

Edward Decker, as president of Northwestern National Bank of Minneapolis, headed a large and healthy regional bank with a strong correspondent banking clientele, and was in a unique position in 1928 to start a holding company. Decker was a man of vision who, assisted by others among his bank's officers—including J. Cameron Thomson, David West, and Henry J. Thrall Jr.—determined the form of the proposed corporation. The plan was to offer prospective affiliates an exchange of Northwestern $50 par value common stock for shares of the acquired banks. The stock offer could be supplemented by a partial cash offer to satisfy those shareholders who either didn't approve of the acquisition or chose not to exchange their stock.

The first banks to be contacted—under extremely confidential conditions—all were outside of Minnesota. With frequent changes in state and federal regulations affecting branching and group ventures, Northwestern wanted to establish a priori bridgeheads across state lines as soon as possible. The exploration began with the First National Bank and Trust Company, a $7 million deposit institution in Fargo, North Dakota, then continued with the First National Bank of Mason City, Iowa, and the National Bank of La Crosse, Wisconsin. Each expressed interest in joining the group. Then, just before Christmas in 1928, Decker met with Louis W. Hill to see whether the First National Bank of St. Paul could be added to the new venture. Hill was open to the suggestion and wrote a letter to his bank's president, Cyrus Brown, with his interpretation of the proposal:

In principle [the matter] seems very sound and logical to me, and quite advantageous to our institution—giving St. Paul greater advantage than I supposed we could obtain in such a situation.

Mr. E. W. Decker is convinced that, with consolidations going on as they are in New York, Chicago, St. Louis, Seattle, San Francisco, and in practically all financial centers, we must expect it here, and he wants to take advantage of the situation by getting the choice of the field for his associates, and, if we do not join, it is natural that our next competitor [presumably Merchants National Bank] would likely to at once have the opportunity, and our second choice would be the First Minneapolis for the next grouping, which would not be as favorable for us.

Edward Decker (ca. 1908) became the first CEO of Northwest Bancorporation in 1929.

As I understand it, the plan is not a consolidation and does not affect the directors or management, but contemplates forming a holding company which would hold a majority of stock in various banks. This holding company [is] to be controlled by a voting trust in which St. Paul and Minneapolis would have equal representation.

This is more appealing to me than any form of consolidation would be and would, in my opinion, strengthen our institution in the entire country as well as our Northwest territory. . . .

I have refrained from seeing Mr. Decker and I know he understands I am waiting for an opportunity to go over it with you. If we decide to go ahead, of course, there are a lot of details to be worked out. Of course, if any deal is made, I am assuming that it will be on a basis fair to our institution.[46]

Initially taken with the proposal, Hill discussed it with other of his confidants, including Ralph Budd, president of the Great Northern Railroad, and his friend Oscar Kalman, the investment banker, both of whom served as directors of the bank. Hill also asked the owner and publisher of the *Saint Paul*

Dispatch what they thought. The letter he received from publisher L. E. Owens the day after Christmas was also sent to E. W. Decker:

> I fear that we have left you under the impression that we were in accord with your thought that it would be a good thing for St. Paul for this merger to go into effect.
>
> The plan which you outlined . . . of placing the stock in a trust agreement under which the representatives of the St. Paul institution would always have an equal vote . . . appeared to be a satisfactory solution, but we have since secured an opinion from our counsel that the Courts have held . . . that such an agreement can be upset at any time by the majority interest. . . . It would therefore seem to us that if this plan went into effect, control would rest with the institution having a controlling stock interest, which in this case would be the Northwestern National Bank of Minneapolis.
>
> While we realize that this is not a matter of interest to the stockholders of the banks who are involved in this plan, it is a serious matter to the city of St. Paul. The stockholders of the bank may well view it as a personal institution, but we cannot help but feel that the influence on the prosperity of the city, which is wielded by its largest banking institution, is so great that its ownership becomes a matter of public interest and should largely be vested in the hands of people who have the best interest of St. Paul at heart.
>
> The fact that the First National Bank of St. Paul is its largest banking institution is an evidence of the confidence which the citizens of St. Paul have had in the ownership and management of the bank. We do not believe that this confidence should now be capitalized for dollars to the detriment of the very people who have made it possible.
>
> We are firmly convinced that it would not be for the best interests of the city of St. Paul to have its largest banking institution pass into control of Minneapolis bankers, and therefore we think it is only fair that we should let you know in advance that we will vigorously oppose the consummation of this plan.[47]

Hill took the response from Owens to heart, along with similar counsel he received from Kalman, Brown, and others. His letter of January 2, 1929, to Ralph Budd concluded the overture, although not the concerto to follow:

> I am obliged to you for your note regarding the conversation you had with Mr. Owens of the Dispatch, as to the bank situation. I have learned that the matter is not likely to proceed any further at present so I do not believe we will be further embarrassed by requests for statements. I think the press was very considerate in having withheld the matter as long as they did. As it appears now nothing may come of it, so I think it is much better that they did not make any guesses at it.[48]

There is no doubt that George Prince and Dick Lilly at Merchants National Bank were aware of this brief but portentous courtship. Their reactions must have included several levels of consternation at the proposal and elation at the outcome. Rejection of Decker's proposal would now give them the opportunity to create their own regional banking history.

THE BIRTH OF NORTHWEST BANCORPORATION

Undaunted, Decker forged ahead. Even though the First National Bank of St. Paul had demurred and the National Bank of La Crosse was slow to make a decision, Northwestern National Bank of Minneapolis announced on January 8, 1929, the Delaware incorporation of Northwest Bancorporation, or Banco. The initial membership consisted of Northwestern, the First National Bank of Fargo, and the First National Bank of Mason City, Iowa. Shareholders of the three banks had agreed to exchange their stock for $50 par value shares in the new company. The Weiser family in Fargo and the MacNiders in Mason City influenced enough of their fellow shareholders to ensure that those banks would participate. The mere announcement of the new holding company was enough to bring the La Crosse bank into the fold, and the acquisition race was on. Banco managers were certain that competition, although not then visible, would soon appear, and that they should move with haste to sign up as many of the better banks in the territory as they could. The initial members

provided a buffer to the south and east, so subsequent moves were toward western Minnesota and the prairie states.

Banco thus found itself opening the First National Bank of Moorhead after that area's primary bank, First and Moorhead National Bank, failed in December 1928, a victim of disastrously low prices for potatoes, the region's dominant crop. Banco incorporated the new Minnesota bank, in which it owned 100 percent equity, in response to a distress call by the town's business leaders. As part of the transaction, Banco bought 50 percent of the assets and liabilities of the failed bank. The strategy, known later as the Moorhead Plan, allowed the holding company to assume ownership of the healthy assets from the receiver, and the former bank customers were allowed immediate access to 50 percent of their deposits, with the balance subject to workout.

Moving briskly, Banco announced on February 19 that the First National Banks of Deadwood and Lead, South Dakota, would join the holding company; on February 20, it reported that the Security Bank in Faribault, Minnesota, had also signed up. On the same day, Banco announced it would sell 100,000 shares of its $50 par stock to the public. The proceeds would be used to buy minority interests in acquired banks whose holders chose not to accept a stock-only exchange. This initial public offering was instantly successful—investors apparently stood in line to sign up—and the stock promptly went to a premium.

The Stock Yards National Bank of St. Paul was one of ninety banks bought by Banco in 1929, the holding company's first year of existence.

Minnesota's Fergus Falls National Bank was also acquired by Banco in 1929.

The success of the IPO helped Banco's acquisition plan move rapidly west.

The job of making offers to acquire regional banks for Banco fell to Robert Macgregor, Northwestern National Bank's correspondent relations officer. Since he and his staff maintained account relationships with most banks in the Ninth Federal Reserve District, they could easily identify the best prospects and offer the owners Banco shares in proportion to the value of their individual institutions. As Banco stock was selling well above its stated $50 par value, the purchases were relatively favorable both to the holding company and to the sellers. In effect, Macgregor could peel off stock certificates until even a hesitant seller would concede. In April in South Dakota, he negotiated the acquisition of two banks in Watertown—the Citizens National and the First National—and the Security National in Sioux Falls. In North Dakota, he lined up six small banks owned by the Wells family in the Jamestown area and merged them into the largest one, the James River National Bank. Capping the month's transactions on April 29 was Minnesota's Fergus Falls National Bank.

Willis Wyard helped negotiate acquisitions as part of Macgregor's correspondent bank team. Fifty years later, at a dinner meeting of Banco directors and officers in Duluth, Minnesota, Wyard reminisced about the excitement of the holding company's founding times. He suggested that Banco should publish the history of its early days so that people like him might "tell the *real* story of what went on." CEO Dick Vaughan turned to me and said, "We'll publish the story, but not until *after* Willis is dead." Wyard passed on in due course, and if there *were* unusually colorful stories of Banco's early days, they've probably been forever lost.

In May 1929, Northwest Bancorporation's directors decided that their holding company should have its own management, corporate affairs having been administered to that point by senior staff members of Northwestern National Bank of Minneapolis. Ed Decker would continue as the designated CEO; thirty-eight-year-old J. Cameron Thomson, the bank's vice president of new business, was strongly endorsed for a new position as Banco's vice president and general manager but only after he had visited all of the new country affiliates. Thomson would continue in active management of Banco, as president and then chair, for the next thirty years.[49]

Banco's first-year acquisition program peaked in the early summer of 1929, when it welcomed the newly merged First National and American Exchange National Bank of Duluth. Along with that bank came an occasionally tempestuous relationship with the Congdon family, who, as its major shareholders, were reputed to be the largest block of shareholders of the parent corporation as well. Next came the U.S. National Bank of Omaha, Nebraska, and, in a complex transaction, the First

After First National Bank of Duluth (ca. 1915) merged with American Bank in 1929, the newly named First National and American Exchange National Bank became a key acquisition by Banco.

National Bank of Aberdeen, South Dakota. The latter transaction involved a merger between Citizens Trust and Savings Bank, Dakota National Bank, and First National Bank—all of Aberdeen and all in varying degrees of fiscal exigency. The details of this acquisition are particularly illustrative of the challenges facing bankers in the more remote regions of the Ninth Federal Reserve District, and demonstrate the care with which reorganizations needed to be structured to protect the interests of depositors and borrowers. If there were shortfalls at the end, the board and shareholders might easily be found liable for those errors, whether in commission or omission.

On June 12, the First National Bank of Aberdeen bought the Dakota National Bank of Aberdeen. First National paid Dakota National $20,000 and assumed its deposit liabilities, thereby relieving its directors of their legal responsibility to their former depositors. (Remember that a depositor's *asset*—his account—is the bank's *liability*.) Next, Dakota National agreed to pay First National an amount equal to its liabilities in return for its assumption of risk; the payment consisted of all the high-grade assets, securities, and cash, plus a residuary note

George Prince became chair of the First Bank Stock Corporation in 1929.

covering the balance of the liabilities. As the residual assets were worked out or collected, the proceeds would reduce the residuary note to zero or, better still, beyond zero and thus eliminate the remaining obligations of the selling shareholders and perhaps create a modest profit. On June 14, the First National bought the Citizens Trust on similar terms, except that the former stockholders—and seller of Citizens—*paid* the First National $60,000 as part of the residuary transaction. Banco had already arranged to buy the First National if these agreements were consummated. When they were, Banco executed the purchase.

THE BIRTH OF FIRST BANK STOCK CORPORATION

While Northwest Bancorporation representatives were racing across the Ninth Federal Reserve District with briefcases full of blank stock certificates and cash, seeking and securing new members of their organization, the leading executives of the remaining large Twin Cities banks were not sitting and watching. Inspired perhaps by the *Saint Paul Dispatch*'s eloquent persuasion that convinced Louis Hill not to ally with Banco, George Prince and Dick Lilly, the senior

Frank Prince, president of First National Bank of Minneapolis and brother to George Prince.

C. T. Jaffray enjoyed a fifty-year career with First National Bank of Minneapolis.

officers of Merchants National Bank, were shortly on Hill's doorstep with a new proposal: to merge the two largest banks in St. Paul so as to form an institution strong enough to become a real player in an alternative organization to Banco. In a move that foreshadowed the First Bank System/U.S. Bank merger almost seventy years later, Prince and Lilly proposed that Merchants National acquire Hill's First National on a fifty-fifty basis and continue the combined venture under the name of First National. Although Merchants was somewhat smaller than the First, it was growing more rapidly than the older, more conservative First National. Hill had for some time been monitoring call reports that reflected this growth. (The U.S. Comptroller of the Currency requires that all banks publish a statement of financial condition in an appropriate legal journal four times each year on his call. The calls are approximately but not exactly quarterly, except for December 31 each year, so that individual banks are not likely to enter into unusual transactions to load the books.) Hill made pencil notations on these call reports, commenting with admiration on the rate of growth of the smaller competitor, particularly when he deducted the railroad accounts. He was indeed eager to enter into this merger, even though his interests would receive slightly less due to the proposed fifty-fifty consolidation.

On January 29, 1929, the $10 million merger of the two St. Paul banks was announced and notice was given that they would build an office tower next to and integrated with the existing Merchants National Bank to house their combined operations. Cyrus Brown, president of the First, retired and the Prince/Lilly management team took over, with George Prince as chair and Richard Lilly as president and CFO. Louis Hill continued to hold the title of chair of the board, but his authority would be nominal. He later reflected on his lack of direct involvement in a letter to an old banking friend in Boston. The gentleman had asked for Hill's intercession when First National's new management closed its correspondent account with the First National Bank of Boston. Hill responded that new managers were in charge, that they had not consulted him, and that there was "nothing, in their opinion, which a bank in Boston could do for the First of Saint Paul."[50] Though fully engaged in combining the two banks and building the new headquarters that continues to be a St. Paul landmark, Prince and Lilly were also thinking about the bigger picture.

For a long time the First National Bank of St. Paul and the First National Bank of Minneapolis had enjoyed familial relations. Frank Prince, who had managed First/Minneapolis for almost three decades, was George Prince's older brother. The Minneapolis bank, the largest in that city, was a strong, well-run institution, recognized as both a metropolitan bank with profitable commercial relationships and as a responsible correspondent to a substantial roster of country banks.

Paul Leeman managed the country bank business with a personal and proprietary concern that was severely shaken when he learned, in January 1929, that the First National Bank of Fargo would become one of the founding members of Banco:

> Incredible news, indeed. Fargo was First National's oldest customer, and it carried a large average balance. Mr. Weiser of Fargo denied that there was anything personal in the matter. He was just cooperating with the Northwestern National Bank of Minneapolis in organizing [Banco].[51]

At the same time he was swallowing this news, Leeman discovered that others among his better clients in the Ninth Federal Reserve District had accepted offers of purchase/merger from Banco representatives. The continual newspaper headlines announcing "Banco's latest" infuriated Leeman, and he let C. T. Jaffray, chair of First/Minneapolis, and Lyman Wakefield, its president, know about it.

By the end of March 1929, officers of the First National Banks of Minneapolis and St. Paul designed a scheme to compete head-on with Banco and yet to divide the ownership/management of their new venture equally between the two Twin Cities banks. On April 1, less than ninety days after Banco's introductory announcement, the First Bank Stock Investment Company was incorporated with George Prince as chair of the board and Paul Leeman as president; Lyman Wakefield and Dick Lilly were elected vice presidents. Initial capital

of $1 million was subscribed equally by
the two banks. The intention of the incorporators was that the investment company
would pay cash for the capital stock of
appropriate country banks, which would
continue operating under existing management; as joint investors the two founding banks would not themselves be a part
of the new entity. The first purchase transactions, both in April, were two newly
chartered banks. The first, in Valley City,
North Dakota, was the successor of the
First and Security National Bank; the second, in Fargo, was the newly rehabilitated
Merchants National Bank. In the next
ninety days, the First Bank Stock Investment Corporation bought fifteen more
banks in Minnesota and the Dakotas.

Despite these accomplishments, Paul
Leeman continued to be frustrated. The
charter of First Bank Stock contemplated
purchases of bank capital stock for cash
only. Banco, on the other hand, was
offering cash and/or Banco common
stock. Stock was often considered a more
attractive option because it both deferred
capital gains taxes to the sellers and
allowed an equity opportunity in the
ebullient national stock market. By mid-
August, Leeman found he was losing out
on competitive deals. Worse, he had
spent all of the new investment corporation's initially subscribed capital.
Clearly, the first round of funding had
been aimed too low for the market.

The strategy was quickly improved.
Effective August 21, 1929, the company

shortened its name to First Bank Stock
Corporation ("First Bank Stock") and
simultaneously authorized common stock
to be offered as part of further acquisitions.
The first participants in the new exchange
option were the First National Banks of St.
Paul and Minneapolis (setting a clear
example of their commitment to the
cause), followed by three Montana banks
previously owned by Anaconda Copper:
the Metals Bank and Trust of Butte, the
First National Bank of Great Falls, and the
Western Montana National Bank of
Missoula. In September 1929, First Bank
Stock had its initial public offering of
200,000 common shares at $47.50 per
share. This too was an immediate sellout.
Leeman now had a full quiver of acquisition arrows and went back to work.

Although Leeman was widely respected
in the territory, other banks in the Ninth
Federal Reserve District chose to accept
Banco's offers of merger. To keep up the
competitive pressure, Banco raised $5.7
million more in cash through a secondary-
rights offering of one share for each ten
held at $62 per share. The stock had
behaved strongly during the summer and
was trading at $72 when the new shares
were offered. Not surprisingly, the second
equity issue also sold out promptly.

While First Bank Stock accepted several
smaller banks into its fold, Banco tried to
maintain a $1 million minimum level of
deposits as its acquisition threshold. In the
fall of 1929, Banco's focus shifted to the
south as it picked up several Union Stock

Yards banks in South St. Paul, Minnesota, in Sioux City, Iowa, and in South Omaha, Nebraska. The Iowa–Des Moines National Bank and Trust Company—now the largest bank in Iowa after consolidating three troubled but solvent institutions— joined Banco effective September 19, the same date Banco common stock was listed on the Chicago Stock Exchange.[52] The stock had been strong in the market, peaking September 16 at $100 per share in reaction to speculation that the First National Bank of Minneapolis might become part of the Banco group. Lyman Wakefield, president of First/Minneapolis, had listened earlier to such a proposal but turned it down, arguing that First National and Northwestern National were too similar to achieve much synergistic savings and that there could well be anti-trust concentration concerns. As Banco stock slipped to $80 after the decision leaked out, First/Minneapolis exchanged its stock for First Bank Stock shares.

Further merger activity by Banco during September brought in Midland National Bank and Metropolitan National, two midsized banks in Minneapolis; the Great Falls National Bank of Montana; and the Spokane and Eastern Trust Company of Washington State, the westernmost outpost of the Banco empire for fifty years. Metropolitan National was merged into Northwestern National in Minneapolis; Midland was continued as an individual entity. The Union Investment Company also was purchased, with its ownership of thirty-one smaller banks. Some Banco

managers proposed that Union Investment should act as a holding company within the holding company (for smaller affiliates), and that Theodore Albrecht, Union's erstwhile owner, manage the smaller institutions from Banco's Minneapolis office. This condition lasted until May 1931, when the Union Investment portfolio of banks and their employees were folded into the Banco structure.

This flurry of activity once again consumed the bulk of Banco's working capital, so the corporation retained A. G.

Metropolitan National in Minneapolis was merged into Northwestern National as Banco acquired banks for its new holding company.

Becker as investment banker to underwrite a second rights offering—again at one additional share for each ten held, but priced this time at $82.50 per share against a going market of $85. Had all gone well, the sale would have raised some $12 million. But the timing was off. While the market had not yet crashed, by the end of September 1929 Wall Street was beginning to fray and Banco's shares fell abruptly to the mid-$70s. This prompted the underwriters to suggest lowering the offering price to $72.50, and encouraged Becker to expand the underwriting group to some seventy-five national brokerage firms. The rights were mailed to shareholders on October 30, but that timing also was atrocious: the stock market broke sharply on Black Monday—October 28—and Banco's stock fell to $50 per share, wiping out the rights value and making the offering moot.

Banco exercised its legitimate prerogative to put the stock to the underwriting syndicate, forcing it to buy the entire issue at $72.50 per share. The group was still strong enough to meet those commitments and Banco netted $10 million—funds that would prove critically valuable over the next few years. The underwriters managed to place about half of the offering and finally came back to Ed Decker, hats in hand: could he help them with sale of the balance? Decker suggested that a local group might be formed to take the last 72,000 shares off the syndicate's hands at $50 per share. Not only did he locate a sufficient number of local

investors to close the deal, but Decker also took a substantial part of the shares for his personal account—a transaction that would soon take him into bankruptcy. Decker also encouraged other officers and employees of Northwestern National Bank to buy holding-company stock with an attractive, low-interest-rate financing package.[53] Some of those employees finished paying off their loans when the stock was worth far less than they had paid for it. In fact, it was not until 1958 that the price of the stock recovered to its levels of 1929 and the early 1930s.

By the end of 1929, Banco had acquired ninety banks in seventy-five communities, serving about 5 percent of the residents of the Ninth Federal Reserve District. Resources of the associated banks totaled $468.8 million. In 1930, Banco added another thirty-one banks to its group. Twelve were solvent and voluntary acquisitions; nineteen, however, were problematic and likely would have failed without the intervention. The prices paid for the marginal banks were sharply adjusted to reflect the distressed assets. Among the 1930 newcomers was the Empire National Bank, a second-tier player in the St. Paul market but the largest available option remaining in that city.

In 1930 Northwestern National Bank completed its new office building in downtown Minneapolis. With a lobby modeled after the Continental Illinois Bank in Chicago—with its second-level banking floor, midfloor islands for officers, and rows of tellers along the sides—it was a handsome and imposing representation of security and conservative banking. The building would serve as home for both the bank and the holding company for half a century. The Banco family was joined in its new home by two businesses that were professionally close to the bank: Faegre and Benson, its legal counsel, and Campbell-Mithun, its advertising firm.

During 1931, Banco wound up its initial acquisition program with eleven new banks. The First National Bank of Denison, Iowa, was the last of these transactions, completed on August 5. The makeup of Banco was thus set for several decades. About one-third of its assets were Minneapolis affiliates; the balance was geographically distributed from Wisconsin to Washington State. While the non-Minneapolis members included the largest and strongest banks in Iowa and Nebraska, as well as substantial banks in other states, Banco didn't have the secure earnings streams of the Twin Cities' two First National Banks. This difference meant that the Great Depression would prove to be more difficult for Banco than for First Bank Stock.

Toward the end of *its* first year, First Bank Stock Corporation sent a progress report to its shareholders, recounting three months of frenzied activity. The company identified itself as "strictly a Ninth District institution," with thirty-six affiliates in eighteen Minnesota cities, thirteen in Montana, twelve in North Dakota, ten in South

Dakota, and three in Upper Michigan. These seventy-four entities had capital accounts of $49.9 million and resources of $444 million. The report was sanguine and, with a good deal of optimism, clearly underprepared for what was to come:

Although less than three months old and still in the organization and expansion period of its initial development, operations to date of the First Bank Stock Corporation have been most satisfactory and the board of directors has established

Construction of the new First National Bank of St. Paul tower proceeded in 1931. The bank's existing offices are visible in the shaded building in the center of the photograph.

a dividend rate of one dollar a share and declared a quarterly dividend of 25 cents, a share payable January 1 to stock-holders of record as of December 21.

Banks in the group are showing a marked increase in deposits and are winning new customers in large numbers.

Plans for extension of the facilities of the individual banks to afford even greater service to their communities are now being developed.

The immediate future of the Northwest appears bright. Conditions are sound and healthy, and prospects for the coming year are most favorable.[54]

The managing officers for the new company had been slightly rearranged. C. T. Jaffray was now serving as chair, with George Prince as president, Dick Lilly and Lyman Wakefield as vice presidents, and Paul Leeman as vice president and general manager. Prince could not resist the opportunity to end his shareholders' message with a new business plug:

As a stockholder and partner in this system, you are naturally interested in its development and prosperity. Stockholders can aid this development by their patronage of affiliates of the Corporation. Your account will be welcomed by any unit of the group. Their facilities to serve you are unsurpassed.[55]

Before year-end 1929, First Bank Stock would add another eleven institutions to its roster. January and February of 1930 brought in six more banks and the

board—recognizing the increasingly difficult national economic picture—agreed to suspend solicitation of further affiliations. It proved difficult to turn away long-term relationships, however, and another twenty-four banks were picked up in 1930. As C. Sterling Popple noted in his thesis, "In some cases the owners received shares of First Bank Stock Corporation in exchange for their stock; in some they received nothing; and in a few situations they were obliged to contribute cash to cover existing losses. In every instance, however, the depositors were fully protected."[56]

In November 1930, trust operations conducted by the Northwestern Trust Company and Merchants Trust Company were melded into the newly chartered First Trust Company, with Philip L. Ray as president. In 1931, First Bank Stock acquired seven banks, which were the last additions to that enterprise for thirty years. During this period, the assets of First Bank Stock were divided into approximate thirds: one-third representing the First National Bank of Minneapolis, one-third representing the First National Bank of St. Paul, and the balance representing all other banks. The corporate dividend, announced with substantial pride, was well covered by the internal dividends of the two big banks.

Despite the heady days of creation and early rapid growth, however, neither holding company could have predicted the subsequent years of fallout from the 1929 stock market crash. The decade of the Great Depression was just beginning.

THE SCORE CARD – 1930

Northwest Bancorporation		First Bank Stock Corporation
115	Number of Banks	85
$409,965,000	Total Deposits	$384,814,000
$222,905,000	Total Loans	$184,733,000
$66,423,000	Capital & Surplus	$42,193,000
1,674,000	# Common Shares	3,093,800
56½ – 30¾	Market Range High/Low	35½ – 19¾
	Per Common Share	
$3.87	Earned	$1.93
$1.80	Dividend	$1.00
$33.81	Book Value	$13.64
4.1%	Yield*	3.6%
$45,956,250	Market Capitalization*	$58,747,400
	Per 2000 Common Share	
$0.027	Earned	$0.039
$0.013	Dividend	$0.020
$0.303	Market Price*	$0.564

* based on average market price

99

Americans barely had a chance to catch their breath between the deprivations of the Depression and their sacrifices at home and abroad during World War II. But between 1941 and 1945, they showed their patriotism by buying war bonds from local banks. Here, a crowd at Powers Department Store in Minneapolis does its duty.

II
Struggles to Survive
1931–1945

YEARS of TRIAL

THE YEAR 1929 had taken bankers in the Ninth Federal Reserve District on an incredible roller coaster ride. The newly created Minnesota holding companies of Northwest Bancorporation and First Bank Stock Corporation together had signed up 150 banks in eight states with total assets of some $800 million. Yet the regional banking environment continued to disintegrate, while the national economy showed the leading edge of what would become the Great Depression. The stock market was symptomatic of this volatility; the price of Banco's common stock doubled from $50 to $100 per share, only to be sold for $30 per share after Black Tuesday. By the end of 1929, many of the banks becoming available to the holding companies were in trouble, either emerging from mergers or reorganizations or targeted by state banking authorities for the holding companies to help. The hardships of the 1930s would test the fundamental reasons for the creation of the Minnesota twins.

JUSTIFYING HOLDING COMPANIES

Not everyone had thought that the holding companies were a good idea to begin with. In an editorial dated July 19, 1929, the *Minneapolis Journal* described the process as "a revolution in banking" and went on, in tones that would be repeated for decades, to share its concern about the merits of group banking:

> Big things are happening among the financial institutions of the Northwest. Large banks in many communities are becoming members of group systems, headed by gigantic holding companies.
>
> What is to be the outcome of it all? Will branch banking eventually become universal, as in Canada and England?
>
> Is there a future for unit (independent) banks?
>
> The independent banker is asking these questions. The small town businessman also wants to know what is to become of him.
>
> Will it be possible under the group system for the independent merchant, the small manufacturer, to obtain loans as promptly and as adequately as he gets them from the independent bank? Will the touchstone of character lose its potency for the small borrower and his credit?[1]

In a series of articles following the editorial, the *Minneapolis Journal* discussed the pros and cons of group banking, but couldn't resolve the big questions it had posed. "Branch banking" was an amorphous term that haunted the industry, but clearly it was presumed to be malicious, cited by foes of holding companies as being bad for independent banks and, by inference, bad for the community at large. The industry had no rebuttal but "wait and see." History does tell us that Banco and First Bank Stock kept their member banks from failure during the Depression at considerable cost to the holding company's shareholders, while all about them independent banks shut their doors. History would have to add that keeping a bank open in a rural community was almost synonymous with keeping alive the town—that is, the auto dealer, the hardware store, the farm equipment company, the grain elevator.

The Madison *Capital Times,* a Wisconsin daily, also went on record with its concern about Wisconsin Bankshares Corporation,

founded in a defensive response to Banco and First Bank Stock acquisitions in that state. The reporter wrote with more vitriol than his Minneapolis counterpart, but the concern was the same, and would continue to dog Minnesota's twin holding companies:

In the financial world today, there are great grasping forces at work seeking consolidation and monopoly control over the many individual, self-governing financial institutions spread far and wide over our country. Small banks are induced to join these great chains by terms so liberal that they resemble bribery, or credit coercion is used to force them to capitulate to the will of the chain organizations. Once they are in the chain, the heads of the local banks find themselves shorn of their power of acting independently.

When the stock market crashed on Black Tuesday—October 29, 1929—it marked the beginning of the Great Depression. Americans would not place their trust in Wall Street again until after World War II.

It is hard to believe that the purpose of this great movement to found a group of financial empires in the United States is other than to give the great money centers of the country a means to exploit the small communities. The advertisements, of course, broadcast that their purpose is to secure "increased stability, better efficiency," etc., but isn't "increased profits" more likely to be the real result behind these great consolidations?[2]

In the cosmic scheme of things, an increase in earnings is always one measure of the success of a bank holding company, just as it is for any for-profit business. However, in 1929 and in the years immediately following, the claims of depositors were a much higher priority for bank managers and directors, since depositor losses could become a lien against a bank director's personal assets. Thus, any candidate to be acquired by a holding company was analyzed for the quality of its assets and the likelihood that it could cover the liability of depositors' savings. The sellers were likely to have paid the shortfall rather than assume liability for the deposits. They would leave that risk to the holding companies.

One of the hopes expressed by Carter Glass and his fellow Congressmen in establishing the Federal Reserve System was that it would provide those financial reserves deemed necessary to keep the banking industry healthy. In fact, *unless* a bank borrowed from the Fed, the agency had little leverage with which to increase

stability. The central bank was still experimenting to see what effect the few tools it had might have on either liquidity or interest rates. On February 7, 1929, the Fed wrote letters "strongly urging all member banks to refrain from making speculative loans. For a few weeks some restraint was exercised but it didn't last. The boom atmosphere and the fact that paper profits were huge made it impossible for banks and other lenders to say no to customers."[3]

In 1928 and 1929, the Fed acted ambivalently. On the one hand, it sold $275 million in U.S. Treasury securities, sopping up some of the banking system's rampant excess credit. On the other hand, it was lending more than $500 million at the discount window. After the October 1929 crash, the Fed dropped its discount rate from 6 percent to 5 percent on November 1, and again to 4½ percent on November 15. It was then that the system realized that these actions had had virtually no effect. It wasn't that the banks lacked the will or the capacity to lend money, but rather that borrowers lacked the will and the need to borrow. The country was assuming a creeping paralysis, a mantle of despair, and it would take more than an interest-rate carrot to entice clients back.[4]

We tend to think of the stock market "crash" as being the cause rather than a symptom of the Depression. The postwar boom had been running for a decade and had effectively run out of steam. The market, as usual, was somewhat behind the economy, and had risen to a high, measured

Quelling customer fears about secure funds was a priority for banks during the Depression. In this 1933 promotional image, loyal clients line up to deposit money at the First National Bank of St. Paul.

by the Dow Jones Industrial Average, of 352.69 in mid-October 1929. The index dropped steadily in the next two weeks, losing 51.5 points or 14.5 percent, before the market's opening bell on Black Tuesday, October 29. That day the index dropped by 40.6 points to 260.24, or a further decline of 13.4 percent. These were major adjustments, but they were not to be the worst of the market news. Six months later, on June 2, 1930, the averages had worked their way up a bit to 274.45. The next two adjustments were psychologically "the Depression." Business across the country was in malaise; earnings were minimal and dividends often suspended. Unemployment was a concern to private and public organizations alike. The market paralleled the reality of the economy, declining to a numbing

41.22 on July 8, 1932; this was a drop of more than 88 percent from the October 1929 peak. After that nadir, things got better: the Dow doubled in the next year and added 50 percent more in the following six months. This was a partial recovery, however, and it would not be until after World War II that the American people returned to Wall Street.[5]

The general economy worsened in each of the four years between 1929 and 1933, and the business bankruptcies sweeping the country did not spare the Twin Cities. Larger failures occurring locally included Wilbur Foshay's utility holding company empire, the Minnesota and Ontario Paper Company, commercial real estate entity Baker Properties, the Nicollet Hotel, and the Minneapolis Theatre

Ninth Federal Reserve District Loans & Deposits by Area 1929–1933				
Year	City Bank Loans	Country Bank Loans	Country Bank Deposits	Number of Banks
1929	$239,000,000	$696,000,000	$1,180,000,000	2,353
1930	226,000,000	611,000,000	1,082,000,000	2,118
1931	222,000,000	478,000,000	879,000,000	1,816
1932	176,000,000	384,000,000	704,000,000	1,658
1933	177,000,000	288,000,000	616,000,000	1,448
% decline	-25.9%	-58.6%	-48.8%	-38.5%

Company. Smaller bankruptcies were commonplace. Farm prices continued to deteriorate and copper, iron, and coal mines were effectively closed as raw material prices were too low to cover the costs of mining. General business did continue, in limited fashion, with tight managerial controls on inventories, borrowing, employment, and production. Gross farm income in 1932 was the lowest since 1912.

The bad news was universal, but statistics for the Ninth Federal Reserve District demonstrate how much more seriously the impact of the recession fell on country banks as compared to their city brethren. In percentage decline, the country banks suffered more than twice as badly as did city banks. The Ninth Federal Reserve District also saw a continuation of the consolidation and liquidation of banks that had characterized this "overbanked" district from its beginnings. A decade earlier, the area had been home to more than 3,100 banks. The numbers of banks

in these five years alone dropped by almost 40 percent.

Surviving banks outside the money centers faced one of two concerns during the 1930s. The first, and the better known, was problem loans. Country banks in the Ninth District saw their agricultural and mining loans continue to deteriorate and be written off for the balance of the decade. The second but more positive concern—which had an impact on the larger, more urban banks—was an absolute shortage of good earning assets.

The First National Bank of St. Paul, for example, had a sound portfolio of U.S. Treasury securities whose value exceeded total deposits, but the bank was challenged from an earnings perspective. Most of its commercial clientele had cancelled building programs, reduced staff, and cut back inventories to survive the extended Depression, and therefore were borrowing little. But First National's vice president Dick Lilly had earlier invested the bank's portfolio in a little known and even less understood security called Veterans Adjusted Service Certificates. These government-backed notes carried a significantly higher rate of return than traditional Treasury bonds. Lilly's younger brother Leonard became the bank's resident expert on these arcane certificates. During the late 1930s, the First/St. Paul also became a substantial buyer of home-improvement loans issued under Title I of the National Housing Act. The bank gradually earned a national reputation as a lender on nontraditional assets—insurance premium installment loans, barges, airplanes, and diesel locomotives.[6]

Earnings from unusual investment and lending risks at the First National Bank of St. Paul, together with a relatively strong commercial loan base for the First National Bank of Minneapolis, meant that there was an uninterrupted flow of dividends paid upstream to the holding company during the 1930s. The internal dividends supported the overhead of First Bank Stock Corporation, covered its public dividend, and helped rebuild the damaged capital funds of smaller affiliates. The big "1st" sign blinking in red neon atop the newly finished First/St. Paul banking tower was especially symbolic during the Depression as it reinforced the existence of a strong, resourceful bank.

CAPITAL PROBLEMS AT BANCO

Across the Mississippi in Minneapolis, in the equally new, sixteen-story office building of Northwestern National Bank, matters were not so rosy. On the one hand, more banks, many of them troubled, were seeking the shelter that had been offered by Northwest Bancorporation in happier days. Whenever possible, Banco had consummated these acquisitions, but by mid-1931 the till was essentially empty.

On the other hand, the agreement with earlier acquisitions had been that their managers would be left in place with

A uniformed employee greeting customers at the entrance to Minneapolis's Northwestern National Bank added to their comfort level.

nominal supervision and with the expectation that they would keep the holding company apprised of opportunities and problems. As rapidly as it could, Banco brought selected employees of its affiliates into Minneapolis for extra training in credit analysis by corporate auditors who were simultaneously installing a uniform system of accounts so that the corporation would have a consistent information base.

In addition to capital shortfalls among country affiliates, a further challenge in 1931 for Banco was a decline in earning assets, leading corporate management to endorse a policy of making low-risk loans whenever possible. In 1932, it became apparent that things were going to get worse. A suggested schedule of transaction and service fees was proposed to bolster income, while new loans (especially those eligible for discount borrowing at the Fed) were still encouraged. Loan losses among a few of the group member banks, however, were becoming a serious matter. The Bank of Spearfish, a small South Dakota bank with a disproportionate number of cattle-based loans, was a case in point. As the price of beef continued to slide, loan write-offs and the required replacement capital exceeded the total of existing capital, surplus accounts, *and* deposits of the Spearfish bank. As banking historian C. Sterling Popple said:

> Legally the Northwest Bancorporation could have avoided liability by letting the bank fail, paying a $25,000 assessment and washing its hands of the entire

affair. Instead, it stood squarely behind its avowal that no depositor should ever lose a penny in a Bancorporation bank.[7]

Thirty-nine Banco affiliates required a further capital transfusion during this period, more than testing the corporation's reserves. In the fall of 1932, Banco underwent an accounting makeover, writing off intangibles and goodwill, converting its capital stock from $50 par to no par, and establishing a $14 million contingency reserve. The reorganization was timely and necessary, but unsettling to Banco shareholders and the general public.

PANIC TAKES HOLD

In January and February 1933, the country's spasmodic series of bank runs by nervous depositors reached the Ninth Federal Reserve District, and while no affiliate bank of either holding company was to fail, they were not immune from customer panic. Three stories affecting Banco are typical of the times.

The first story begins with a telephone call to Northwestern National Bank in Minneapolis from Security National Bank and Trust Company, an affiliate in Faribault, Minnesota, reporting that several farmers had come to the bank, alarmed about the status of their deposits. Anticipating trouble at the next morning's opening, Northwestern loaded a car with cash and sped from Minneapolis an hour south to Faribault, escorted by police officers. Upon their arrival, announced by sirens blaring and lights flashing, the bankers and the guards ostentatiously carried the large bundles of bills into the Faribault bank and stacked it at the tellers' cages. The run evaporated.[8]

The second tale, involving the First National Bank of Grantsburg, Wisconsin, has a movielike quality. H. A. Anderson, president of the small bank, telephoned Northwestern to report that his depositors were "running" his bank. This time Northwestern chartered an airplane, an unusual event in itself, and had the requisite bundles of cash delivered to Grantsburg about an hour after the call. Again, all those requesting withdrawal of their balances were paid in full.[9]

The third and final story is less dramatic but broader in scope. The Spokane and Eastern Trust Company, Banco's sole affiliate in Washington State and its farthest western outlet, reported by telephone that it was suffering a run. Not only was it low on vault cash, it had also used its collateral with the Federal Reserve for discount borrowings. Northwestern added the necessary collateral to the Fed account and wired Spokane that it was OK. And it was.[10]

During the Depression, many bank customers felt more secure when they kept cash and other valuables stashed in safe deposit boxes, such as those at National Exchange Bank of St. Paul.

First Bank Stock's most dramatic Depression-era rescue was that of the Western Montana National Bank in Missoula. The affiliate had long been recognized in the region as an aggressive lender, but that sort of reputation in 1932 was not necessarily good. In June of that year, a run began that appeared likely to drain the bank's resources. Management wired for cash from the Helena branch of the Ninth Federal Reserve Bank, but was told it had exhausted its collateral. The Fed quickly contacted First Bank Stock, which posted sufficient collateral in Minneapolis to cover all of Western Montana's deposits.[11]

BANKING TAKES A HOLIDAY

In Washington, the Federal Reserve System continued to dither. President Herbert H. Hoover wrote its chair, Eugene Meyer, to say that the Federal Reserve seemed more concerned about the strength of European central banks than about the U.S. banking system. Meyer replied that the Fed "was working on the problem."[12] As in 1929 and 1930, actions taken by the Federal Reserve in 1931 were inconclusive. Although it had purchased securities in the open market to increase liquidity and had lowered the discount rate from 4 percent to 2 percent, neither action had a visible effect on the economy. So in 1932 the Fed sold securities and raised the discount rate back to 3½ percent. Those reverse actions also had no effect.

Before Franklin D. Roosevelt's inauguration in March 1933, President Hoover made one more appeal to the Federal Reserve. On February 22, he sent a plaintive note to the board, saying, "I wish to leave no stone unturned for constructive action." The response was unanimous: "At the moment, the Board does not desire to make any specific proposals for additional measures or authority, but will continue to give all aspects of the situation its most careful consideration."[13] As the picture worsened across the country, several governors declared state banking holidays of varying lengths. They hoped that such "quiet time" would give banks and their clients a chance to regain stability, and that orderly banking transactions might begin again. In Minnesota, however, populist governor Floyd B. Olson declared on March 2 that there would be no such holidays in his state. Still, a general uncertainty existed due to the growing number of states with closed banks.

Congress, the federal government, and the Federal Reserve all had tried anxiously to do whatever they could to help the economy and the banking system, but nothing meaningful happened until Roosevelt's inauguration on Saturday, March 4, 1933. Almost immediately, the new president declared a national bank holiday, from Monday, March 6, through Friday, March 10. It was ironic that the only legal tool his administration could use to order the closings was the Trading with the Enemy Act of October 1917. The legislation allowed the president to proceed on the hypothesis that foreign banking activities were undermining U.S. currency.

While Banco's relieved officers used the weeklong holiday to catch up on reserve allocations, managers of the two principal institutions of First Bank Stock were taken aback. Lyman Wakefield, president of the First National in Minneapolis, had just called on the Minneapolis Fed to confirm that it would continue to accept eligible paper (that is, superior-quality loans) as collateral for discount borrowing. Wakefield was assured that such policy not only would continue but would be further reinforced by Governor Olson's no-bank-holiday pronouncement. M. O. Grangaard of First/Minneapolis thus advised correspondent bankers in writing that the holding company would continue to meet their cash needs without interruption. Those letters were just going into the mail on Friday, March 3, when Minnesota's lieutenant governor announced that the state would declare a bank holiday after all. Grangaard was able to retrieve most of his letters from the post office.

Predictably, the next day, a Saturday, was "a banking nightmare":

> Gordon Murray, still some years from becoming President of First National, and several other young clerks were stationed at the front door to try to placate the throng of angry and befuddled customers. "They were all screaming and demanding their money," he remembers, "and I almost got myself killed—or so it seems now." Evan Johnson, then the Assistant Comptroller, recalled that the holiday decision was

phoned to critical employees around 4:00 a.m. and they were asked to come in by 6:00. "At 8:00 the phones started ringing and never stopped."[14]

Under president R. C. Lilly, the First National Bank of St. Paul built a national reputation as a lender on nontraditional assets.

Dick Lilly had bragged on more than one occasion that the First National of St. Paul would never have to close, so assistant cashier George M. Robbins was astounded to receive a phone call that Saturday at 8:00 a.m. announcing that the bank would not be opening that day. Robbins was particularly confused since the call had come not from one of his superiors, but from a clerk at the Ninth Federal Reserve. Fortunately, Lilly and George Prince arrived before the 9:00 opening hour to confirm that the news was indeed true.

The remainder of the holiday week was surrealistic. Tellers were on duty but permitted to make change only. Staff played bridge and listened to the radio for news of government actions to end the holiday.[15]

President Roosevelt may have had the legal means by which to shut down the nation's banking system, but he had neither the authority nor the criteria for determining how and when to reopen it. On March 9, he called a special session of Congress to ask for the powers and restrictions necessary to reopen the banks as quickly as possible. In just an hour, the U.S. Senate Banking Committee reported a bill into the full Senate, which approved it; the House had already adopted it, although it was impossible that any member could have read the bill in that brief time. On March 10, Roosevelt authorized reopening those banks deemed sufficiently liquid. First to reopen on Monday, March 13, were the regional Federal Reserve Banks themselves. On Tuesday, banks located in Federal Reserve Bank communities were permitted to resume business. They included the Twin Cities' two First National Banks and Northwestern National Bank. On Wednesday, banks in 250 additional communities across the country opened their doors, and the remaining healthy banks were welcomed back on Thursday.[16] Toward the end of the banking holiday, larger banks had been allowed to accept deposits, and by the following Tuesday, things began to return to normal for the holding companies and the state of Minnesota. Well, almost normal:

Everyone came to work early (on March 14). Photo enlargements of the license to reopen were posted throughout the lobby, along with the U.S. Treasury's new warnings about gold and silver hoarding. Tellers were literally buried in money. One downtown store alone brought in over $200,000 in currency. The proof department (of the First/Minneapolis) handled 130,725 items, compared to the usual 50–60,000 daily total.[17]

THE LAWS OF BANKING

After decades of ignoring the banking industry, Congress passed three sets of laws in the early years of the Depression to help solve real and perceived problems affecting banks: the Emergency Banking Act of 1933 and, in late 1933, the Reconstruction Finance Corporation, both preceded by the Glass-Steagall Act of 1932.

Carter Glass, father of the Federal Reserve System, had served as secretary of the treasury at the end of Woodrow Wilson's second term, and since 1920 had been a U.S. senator. Glass had been concerned for some time about bank-financed speculation as a contributor to the market collapse and to the Depression, and was therefore determined that the investment banking components of the larger banks become legally separate entities. The Glass-Steagall bill prohibited national and state member banks from underwriting or owning equity securities and from affiliating with securities dealers. The bill also prohibited interlocking directorates between banks and security dealers, and, to the relief of First Bank Stock and Banco, limited the size of holding company boards to no more than twenty-five members. At the end of 1931, Banco had 132 directors on its board; First Bank Stock had eighty.

The Emergency Banking Act of 1933 prohibited interest payments on demand (checking) deposits; created the FDIC—the Federal Deposit Insurance Corporation—to insure depositor accounts up to $2,500; gave the Federal Reserve authority to impose interest-rate ceilings on time (savings) deposits; and reinforced the Open Market Committee to regulate member bank transactions in government securities. It also extended the authority of the bank examination process to include affiliates. One observer commented that the Banking Act was belt-and-suspender legislation—that if the examination process were managed well, the insurance provision would be moot.

Instrumental in writing the Emergency Banking Act was Marriner Eccles, whom Roosevelt appointed as chair of the Federal Reserve System in November 1934. This strong-minded Mormon served until 1948 and gave the Federal Reserve a firm sense of purpose as new legislation was implemented. Eccles was the first Federal Reserve president to have a decisive impact on the banking and securities industries. There would be no more dithering.

The Reconstruction Finance Corporation was the third leg of Congress's efforts to restore the U.S. banking system. Funded by the government, the RFC had the power to make direct investments in qualifying but struggling businesses, including banks and bank holding companies. The expectation was that enabling these companies to rebuild a necessary level of capital strength would then help them regain profitability and thus repay RFC advances. In return, the RFC staff could look over management's shoulders and make suggestions as to how to run the business.

Federal regulators had advised Banco that its banks would not qualify for the new FDIC depositor insurance unless and until the banks had capital funds equal to 10 percent of their deposits. Few Banco banks could meet that test. In September 1933, the Banco board authorized creation of an ad hoc committee, to be chaired by J. Cameron Thomson, the holding company's president, and supported by directors John Crosby and Frank Heffelfinger, to prepare a plan for submission to the RFC. In December, Thomson reported back to the board that an arrangement had been made with the RFC—supposedly the most complex agreement that body had yet approved. The essence of the plan was that all Banco member banks would write down their assets to bedrock values, charge off those write-downs against capital, and then sell a special issue of preferred stock to the RFC to restore the necessary level of capital. Under terms of the agreement, Banco affiliates were required to apply 40 percent of net earnings to retirement of the RFC preferred stock, and no dividends were allowed on Banco common stock without the RFC's consent. The accompanying table (below) reflects the substantial decline in Banco's capital position during the 1930s as the result of write-downs and charge-offs.

While the RFC invested more than $25 million in Banco's special preferred stocks, the table also reflects the holding company's inherent strength as deposits had already begun moving up in 1934–1935 and corporate earnings were already allowing substantial repayments to the RFC. Per-share dividends on Banco common stock, which had been initiated in 1930 at $1.80 per share, were reduced to $0.80 in 1932, then suspended until 1939 when the last of the RFC investment had been repaid. The $1.80 per share dividend level was not reached again until 1951.

On balance, the case of Banco demonstrates that the Reconstruction Finance Corporation approach was effective, and that the bank holding company regained its fiscal health relatively promptly.

Echoes of this sort of success must have encouraged Congress in the 1970s when it created the Resolution Trust Company to address the fiasco of the savings and loan industry. The Resolution Trust Company was far more hands-on and draconian than the RFC, in that its principal weapon would be foreclosure and liquidation of the damaged thrift entities.

HOLDING COMPANIES ON TRIAL

By the close of the 1930s, Banco and First Bank Stock would see light at the end of the fiscal tunnel as deposits recovered and loans and earnings soon followed. Politically, however, challenges remained. Minnesota governor Floyd B. Olson was convinced that the holding companies were, in the words of the Independent Bankers Association, engaged in "outrageous financial debauchery." It has long been a political no-brainer to attack the banks—and bank holding companies—as enemies of the people, gouging the little man and evicting widows and orphans. It is equally easy to overlook matters

RESTORING BANCO CAPITAL WITH RFC ASSISTANCE

Year	Deposits	Capital	RFC Invest	Combined w/Minority	% of Deposits
1930	$409,965,000	$66,423,000	0	$68,923,000	16.8%
1931	342,398,000	49,854,000	0	52,465,000	15.3
1932	290,210,000	29,259,000	0	31,700,000	10.9
1933	290,282,000	10,319,000	$25,534,000	37,384,000	12.9
1934	358,734,000	11,849,000	24,979,000	38,393,000	10.7
1935	360,381,000	19,155,000	16,970,000	37,657,000	10.4

perceived to be of remote interest to the voter, such as shoring up the region's banking system, facilitating home ownership, and enabling business development.

So it was with Olson's blessing that the State Commerce Commission initiated an investigation of Northwest Bancorporation in November 1933. The inquiry was based on a charge filed by Herman Bosshard, who had bought Banco stock in December 1931. Bosshard was distressed that his stock had gone down, not up, and that the dividend had been almost immediately reduced. The grand jury refused to indict since it could find no evidence of fraud. Yet Bosshard was prevailed upon to swear out a warrant for the arrest of twenty of Banco's officers and directors and bring them to trial on charges of fraud.

Governor Olson's strategists had selected the agricultural town of Moorhead as the trial venue, thinking that a jury of aggrieved farmers would be likely to accept the accusations. The first defendant was Banco president J. Cameron Thomson. Bosshard was represented by the state attorney general's office. The matter was covered flamboyantly by the press, who failed to note that the defendants, all of whom were more substantial investors in Banco than Bosshard, had lost far more than their accuser in the Depression. Over several weeks, the prosecution presented a galaxy of witnesses offering expert testimony on fraud, accounting techniques, stock investment, and many other matters, relevant or not. When counsel for Thomson, Frederick

Governor Floyd Olson of Minnesota was not a fan of holding companies and accused Banco and First Bank Stock of "financial debauchery."

H. Stinchfield, finally took the floor, he summarized the trial to date, announced he had no need to call witnesses since the state had not proved anything, and turned the case over to the jury. After a night's worth of deliberation, the panel agreed with Stinchfield and on January 24, 1935, found the defendant not guilty.

The second defendant was Ed Decker, probably the most key individual in the creation of Banco, but he had just retired from his position as CEO of Northwestern National Bank of Minneapolis and subsequently was of little interest to the media.

Banco's Ed Decker (left) and First Bank Stock's C. T. Jaffray at a 1955 event, long after leading their respective bank holding companies through the Depression and war.

Olson attempted to designate a new judge to hear Decker's trial, but the Minnesota Supreme Court advised him that he did not have that authority. Although Olson would not accept that the holding companies held the regional banking structure together during the Depression, the facts spoke for themselves and temporarily put to rest the notion that branch banking was, inherently, some kind of generic bad guy. Even independent bankers finally agreed that holding companies were not only fair competition but good citizens.

MOVING FORWARD

The latter years of the 1930s brought a period of tightly controlled fiscal discipline. All banks were rigorously reviewed by state and national examiners, and those with perceived terminal cancer in their loan portfolios were ruthlessly merged, sold, or closed. Banco had held 132 banks at its peak in 1932; by 1940, the number had been whittled to eighty-three. Managers of First Bank Stock had similar goals and results, so that the latter half of the decade saw a steady improvement in capital and earnings for the holding companies.

Several of the early players in this saga exited during these years. Ed Decker, president and CEO of Northwestern National Bank and president and first chair of Northwest Bancorporation, retired in 1934. It was a bittersweet retirement: sweet with recognition for a long, successful career that included putting Banco on the map, bitter with personal bankruptcy when he couldn't repay the loan he used to buy Banco stock before the stock market crash. The price per share had fallen from a high of $100 to $30 in 1929 and to a low of $3\frac{7}{8}$ in 1934. Even so, family history records that he was supported in retirement by mysterious periodic payments from Banco.

George Prince died in his office on October 3, 1933, after having served as chair of the board of Merchants National Bank in St. Paul from 1912 until the 1929 merger with First/St. Paul, then as chair and CEO of the combined banks, and later, first chair of the First Bank Stock Investment Corporation. First Bank Stock chair C. T. Jaffray retired to his beloved golf game. Their successors, at least for the balance of the decade, had little choice but to follow their established course.

THE SCORE CARD – 1940

Northwest Bancorporation		First Bank Stock Corporation
83 (-32)	Number of Banks (change since 1930)	73 (-12)
$343,000,000 ($67,000,000)	Total Deposits (change since 1930)	$384,814,000 ($56,186,000)
$161,000,000	Total Loans	$184,733,000
$37,200,000 ($29,200,000)	Capital & Surplus (change since 1930)	$42,193,000 ($1,007,000)
1,557,000	# Common Shares	2,920,500
12 – 7¾	Market Range High/Low	12¾ – 9¾
	Per Common Share	
$1.83	Earned	$1.02
$0.20	Dividend	$0.60
$23.90	Book Value	$15.49
2.0%	Yield*	5.3%
$15,375,375 ($57,653,000)	Market Capitalization* (change since 1930)	$34,315,875 ($51,150,350)
	Per 2000 Share	
$0.013 ($0.014)	Earned (change since 1930)	$0.021 ($0.018)
$0.001	Dividend	$0.012
$0.069 ($0.234)	Market Price* (change since 1930)	$0.240 ($0.324)

* based on average market price

REBUILDING the ECONOMY

ALTHOUGH THE NATIONAL economy was still shaky, and the Damocletian sword of potential but undefined disaster hung over the banking world, the 1930s were ending on a relatively tranquil note for Northwest Bancorporation and First Bank Stock Corporation. Deposits grew back to the levels of the late 1920s, and earning assets—particularly loans—were recovering. Net earnings also improved, assisted by diminishing loan charge-offs and write-downs, so that the capital accounts of the holding companies' affiliate banks were substantially restored. In 1939, with all of the Reconstruction Finance Corporation advances repaid, Banco directors again voted a modest dividend on its common stock.

In the late 1930s, recovery of the American farm economy was stimulated by side effects of the expanding war in Europe, namely the disruption of agriculture overseas. Farm prices firmed and rose, and country banks began once again to solicit agricultural credits, although cautiously. As an admirer of Winston Churchill, Franklin D. Roosevelt was prepared to join England in its fight against Germany and Adolf Hitler. Congress approved America's Lend Lease Program, which not only provided the

European Allies war materials as needed but also deferred payments. Fulfilling orders for these basic materials began to drive a recovery of heavy industries in the United States, which in turn improved demand for commercial loans. As World War II escalated, however, opportunities for good loans again began to dry up. Capital equipment, steel, and manpower were in such short supply that virtually all nonmilitary business expansion was postponed to a future "after the war."

BANKING AS A STEADY JOB

On the homefront in the 1940s, a bank—particularly one of the holding company banks—was a good place to work. The pay was never terribly high, yet banks that remained open through the Depression were fair in giving annual increases to long-term employees—perhaps as little as $5 per month, but still something. Benefits were equally modest, although Minnesota's holding company banks were among the nation's leaders in establishing pension and health insurance programs.

A sense of performing a public service provided some psychic compensation to supplement cash wages. Part of this job satisfaction, particularly for managers, was derived from the extraordinary

The clock on the Soo Line–First National Bank Building—seen here in *Downtown Minneapolis, 1940* by Edwin Nooleen—has ticked through many reconstructions and relocations of bank headquarters.

THE FARMERS AND MECHANICS SAVINGS BANK OF MINNEAPOLIS

SIXTH AND MARQUETTE — MINNEAPOLIS 2, MINNESOTA

Farmers and Mechanics Bank moved in 1941 into its new home, an example of the Moderne style as rendered by the architectural firm of McEnary and Krafft.

amount of information a banker had at hand about business affairs in his community—knowledge that was treated confidentially, yet fit into the general pattern of being involved. Darrell Knudson, who would retire in 1990 as vice chair of First Bank System, expressed such sentiments when late in his career a reporter asked him why he went into banking. "Well," Knudson said, "at the time it wasn't the money." Then he added, "I liked the idea of working with people. I liked the idea of being at the center of commerce in the community and the impact it has on social and economic development. To have a positive influence on the economic well-being of a community was a very attractive prospect to me. It is to this day."[18]

Job security at a bank was high. Following an internal change in job assignments in 1933, the management of the First National Bank of St. Paul identified sixty-five "redundant" employees on staff. Rather than lay them off, president George Prince elected to have them absorbed over time by turnover, retirements, and newly opened positions—a humanitarian decision that took almost five years to realize. (History would repeat this policy sixty-five years later as Norwest Corporation, Banco's successor, combined operations with Wells Fargo. Although it appeared that several hundred Minnesota employees would be redundant within Wells Fargo, management pledged that as many as possible would be retrained for new positions. A prescient move, perhaps: within two years, Wells Fargo would be seeking additional Minnesota employees in what had become a tight labor market.)

World War II marked a permanent change in the makeup of the nation's workforce. When women came to banking and other industries to replace men serving in the military, they became the larger percentage of the payroll. Diverse jobs benefited from their skills, and many women continued in banking careers even as returning veterans resumed their prewar jobs. Banking was no different than the rest of the American business scene, however, as women found promotion to officer ranks to be delayed and difficult.

The number of new bank hires during the nation's postwar return to "normalcy" did not increase substantially until well into the 1950s. The lack of inductees into Northwestern National Bank's Covered Wagon Club during the 1960s illustrates the point. Once an employee had completed twenty or more years of service with the bank, he or she was inducted into the club, whose name derived from the early corporate seal (and foreshadowed the relationship with Wells Fargo) as well from the hokey covered wagon that transported each year's initiates to a dinner celebration. In the 1960s, very few club members were on hand to represent the annual hiring done between 1940 and 1950. Two to five new members per year was typical.

The February 1936 Twenty-Year Club banquet for long-term employees of Northwestern National Bank of Minneapolis shows only a handful of women. The group later changed its name to the Covered Wagon Club and expanded its membership to include most of Northwestern's Twin Cities affiliates.

The men's basketball team from First National Bank of Minneapolis became 1928 champions of a league whose members were other downtown banks and businesses. The games were probably played at the Minneapolis Athletic Club, with personnel department employees often doing the coaching.

SOCIAL LIFE

The banks sponsored employee golf leagues, softball teams, choruses (with performances at Christmas and other special occasions), even marching units and bands. During community events such as the St. Paul Winter Carnival and the Minneapolis Aquatennial, larger employers fitted their bands with special tunics or matching storm coats to wear during parades. (Bill Jason, who racked up a remarkable fifty-six-year career with Northwestern National Bank, claimed that he had cinched his teenage employ-

ment as a messenger at the Minneapolis bank with his cornet skills.) The office Christmas party featured dinner and a show, usually at a downtown hotel, with the main event preceded by departmental cocktail parties—and often followed by recrimination, but never retaliation. Banco paid a $20 Christmas bonus to every full-time employee, from the chair of the board to the night watchman.

THE BABY BOOM ECONOMY

A fundamental social change occurred in the United States during the 1930s and

1940s. The Depression had leveled and lowered barriers between the working class and the white-collar populace, while the war and its aftermath raised economic and living standards and promoted a college-level education for millions of returning veterans. The postwar boom, reflected in a dynamic expansion in housing and automobile sales, created and embraced the baby boom, which would dominate and revolutionize the nation's educational systems, job markets, and leisure activities for the balance of the century. The new American family

In addition to funding sports teams, banks participated in civic adventures such as the Winter Carnival in St. Paul and the Aquatennial in Minneapolis. These women from Farmers and Mechanics Savings Bank formed a marching unit in the 1940 Aquatennial parade.

In July 1949, Minnesota state treasurer Julius Schmahl (third from left) accepts an $84 million check from Howard Sheperd, president of National City Bank of New York, for an issue of Minnesota Veterans Adjusted Compensation Bonds. This type of unusual financing was a particular specialty of the First National Bank of St. Paul, represented here by vice president Walter Hoinebrink (far right).

would conduct business affairs in new ways using new services from all vendors, but particularly their financial intermediaries—that is, their banks.

Commercial accounts were still the backbone of business for the larger banks in the money-center cities, but the retail/consumer customer was becoming a major market opportunity for banks throughout the rest of the country—a widely sought client for both deposit and lending services. Incentives to attract such customers were both conventional and novel. In 1942, First National Bank of Minneapolis introduced the Dime-a-time[19] checking account, a pay-as-you-go product that was convenient and popular, and which became widely adopted across the

country. Carried away with that success, First/Minneapolis introduced special checking accounts in 1944 for left-handed persons; the cheering was muted. New products were offered on the credit side as well, with installment loans for buying cars and making home improvements.

Although the average customer would still have had a difficult time opening a checking account at the Morgan Guaranty Trust on Wall Street, smaller banks were beginning to deal with the challenges of multiplying accounts and the strange new worlds of marketing and customer relations. The concepts of change and adaptability, however, were alien in an industry accustomed to looking to the past rather than to the future for inspiration.

THE SCORE CARD – 1950

Northwest Bancorporation		First Bank Stock Corporation
70 (-13)	Number of Banks (change since 1940)	75 (2)
$1,341,000,000 ($998,000,000)	Total Deposits (change since 1940)	$1,140,000,000 ($699,000,000)
$443,000,000	Total Loans	$373,000,000
$69,000,000 ($31,800,000)	Capital & Surplus (change since 1940)	$82,300,000 ($39,100,000)
1,548,000	# Common Shares	2,831,200
33½ – 25⅞	Market Range High/Low	22¼ – 19¼
	Per Common Share	
$3.90	Earned	$2.57
$1.20	Dividend	$1.10
$44.57	Book Value	$28.02
4.0%	Yield*	5.3%
$45,956,250 ($30,580,875)	Market Capitalization* (change since 1940)	$58,747,400 ($24,431,525)
	Per 2000 Common Share	
$0.027 ($0.014)	Earned Change since 1940	$0.054 (0.033)
$0.008	Dividend	$0.023
$0.206 ($0.137)	Market Price* Change since 1940	$0.432 ($0.192)

* based on average market price

The Federal Reserve had no public depositors who might worry about their accounts; its depositors were banks. The Fed's promotional messages thus dwelt on large amounts of cash and currency. Here, Ninth Federal Reserve employees fill and stack bags of coins.

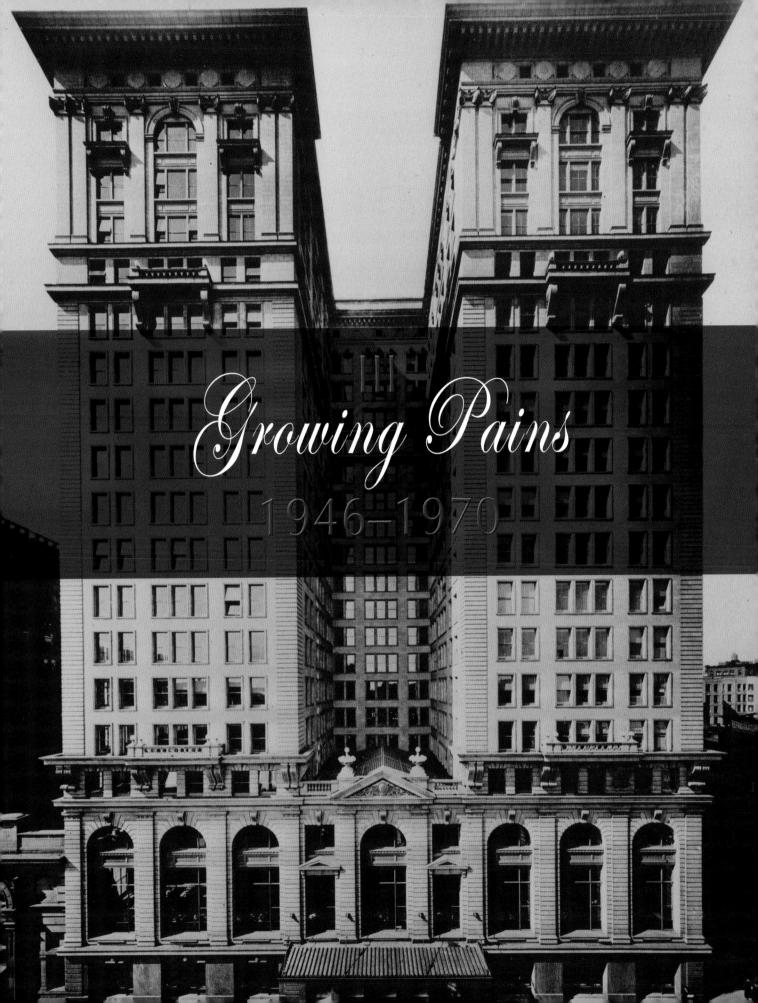

Growing Pains

1946–1970

EVOLUTION of the SPECIES

A RETURN TO THE GOOD old days of banking in the Upper Midwest would not be the reality of postwar times. In the first place, the good old days were, at least for Northwest Bancorporation and First Bank Stock, a myth. The decade preceding their conceptions was marked by a steady decline in the numbers of banks in the Ninth Federal Reserve District, plus a progressive weakening of even the strongest of country banks; their births were followed by the stock-market crash and the Great Depression, eased only by a booming wartime economy. In the second place, the postwar recovery had initiated irrevocable changes in the American business scene: changes in the character and needs of the consumer, represented by a dominant, educated, and empowered middle class, and changes in the nature of banking, whose legislated, inequitable playing field both distorted historic banking methods and opened doors to unimagined competition.

From the beginning, bank management was slow to recognize and accept such changes, with older staff hoping that the new dynamics would go away so that they could get back to a world they believed they could control. Younger staff, on the other hand, understood that they were living in a world of rapid evolution and accepted that "continuous change"—soon to become a corporate catchphrase—was the new reality. The dichotomy between these two groups would cause internal friction and slow development as the two holding companies moved into the 1950s. Indeed, the phenomenon of change, and the ways Banco and First Bank Stock reacted and coped with it, defines their history throughout the second half of the twentieth century.

THE OLD GUARD

Not only did the methodology and philosophy of banking transactions change, so did the people implementing those transactions. Old-school bankers were so stylized they were almost caricatures. They wore dark three-piece suits, white shirts, conservative neckties, and shined black wingtip shoes. (John Moorhead, chair and CEO of Northwestern National Bank from 1956 to 1973, bought a navy blue suit every year and kept six identical suits in his closet, allowing for a daily rotation with one suit at the cleaners.) The old timers smelled of cigars and Aqua Velva, and were regular customers of the nearest barber. A vanishing handful could even be spotted early in the day getting a shave.

Exercise was not a significant activity for old-time bankers, unless you count a round of golf on Sunday and perhaps a midweekly round with valued customers. The average banker was hale, Club to Charlie's Café Exceptionale to the Flame Room. Very senior managers enjoyed lunch at the Skylight Club in the select upper reaches of the Minneapolis Club.

Senior banking officers in Minneapolis enjoyed business lunches at exclusive restaurants such as the Flame Room in the Radisson Hotel, depicted here by artist Syd Fossum.

hearty, and a little heavy, his heft slightly magnified by the business lunch, which, often enhanced by a drink or two, was a staple of the day's schedule. The non-business—or, more strictly speaking, the noncustomer lunch—ranged from a brown bag in the employee cafeteria (usually a small, smoky room with a hot plate and coffeepot) to the Five O'Clock Bankers loved to travel, visiting their correspondent banks and calling on customers to inspect new plants and offices, to check on the collateral of loans, to meet second-level managers, and to share the congeniality of the bank's senior staff. There was a truism in banking "that money flowed downhill"—that, all other things being equal, clients thought

Charlie's Café Exceptionale in Minneapolis, ca. 1942, was a favorite watering hole for Twin Cities bankers and businessmen.

politan institutions of the East Coast called on and solicited the banking or trust business of individuals, corporations, and other banks. These representatives had to be discreet, polite, and careful not to be considered the rustlers they actually were. They enjoyed ample expense accounts, which they used to benefit and charm customers, whether in New York or the Twin Cities. Lunch in a paneled bank dining room forty or more floors above Lower Manhattan always impressed the midwesterner, but there were still higher levels of prestige. Marcel Malenfant, then an officer in the Paris office of J. P. Morgan, hosted the most exotic bank lunch I've experienced: *extraordinaire* cuisine (although *le chef* leaned heavily on *le fromage bleu* in the soup, salad, and dessert), nice *vin*.

it was a big deal to be a customer of a Chicago or New York bank or trust department. It was a good deal more prestigious in Minot, North Dakota, to say you had been visiting your bank in New York rather than in St. Paul. Bankers also loved to attend the annual American Bankers Association conventions, where members traveled to cosmopolitan cities like Miami, New York, San Francisco, or (every five years) Honolulu.

The polished young men, and eventually women, who represented the large metro-

Bankers were streetwise in the manner of the self-trained, and thus not particularly adventuresome or risk-assumptive. Bank owners were often able to amass personal fortunes by investing in a client's business. Non-owners were not often wealthy—respected and admired, surely, but neither willing nor allowed to take advantage of their knowledge of community business affairs. Confidentiality—and the potential conflict of interest—has always been a primary moral and legal canon in hiring and mentoring employees. Even apparently minor violations were almost always cause for instant dismissal without recourse. Those who cheated, whether embezzlers of bank or client funds or traders on confidential bank files, were sent to prison or banished from their community.

Despite the caricature, and contrary to public opinion, bankers did not delight in calling loans or foreclosing mortgages. A live, interest-paying relationship was much preferred to the bad press one might get for putting a widow and her scant belongings out on the curb.

CLIMBING THE LADDER

Historically, banking was a field where a person could (and often did) find a job right out of high school as a messenger or runner. It was always a celebrated accomplishment, but not an unusual one, for a bank's top officers to have climbed from

Farm owner Rudy Oppegard (left) of Detroit Lakes, Minnesota, shows Keith Isaacson of the Norwest Agricultural Group his computerized dairy operation. The Holsteins were really impressed.

Two bankers from Northwestern National of St. Paul visit John Maxson of the Maxson Corporation in the railcar construction facility.

the holding company board for another three years for a grand total of forty-nine years of service to Banco. Although he never talked about it, Rutledge must have been proud of having accomplished his successful career without the benefit of a college degree. Midsized, squarely built, slightly jowled, he did look like a banker—a regional banker, perhaps, rather than a big-city financier, but a banker all the same. Rutledge had the ability to deal with people at all levels, and although he smiled frequently, he didn't always look as though he meant it. He died in 1998 at the age of eighty-five.

Donald Grangaard, Rutledge's counterpart at First Bank Stock, accomplished a similar career. Starting as a clerk, Grangaard earned a degree in accounting while on the job in Grand Forks, North Dakota, and added a law degree after transferring to the Twin Cities. His fifty-year career culminated in 1970 with the title of president and CEO and later as chair of the board. Grangaard retired in 1983 and died in 1999.

the bottom of the corporate ladder over a forty- or fifty-year career—and always with the same employer.

Henry T. Rutledge and Donald Grangaard were two such success stories. Rutledge's career with Northwestern National Bank of Minneapolis began in 1931 when he hired on as a messenger and ended in 1977 when he retired as chair and CEO of Banco, the bank's parent organization. After retirement, he continued to serve on

Managers such as Rutledge and Grangaard were intelligent, patient, and diligent. They were also, as noted by one outside observer, treated like gods—perhaps, as suggested by the same person, because they had a life-or-death power over many of their clients, from granting a home mortgage to establishing a capital line of credit. In general, a bank's directors were willing to accept a modest megalomania in their bank CEO as long as the books balanced.

Because many of their employees in the 1930s and 1940s hired on directly out of high school, banks developed several levels of training to help employees improve their technical skills and advance their careers. By the 1950s the American Institute of Banking, founded at the turn of the century by Joseph Chapman of Northwestern National Bank (among others), had become a nationwide training resource. Its purpose was to offer courses in such office basics as accounting, shorthand, filing, and bookkeeping, and, more recently, computer training and management skills. Professional courses in credit, trust administration, and portfolio management were added as well. Attendance was seen as a plus in personnel files, and because most students were eligible for tuition reimbursement, enrollment was generally high. AIB courses were offered in the evening, and the faculty was generally chosen from junior and senior managers of the participating banks. These instructors took a personal interest in the success of their students, with whom they shared their perspectives and, at the same time, their parochialism.

Even at more advanced levels, training programs tended to maintain a professional insularity. Workshops and seminars sponsored by the American Bankers Association typically featured only bankers as presenters and panelists. Credit specialists had their own school and trade association—Robert Morris Associates—while trust officers attended their special schools at Beloit College and Northwestern University.

Northwest Bancorporation was an early participant in a Twin Cities cross-corporate training project called the Four Company (later Five Company) Management Program. As the project began in the late

Personnel from Northwestern National Bank of St. Paul visit a gravel pit operator.

133

1960s, the involved executives—CEOs, COOs, and others at the top of their career ladders—shared ideas in a meaningful way, with meeting agendas tailored to address generic management issues. Gradually, as the program included the next rank of managers and tried to put them on equal footing, a massive gap developed. After all, what ground could a Honeywell regional manager from Italy, a General Mills product manager from Minneapolis, and a bank president from Montana find in common? The size and shape of the world and its challenges were vastly different for those people as well as were their training needs.

BECOMING AN OFFICER

It took a minimum of four, perhaps five years of meaningful employment to become a bank officer. Officers dealt with clients on significant and confidential business matters and supervised division managers. Titles were formal and derived from traditional organization charts: president, vice president, secretary, and cashier. Larger banks introduced the concept of assistants, such as assistant vice presidents and assistant cashiers. As management structures became more complex, the titles of executive vice president and senior vice president added branches to the organizational tree. The trust department created an extra tier of titles, with the addition of the trust officer and assistant secretary (the equivalent of an assistant cashier on the commercial side) and assistant trust officer (entry-level officer). Later, the trust department moved broadly into functional titles,

such as investment officer and assistant investment officer.

Junior officers were expected to "walk the deck"—patrol the bank lobby—on an assigned schedule around the noon hour to greet bank customers and assist in minor emergencies. Young officers from the trust department found this a difficult assignment because most of them were not familiar with commercial bank clients—they generally stood in awe of such recognizable customers—and would hardly know a banking emergency if they saw one.

To be a senior bank officer had its advantages, both professional and social. As a new teller at First National Bank in Minneapolis, Harvey Peterson was well aware of the class differences:

> Officers of the bank had to be addressed, always, as "Mister." And only they rated cuspidors beside their desks; for employees, cigar and pipe smoking was permitted only after hours, cigarettes never.[1]

Officers were awarded four weeks of annual vacation, twice the time allocated to the rank and file. (In fact, officers were *required* to take one vacation of at least two consecutive weeks each year—believed to be a sufficient amount of time for any possible hanky-panky with their accounts to surface.) Officers also carried the almost mystical capacity to make binding commitments for the bank. If, for instance, a junior officer in the trust department were so foolish as to promise a customer a $100,000 loan without going through proper channels, the bank would issue the check first and deal with the junior officer later. This particular authority was so special that no one abused it, although there were moments of fantasy at coffee breaks. ("If I authorized a $500,000 loan to your brother, do you think he would split it with me?")

A special advantage of being an authorized bank officer was to be listed in the national directory of facsimile signatures. This thick volume was found in almost every bank, and it gave the bank in Peoria a way to instantly verify the signature on an order or direction from a bank officer in Minneapolis. The directory also came in handy when a corporate client split its stock or issued a stock dividend and the bank handled the stock-transfer functions; junior officers would countersign stock certificates for days on end. The availability of the signature book also made it possible for bank officers to facilitate cashing their personal checks in a strange town and bank, since their signatures were on file and readily accessible for verification.

Banks tended to promote internally, with the best and brightest rising to the top as the result of hard work, luck, and the occasional lightning effect. Since the commercial loan function was the most visible and, presumably, the most profitable department for most banks, the better loan officers frequently ended up as senior managers and CEOs of the

institution. This followed national models of succession, in which the best car sales rep or life insurance sales rep would become president of his company, with little or no opportunity for the production

It took decades for women to make their way from receptionist to officer in Twin Cities banks. In this photo, a member of the First National Bank of St. Paul's 1936 bowling team shows off her new uniform.

Joseph Chapman established Minneapolis's American Institute of Banking in the early 1900s to offer advanced training to bank employees.

manager or an actuary. Bank operations officers everywhere thus cheered the 1978 election of Charles Arner, long-time manager of operations, to the position of chair and COO of the First National Bank of St. Paul. (The irony, of course, is that he was also the last person to fill that slot, thanks to institutional restructuring.)

If all "real" bankers knew the five C's of credit, then it was self-evident that those who did not know that mnemonic exercise were outsiders.[2] It took a long time, therefore, for "outsiders" to become accepted as viable candidates for senior bank management positions. Viable did not necessarily mean acceptable. The

announcement that George H. Dixon would join the First National Bank of Minneapolis as president and chief administrative officer in January 1968, for instance, caused a major ripple. Although he had enjoyed a career with Brown Brothers Harriman, the old-line New York investment bankers, Dixon had served as vice president of finance for Sperry and Hutchison, the Green Stamp incentive marketers. Despite raised eyebrows at his nonbanking background, Dixon served as president of First/Minneapolis for eight years before accepting a two-year stint as deputy secretary of the U.S. Treasury. When he returned in 1978, Dixon moved upstairs as president of First Bank Stock to work with Don Grangaard, chair and CEO of the holding company. The move was subtle but significant, as it marked a tectonic shift in the management of affiliates from the individual bank to the parent corporation.

D. H. (Pete) Ankeny Jr. was also considered a nonbanker when, on February 9, 1976, the board of the First National Bank of Minneapolis elected him as their next president. Although Ankeny had been with the organization for almost a decade, he came in by way of the trust and investment side—not considered true banking functions. Before launching his career with First National, Ankeny also had been a beer salesman, and an excellent one at that. (He brought a unique perspective to First National with a maxim about marketing beer that always seemed to have a broader value: that a younger generation whose family refrigerator is always filled with Brand X beer would *not* be good customers for Brand X by the time they reached the buying stage. This attitude was apparent in the younger customer's opinion about trust services and other banking options as well.)

While there were a few noted exceptions, Northwestern would neither recruit nor hire an employee of a First Bank and vice versa—a far cry from today's "plug and play" opportunists whose resumes are always current.

WHO IS IN CHARGE?

The relative roles of the CEOs of the two holding companies and their larger affiliates were not determined, at least on paper, in the 1950s and 1960s. From the beginning, the organizational position of Northwest Bancorporation on its own chain-of-command ladder was functionally subordinate to the status of its largest bank, Northwestern National in Minneapolis. Henry Rutledge was the third of four consecutive CEOs of Banco to be promoted from the position of executive vice president of Northwestern National and to receive his banking indoctrination and training from that organization.[3] Each of these executive VPs worked with and for the continuing manager of the big bank. In Rutledge's case it was John Moorhead, long-time chair and president of Northwestern. Moorhead believed deeply that it was *his* responsibility to manage the main bank so that its resources would be sufficient and liquid

enough to save the holding company should the latter get into trouble. The corporation compounded the chain-of-command confusion by paying Moorhead and Rutledge the same salary to the penny.[4]

The situation at First Bank Stock was similar but with a twist: there were two large, discrete banks that acted autonomously. The corporation temporized for years, allowing the First National Banks in Minneapolis and St. Paul to go their philosophically different ways and directing corporate attention to other affiliates.

Early on, aside from the technicalities of ownership, the holding company provided a uniform accounting structure for all affiliates; trained the necessary staff to direct a regular, comprehensive corporate audit program; and selected the managing officers (in coordination with individual boards of directors) for all but the largest bank. The board of Northwestern National Bank of Minneapolis, in terms of community and corporate recognition, was arguably more prestigious than that of its owner, and was accustomed to making decisions about its membership and executive management with little more than passing conversation with Banco.

From 1945 until the 1960s, the affiliates of Banco and First Bank Stock Corporation were effectively as autonomous as they had been before the holding companies were born. Beyond the few parameters established by headquarters, managing officers and board members acted independently, electing and promoting officers as well as approving policies and reviewing daily operations. The first emergence of real authority from the corporate office occurred during Rutledge's administration, with his "clarification" of matters related to the corporation's undisciplined computerization efforts.

Autonomy was not only an extension of the founding principles of both holding companies, it was also a product of banking and antitrust regulation. Ownership was not deemed sufficient justification to breach walls of confidentiality about customers, even between commonly owned institutions. (To this day, the Great Wall of banking confidentiality limits and protects information about trust clientele from commercial bankers in the same company.)

Field officers from the bank holding company headquarters were designated for each affiliate. The reception given to the corporate representative ranged from genuine welcome to genuine disdain, with certain affiliate managers feeling autonomous enough to treat the corporate representative as a messenger boy. Politics were such that only the CEO of the holding company might be the representative to the largest affiliates, and was likely to sit on their boards.

The corporate representative was responsible for communicating company strategies, ensuring timely upstream reporting, and serving as ombudsman for his

banks back in Minneapolis. With the affiliate manager, the representative reviewed the performance of the regional bank's officers each year, identified those with succession potential, and met annually with the board of the affiliate in executive session to share corporate information and to review the performance of the local CEO. Salaries were set locally, although corporate guidelines were eventually made available, recommending consistent and equal pay for equal work or responsibility.

Bookkeeping structures and policies for the holding company and its affiliates had been standardized from the beginning, with an intense focus on credit quality. In each of its banks the holding companies trained and installed disciplined credit officers, who were expected to report challenges both to their own board and to the staff of the holding company. By the 1960s, each affiliate was expected to prepare one- and five-year plans to be reviewed and approved by headquarters. Each affiliate manager was expected to meet and accommodate corporate goals and expectations as a part of his affiliate's plans.

In 1945, the majority of senior employees and board members of the holding company affiliates could still remember the days preceding the assemblage of the companies. In their subconscious minds lingered certain suspicions, primarily that managers in the Twin Cities didn't understand their problems and that any proposed joint venture, whether sharing loans or selling securities, was a scheme designed to help the bigger banks in the Twin Cities at the expense of their country brethren. By the 1970s, even though many of these suspicions were fading as older employees retired, a major degree of autonomy in the field and varying levels of sympathy or concern for that spirit lingered at headquarters. At Northwestern National Bank, for instance, a venture named BancNorthwest was created to underwrite and sell securities (U.S. Treasuries, federal agency bonds, and certain tax-exempt bonds and notes) through an office in Chicago. Banco politics determined that the four next-largest affiliate banks in the company should be partial "owners" of the venture to enhance "corporate unity."

CHANGING OF THE GUARD

Both Minnesota holding companies were built by old-school bankers who held their organizations together through difficult decades and saw their banks into the dynamic latter decades of the twentieth century. In anthropological terms, however, they were mastodons. As they neared the end of their careers, Rutledge and Grangaard often disagreed with new banking strategies and management styles. It's difficult to differentiate the style or culture of First Bank Stock or Banco at that time, although the former might have been characterized as Ivy League and the latter as state university. Certainly First Bank Stock was respected as being cool-headed and deliberate while Banco was considered

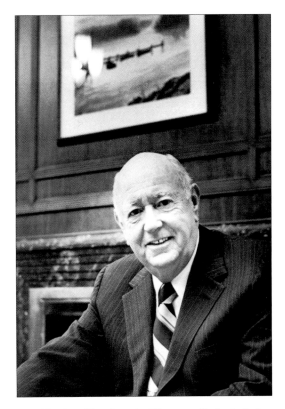

Old-school bankers in Minneapolis included John Moorhead, whose fifty-year career at Northwestern National culminated in his role as CEO from 1956 to 1973.

somewhat headstrong and proactive. In either case, it was becoming evident that homegrown talent might no longer be sufficient to meet the emerging challenges.

Rutledge and Grangaard and others like them inevitably recognized that change was critical to survival. (Significantly, Banco was retitled Norwest Corporation in 1981, Rutledge's final year as a director.) Both holding companies were well into the early phases of evolutionary transition to new and different characters—reflective of a changing world, an inflationary economy, and vastly empowered competition.

THE BOARD

A BANK'S BOARD of directors has always differed from those of other corporations. More than in most businesses, members of the bank board face a perpetual conflict of interest between owner/managers as well as suppliers (depositors) and consumers (borrowers). At one time, most directors were arguably all three, that is, owner/managers, depositors, and borrowers. Even though borrowers had the greatest concern about the bank's survival, state and federal regulations addressed the safety and security of depositors. Rarely was it appreciated that the interests of both sides of the balance sheet ran parallel to the third area of interest: shareholder value. That value is what makes bank directors unique among commercial enterprises; they can be held personally liable for losses to depositors resulting from malfeasance on their watch and for losses resulting from fraud or violation of federal or state law.

It was critical that clients perceive a bank as a secure depository so it could attract funds, which in turn could be invested or loaned out. Earnings from those investments and loans paid the interest on several varieties of deposits, plus the bank's operating expenses. The hope was that the gap between earnings and expenses would be sufficient to build reserves *and* to pay dividends to the owners. The Federal Reserve System, as originally conceived, was committed to the security of depositors. Over time, however, it realized that its focus needed to be on the competencies of a bank's management. The Fed's oversight of loans and other investments was critical because the quality of those practices moderated or extended risk to the depositors.

TWIN CITIES BANK BOARDS

In Minneapolis and St. Paul, the boards of the three larger banks numbered between twenty-two and twenty-five members, the latter being a statutory limit imposed by the Glass-Steagall Act. A seat on the board was a community plum, and each of the banks had relatively large numbers of traditional or implicit ex officio seats that went, for example, to the chair of General Mills for one of the Minneapolis banks and to the president of General Mills for the other Minneapolis bank. Lesser titled officers of high potential at that company might be offered seats on an affiliate bank's board or on a trust committee for what was understood to be farm-team

The First Trust Company—a Minnesota chartered bank whose assets and earnings were carefully enfolded within those reported by First National Bank of St. Paul—enjoyed a prototypical (that is, homogeneous) board of directors in 1950.

training for the major league board. Descendants of the Twin Cities' founding families—some of whom represented arcane businesses, personal holding companies, or substantial trust funds—would have quasi-hereditary seats. A member of the Dayton family—founders of the namesake department store head-quartered in downtown Minneapolis—was always a welcome addition. The president of the University of Minnesota or of one of the area's strong private colleges might be offered a seat, as would a senior partner of the bank's primary law firm. Women were no later arriving in Twin Cities bank boardrooms than they were in the lobbies of the private Minneapolis or Minnesota Clubs. Often enough, the search for appropriate and eligible women to sit on boards would end with nominees who were wives of clients or community icons.

The careful alignment of the banks' board of directors—split impartially among managing officers of leading businesses—reflected a tacit community preference for two banking systems, approximately equal in size and capability, to support the Twin Cities' financial needs. It meant that if a credit accommodation were needed, one or the other bank

The First Trust Company developed a reputation for managing western timber properties, including that of Timber Service Company, whose board of directors included lawyers, trust officers, and family owners.

would provide it, and the presence of a peer competitor meant that terms and rates would be fair and reasonable in the marketplace.

Larger Minnesota corporations were sophisticated in handling this banking environment, often anticipating and forestalling solicitations from smaller banks. This was particularly true in St. Paul, where Northwestern National Bank, Banco's largest presence in that market, was but one-fifth the size of First National of St. Paul. Leaders of the city's larger firms sat on the board of, and did the bulk of their banking business with, the dominant First National. So even though Northwestern had long enjoyed a 3M representative on its board, the

company did only nominal business with the bank; periodic repeat solicitations never met with much success. Even when a new president of Northwestern National Bank was invited to 3M headquarters for lunch in 1974 with its financial officers, 3M's treasurer made a few welcoming remarks, noted that Northwestern enjoyed an inactive $100,000 certificate of deposit from 3M as well as a board representative, and stated that there was no point in the bank soliciting further business. The bank president thanked them for the lunch and left empty-handed.

Board meetings were generally more interesting in their context than in their content. Bank boardrooms were large and elegant, with portraits of several generations of bank presidents staring puritanically and dyspeptically down at the meeting. Cigars were passed—at least until they were replaced with dishes of hard candy—but few were lit during the meeting. Coffee was served in delicate china cups or heavy paper mugs. Leather wingback chairs surrounded a massive table (or tables), with the seating arranged to emphasize the slightly larger chairs reserved for the board chair, the president, and often the controller. Contemporary technology was de rigueur. During the meeting, presentation screens descended from the ceiling or emerged from behind sliding panels while drapes automatically closed to darken the room.

After minutes of the previous meeting were presented for approval, the controller would report the financial results. This was serious business, but the only numbers that made sense to most of the board members were the totals of loans and deposits: these numbers measured size, and size equaled strength and market position. The size of Northwestern National in relation to the First National (and vice versa) was a major agenda item at the meetings in Minneapolis, although the relative sizes of the holding companies themselves were not.

Earnings were a particularly arcane and meaningless number. The results of earnings, which increased the bank's capital accounts (and thus its lending limit[5]),

were diligently reported, but actual pretax earnings weren't discussed as such. Both the tax-exempt bond portfolio and designated reserves for loan losses were managed to minimize taxes. At one meeting of the Northwestern National Bank's board, Kenneth Dayton, a senior executive at the Dayton Company, with typical perspicacity asked chair John Moorhead just what the pretax earnings of the bank had been in the preceding year. Moorhead responded cautiously, but with a degree of satisfaction, "About $1,800." Perhaps management was subconsciously embarrassed to admit that Northwestern was not a significant taxpayer among an audience where almost all present, corporately and personally, were. Perhaps the topic was too complex to manage in the context. At any rate, it was neither difficult nor expensive for a bank to be a member of the Twin Cities' corporate charitable giving clubs. Two percent or 5 percent of pretax income was the minimum target established for contributions by the leading corporations.

Bookkeeping aside, these remarks aren't meant to denigrate the charitable intentions of Twin Cities banks. These financial institutions were serious about supporting their communities, and to that end the larger banks established and funded charitable-purpose trusts that permitted making substantial contributions to meaningful organizations despite fluctuations in earnings. In addition, management encouraged bank employees to volunteer to help these needy entities, with the United Way given distinct priority.

Board meetings and committee activities supported two important functions of the bank: monitoring major corporate loans and reviewing trust activities. Both responsibilities gave directors an opportunity to know a good deal about current affairs in businesses (often competitors' businesses) with loans or credit lines at the bank. They could also peek over the shoulders of trust officers for a glimpse at large family investment accounts. Of course, directors were expected to treat such information with the greatest discretion—and they did. Of far greater value to the bank and the region was the chance for the bank's directors and managers to share information about the state of their community—to speak in relative confidence about challenges they might face or opportunities they might meet. Not often cosmic dialogue, but always good civic maintenance.

Holding-company consolidations of Twin Cities affiliate banks in the 1980s were intended to reduce the overheads of management and the vestigial boards of directors. An unintended effect of dissolving these boards became a matter of major consequence to the city of St. Paul, where the First National Bank's boardroom had been the center of general community business conversation for more than fifty years. As others of St. Paul's businesses merged, moved out of town, or relocated to suburbs, the First National/First Trust

boardroom remained the ad hoc decision-making center that helped to shape and maintain the city. There was no replacement.

HOLDING-COMPANY BOARDS

When it came to requirements and activities, the early boards of Banco and First Bank Stock were far less dynamic than those of the banks. Nevertheless, directors of the holding companies were equally respected citizens, often represented by a broader geographic diversity that paralleled their regional affiliate relationships. They were given similar reports of institutional size and growth, and substantially more meaningful statements of composite earnings and dividends on a per share basis. Wall Street's machinations were much more an issue for the holding companies as both had debt and equity traded in the general security markets. Politics and the Federal Reserve System were also regular agenda items for Banco and First Bank Stock boards. Political winds shifted regularly and Congressional actions occurred unpredictably, with the Fed's efforts to protect and level the playing field sometimes leading to greater and/or less restrained competition—both within the banking system and without.

Back in the boardroom, holding-company directors took a keen interest in management succession in the affiliate banks as well as in the parent company. Banco and First Bank Stock had finally initiated formal management training programs in the 1970s at the corporate level and had warily begun recruiting MBA graduates of eastern universities. There was, however, a sense of detachment in the "upstairs" boardroom. The red meat of the business remained in the banks downstairs and in the field.

In general, the affiliate manager was required to clear the names of proposed directors for his board through the main office. Headquarters also generated nominations of executive officers, and usually gave the affiliate board a slate of candidates for the position of president/CEO for their (semifinal) approval.

As state and federal regulations moderated and holding companies were permitted to consolidate banks not only within but between states, it was clear that the process was driven by the economies of increased computer efficiencies and by the merits of marketing similar products under consistent brand names. This process could be coordinated and managed only by a shift in working control from the banks upstairs (in both cases *literally* upstairs) to the holding companies. This shift changed the agenda, authority, and responsibility of the holding-company boards.

In 1975 back Kenneth Dayton wrote the book on governance ("the purpose of governance is *governance*"), and the parameters he outlined still guide many corporate and not-for-profit boards of directors in the Twin Cities. Dayton's

general philosophy on the subject was typified at a Northwestern National Bank of Minneapolis board meeting in the early 1970s, when the topic of a corporate matching-gift program for employee charitable contributions was proposed. Dayton listened to the rationale and then asked John Moorhead, the board's chair, in all seriousness, "Why does *management* need its employees to tell it where to give its money?"

Ken Dayton, longtime Northwestern National Bank board member, was a leader in the Minneapolis business, arts, and philanthropic communities.

In the late 1980s, Honeywell, among many other local companies, adopted a comprehensive restatement of Dayton's governance paradigms for the contemporary corporate board.[6] Overall, the guide calls for a Nominating and Governance Committee to oversee the evaluation and succession of the CEO, as well as the evaluation of the board as a whole, and to establish compensation benefits and stock-ownership plans for members. In addition, the guide empowers the board to determine its size, its composition, and (with input from the chair and CEO to prevent conflicts of interest) its membership and their retirement, as well as to monitor the institution's performance, financial goals, operating plan, and long-range strategic plans. Last, the guide states that the chair and CEO will solicit ideas from board members for establishing meeting agendas. Honeywell's guide emphasized far more stringent and specific expectations of a contemporary board of directors compared to the more laissez-faire approach of former years.

The comparisons of board responsibility then and now are even more germane as directors and managers have become ever more focused on enhancing shareholder value via the performance of the company and its CEO. In the immediate postwar years, it was difficult—impossible, really—to evaluate a CEO's performance without criteria or hurdles to review. Back then, there weren't long-range plans or strategies to approve or monitor. Since board members were often inherited or recruited by the managing officer, there was a pervasive atmosphere of "If it ain't broke—and we have no way to measure if it is or isn't—why try to fix it?" Members of boards in the latter twentieth century became much more focused on planning and the bottom line—and the directors' performance (and stipend) is ever more closely related to the accomplishment of such goals. The current and common practice of granting stock options to board members gives them an incremental incentive to be prepared for and proactive during board meetings. Long-distance telephone and television-enhanced board meetings can be called on short notice and at odd hours to discuss matters of urgency, and—for bank holding companies, at least—attendance is monitored by the regulators to ensure compliance.

The boards of directors of both Banco and First Bank Stock found occasion in the last two decades of the twentieth century to step up and take charge of a temporarily foundering enterprise. In both companies, those moments of extreme action proved to be watershed events in the history of banking in the Ninth Federal Reserve District.

THE SCORE CARD – 1960

Northwest Bancorporation		First Bank Stock Corporation
77 (7)	Number of Banks (change since 1950)	87 (12)
$1,779,000,000 ($438,000,000)	Total Deposits (change since 1950)	$1,655,000,000 ($515,000,000)
$997,000,000	Total Loans	$899,000,000
$165,700,000 ($96,700,000)	Capital & Surplus (change since 1950)	$156,500,000 ($74,200,000)
5,321,000	# Common Shares	3,470,400
41½ – 29	Market Range High/Low	53 – 46½
	Per Common Share	
$2.90	Earned	$4.70
$1.20	Dividend	$1.95
$31.14	Book Value	$45.08
3.4%	Yield*	3.9%
$187,565,250 ($141,610,000)	Market Capitalization* (change since 1950)	$172,652,400 ($113,905,000)
	Per 2000 Common Share	
$0.060 ($0.033)	Earned (change since 1950)	$0.098 (0.046)
$0.025	Dividend	$0.041
$0.734 ($0.528)	Market Price* (change since 1950)	$1.036 ($0.636)

* based on average market price

THE AGE of COMPUTERS

BANKERS HAVE ALWAYS used state-of-the-art equipment to handle the numbers of their business. Four thousand years ago, the abacus was among the first tools used to tote up sums greater than one person's fingers and toes. Then as now, speed and accuracy were obligatory in

balancing clients' accounts and the bank's own books. During the nineteenth century, adding machines and other inventions made the work of moving massive quantities of numbers easier and faster. The adding machine was a mechanical extension of ten fingers in doing sums. The calculator added the next steps—multiplication (which was many additions of the same number), subtraction (or negative addition), and division (multiple subtractions).

In 1888, Herman Hollerith and his associates converted numbers to punched holes in uniform pieces of stiff paper. The cards could be collated and processed (that is, read) at ever increasing speeds—very fast for their times, intolerably slow today. Hollerith's invention, available in time for analyzing the 1890 census, was the first mechanical sorting system that could accumulate number-handling processes. In all of its generations, however, the Hollerith card could handle only as much information as the number of columns on its face. Each column had ten possible locations for a punched hole, and thus could manage ten numbers, from 1 to 9 and 0. To save space, a year was allotted only two columns on the cards—a limitation that some 110 years later caused

Herman Hollerith invented the punch card, the first mechanical data-sorting system.

considerable anxiety surrounding Y2K. The critical question was whether there was enough information in the data banks contaminated by prehistoric Hollerith processing to record years by their last two digits only, and not the century or the millennium, to stop the data-processing world. The answer was that there was not.

Think of a hole in a punch card as being an "on" or "off" indicator. When light shines through a hole in any given spot, that bit of information is "on" as the light activates a counter. No hole, no information. Then imagine that the holes and light are replaced with an electrical circuit and a metallic chip, perhaps silicon, which serve the same purpose: switch "on" means data, switch "off" means no data. The introduction of the electrical circuit and the ability to store on/off signals in ever more compact form—from doughnut-size magnets to atom-sized bits of Pentium—is the oversimplified evolution of the computer.

During World War II, office equipment companies joined other manufacturers in designing complex electric/optical systems such as bomb-sights and communication links. John W. Mauchly and Presper Eckert of the University of Pennsylvania designed an integrated data-sorting system they called ENIAC (for electronic numerical integrator and computer) to calculate trajectories for WWII artillery. They also dubbed their invention a "giant brain"—"the first digital, general purpose, electronic computer." In *The*

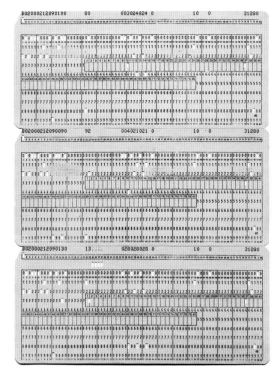

In punch card technology, data was conveyed when light shined through holes. No holes meant no data. The storage of similar "on/off" signals, combined with electrical circuitry, led to the creation of the computer.

Triumphs and Tragedies of the World's First Computer, Scott McCartney describes this early machine as "a bus-sized mousetrap of 40 nine-foot-tall cabinets filled with nearly 18,000 vacuum tubes and miles of wiring."[7]

After the war ended, it was clear there would be civilian applications for this sort of technology, but access to such opportunities was not clear. Luck, co-incidence, and a few bright young engineers turned the Twin Cities into a major hub of the emerging computer industry. William C. Norris, Howard T. Engstrom, and Ralph L. Meader incorporated Engineering Research Associates in January 1946, and set up shop in idle buildings that once housed glider manufacturing near Wold-Chamberlain Airport (now the Minneapolis–St. Paul International Airport). There, ERA built the Atlas, its first large, general-purpose, non-military computer, and installed it at the National Security Agency in 1947. Most early systems were built for federal entities—the National Weather Bureau, the Census Bureau, and other large generators and analysts of similar numbers. As customers, the government had both a sizable need and the money to buy this new technology.

Sales of computer systems were steady and growing at ERA, but the small organization needed working capital. In December 1951, Remington Rand, a manufacturer of typewriters and mechanical calculating systems, acquired ERA, which continued to assemble computers in the old glider plant. The cash squeeze got steadily worse since most of the new systems were leased so that ERA was essentially selling its products to its own balance sheet. The Sperry Gyroscope Company, which had designed and produced the world's most successful bombsight, had a substantial postwar bankroll and merged with Remington Rand in June 1955. The newly formed Sperry-Rand labeled its computer division Univac and appointed William Norris manager. The Univac group, as its name implies, was the country's early postwar

leader in the design and construction of commercial data processing systems using vacuum tubes as the off/on switch.

In 1957, suffering from corporate claustrophia, Norris and his closest associates left Sperry-Rand to found the Control Data Corporation. Their new enterprise became the role model for a generation of startup electronics ventures in and around the Twin Cities. CDC earned a national reputation for its successful challenge to the data-processing establishment and for its enormously successful IPO (another new term for the times). As reported by Don Larson in *Land of the Giants,* Control Data's initial public offering fomented a 1960s boomlet in dollar stocks in the Twin Cities.[8] The legend of CDC—the stock even more than the company and its products—grew from the first public sale of stock at one dollar per share to $32.50 per share eighteen months later.

Encouraged by enthusiastic (if not always ethical) securities dealers, the descendants of long-established controls companies, hearing-aid manufacturers, and burgeoning mini-electronics companies joined CDC in creating a local stock market that resembled the seventeenth-century Dutch tulip mania. Nearly fifty years later, a few survivors and their heirs of that first wave of penny-stock electronics companies, including fragments of Control Data itself, continue to form part of the core of Minnesota's version of a Silicon Valley. Control Data alumni who, like their former boss, chose to take their ideas and energies to the public forum, founded many of these ventures.

In those early years, International Business Machines was selling primitive modifications of its Hollerith line of card sorter/readers and lagged behind Univac in technology. But IBM had an aggressive sales organization and an extensive service network, and thus established and maintained industry dominance in medium- and large-scale systems. In the 1960s, IBM built a plant near Rochester, Minnesota, and became another member of the state's computer community. Minneapolis's Honeywell rounded out the roster of major U.S. computer manufacturers in Minnesota as it executed what was, initially, a joint venture and later an acquisition of the computer activities of Machines Bull of France.

William C. Norris, founder of Control Data, helped give the Twin Cities the edge in the fledging computer industry.

While many corporations used the new computers in specialized tasks such as controlling inventory, processing mailing lists, and maintaining personnel records, the banking industry's needs were unique in that numbers management was its entire business. Knowing where their dollar inventory was became a measurement of profitability, so banks were often ahead of the curve in their computer usage. They would order and install prototype systems, switch to electronics before the books had been stabilized and balanced on the new equipment, and—in the inevitable environment of a system failure—be at the mercy and good graces of the owner of a similar system that might

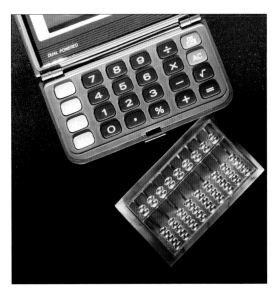

The abacus predated adding machines, which were replaced by calculators, then by computers.

Martin Peterson analyzes 1960s computer circuitry at the IBM (International Business Machines) plant in Rochester, Minnesota.

be 3,000 miles away and operating in a different mode.

Bank customers frequently heard the phrase "The computers are down," and while it was true more often than not, the customer was rarely informed about the degree of "downness." In some conversions from one system or computer program to another, the accounting records could be out of sync for more than a year, as was the case with the simultaneous combination of recordkeeping for the First Trust Company and for the Trust Department of the First National Bank in Minneapolis. From a consumer's point of view, the situation was no worse than

having an unbalanced checking account, since day-to-day business goes on regardless. A banker, however, especially one with a compulsion for accuracy, would agonize over not knowing what transactions might have been lost or entered in error. (The Federal Reserve examiners have always been unhappy about "out of balance" systems.)

System capacity was an ongoing priority for early computers, both in processing speed and in storing large volumes of data. Because they still used vacuum tubes, the more primitive machines suffered both from size and from heat generation. Special suites that were air-conditioned for coolness, filtered for cleanliness, protected by Halon fire-suppression systems, and guarded against competitors and terrorists began to consume the same banking space that had been emptied by technologically redundant bookkeepers and accountants. It was evident that computer systems would keep growing, and that it would be more effective (and secure) to create special-purpose centers than to continue remodeling floors of the bank building.

It was symptomatic of Banco's management style of the time that whether to use computers as a bookkeeping tool was a matter for each affiliate to decide. Thus, in 1963, Goodrich Lowry, then president of Banco, initiated a survey to determine the level of computer usage in his own corporate backyard. The report came back that fourteen of the seventy-plus affiliates had ordered or were using computers; these systems represented eight manufacturers, and none of the fourteen installations was compatible with any others. Lowry recognized that the survey revealed serious inefficiencies in Banco's basic management structure. As he saw it, fixing those inefficiencies would require a complete overhaul of Banco's historic

parameters of corporate management. That was more of a task than the introverted Lowry cared to assume. He went downstairs to the Trust Department, consulted with his investment adviser, and immediately arranged his early retirement.

Henry Rutledge, executive vice president of Northwestern National Bank of

Virgil Dissmeyer and Peter Gillette of Northwestern Bank (from left in reflective glass of the new Northwest Operations Center) congratulate Frank Powell, CEO of the detached computer services facility. The center proved a business saver when the main office was destroyed by fire in 1982.

Minneapolis, succeeded Lowry in 1963. Rutledge moved upstairs to Banco knowing that reining in the emerging data-processing challenge and the apparent management gap was his first priority. He addressed the problem by creating a separate entity, Northwest Computer Services, which would provide data-processing services to all of the affiliates. Banco designed and built a specialized facility for NCS, which opened in 1968. Significantly, NCS employed staff primarily transferred from Northwestern National, but it was an operating subsidiary of the holding company. One by one, the disparate corporate computer systems were wound down and functions consolidated, at first regionally and later in Minneapolis. Of course, it wasn't *that* easy: never in Banco history had the main office so massively overridden decisions made in the field and ruffled feathers that had hardly been disturbed since 1929.

Even though the hardcore decision-making process had been centralized (for computer systems at least), some of the considerations as to which manufacturer Banco would select for lease/purchase commitments of its mainframe computer were still made in the context of traditional bank strategy. Rather than look only at technical competence, service capacity, and numbers of systems in the field, Banco chose to analyze the location of provider plants. Were they employers and investors in the community?

Was the potential supplier a historic or continuing customer of the bank (with compensating balances, payroll processing, and a pension trusteeship)? Such secondary influences often overrode decisions made at a lower level on the basis of technical competence and system capability.

As a result, Banco's choice in 1968 of General Electric as the first supplier of corporatewide central-computing capacity seemed almost *deliberately* different, as if manufacturers were ruled out if they were from Minnesota, had a long history in the business, or had established service networks. In the cosmic scheme of things, it's no longer important that Banco's order was the first large-scale integrated banking system produced by GE. What mattered was that no similar systems were installed nearby that could serve as back-up during the relatively common disaster of a system failure. The closest such system was in St. Louis, which was not a major airline link from the Twin Cities. As a result, there was more than one occasion in those early years when Northwestern National Bank and Banco were out of balance, occasionally for days, prompting nightmares for auditors and lawyers alike.

Technology was moving so fast that the GE system was becoming obsolete even as it was being installed. The experience was a good lesson: The next computer-system buy for NCS—coming imminently— would be more mainstream.

THE SCORE CARD – 1970

Northwest Bancorporation		First Bank Stock Corporation
78 (1)	Number of Banks (change since 1960)	88 (1)
$3,393,000,000 ($1,614,000,000)	Total Deposits (change since 1960)	$3,684,000,000 ($2,029,000,000)
$2,237,000,000	Total Loans	$2,297,000,000
$336,000,000 ($170,300,000)	Capital & Surplus (change since 1960)	$297,000,000 ($141,300,000)
11,537,000	# Common Shares	7,313,600
36¾ – 27	Market Range High/Low	61½ – 45
	Per Common Share	
$2.94	Earned	$5.58
$1.30	Dividend	$2.20
$24.97	Book Value	$45.24
4.1%	Yield*	4.1%
$367,741,875 ($180,176,625)	Market Capitalization* (change since 1960)	$389,449,200 ($216,797,200)
	Per 2000 Common Share	
$0.123 ($0.063)	Earned (change since 1960)	$0.233 (0.135)
$0.054	Dividend	$0.092
$1.328 ($0.594)	Market Price* Change since 1960	$2.219 ($1.183)

* based on average market price

Cass Gilbert's Beaux Arts version of the Ninth Federal Reserve Bank in downtown Minneapolis was replaced in 1973 with a modern structure designed by Gunnar Birkerts and Associates. In 1997, the Ninth Federal Reserve Bank relocated yet again (at right), this time on the Mississippi River in a $100 million building designed by Hellmuth, Obata + Kassabaum.

IV

Coming of Age

1971–1985

REGULATION and INFLATION

BANKERS NEEDED A NEW dictionary to cope with the decades of change. "Disintermediation," one word that flowed into the industry's vocabulary in the late 1960s, described the process that

The Home Loan Department of the First National Bank of Minneapolis was crammed into temporary space with an appropriate front stoop.

encouraged traditional depositors—owners of demand (checking) and time (savings) accounts—to transfer their funds to other types of financial intermediaries that offered ready accessibility and higher rates of return. Some alternatives were less secure than banks, but the desire for a higher return blunted caution. Banco and First Bank Stock took on these nontraditional competitors, but Federal Reserve regulations and double-digit inflation made that challenge especially difficult.

COMPETING INTEREST RATES

Early in the Great Depression, to prevent dangerous speculative competition between banks, Congress ordained a 5 percent limit to the interest rate banks could pay on consumer savings accounts and prohibited payment of interest on checking account deposits. Back then, it seemed improbable that any bank could ever want or need to pay as much as 5 percent on savings accounts. Besides, regulators feared that competition based on paying interest on checking accounts could harm the less well-managed bank.

Congress authorized those financial organizations whose purpose was issuance of home mortgages—the home-loan banks, or "savings and loans" (*real*

Christmas savings clubs (such as that at Third Northwestern National Bank in Minneapolis) encouraged depositors to anticipate holiday expenses with weekly or monthly deposits throughout the year.

bankers would never refer to such institutions as *banks*)—to pay a slightly higher rate (up to 5¼ percent if necessary) due to the greater risk exposure of a mortgage-based institution.[1] As savings interest rates crept incrementally higher in the 1950s and 1960s, depositors began to react to the rate differentials between savings institutions and banks. An early loser in the competition for customers was the Christmas Club account, a low- or no-interest savings account that was used for setting aside money during the year to spend on the upcoming holiday season.

As interest rates rose, overnight balances on corporate books began to generate earning power. Thus, large corporations were the first to turn to investment bankers for such investment alternatives as overnight "repos," or short-term commercial paper transactions.[2] Bankers soon

began to offer corporate clients a similar type of transaction through their bond department, or that of their correspondent bank, later labeled "the money desk." Since commercial paper—short-term notes sold by corporations as interim borrowings—was interpreted to be a corporate security under Glass-Steagall limitations, banks weren't allowed to sell that investment as a principal (that is, as an owner). A bank could sell such paper as an agent, but the spreads were either too low or the fees too high to make it a broadly useful product for either the banks or their clients.

As the first signs of the long-delayed post-war inflation began to erupt during the 1960s, the need for bank credit to meet expanding commercial-loan demand caused bankers to initiate basic strategic thinking about their own sources of funds. A phenomenon of the times was formation of an ALCO—an Asset and Liability Committee—in the larger banks. These entities developed creative ideas about the volatility of assets and liabilities, of risk and time horizons, and of offset (or matched) categories of assets (loans and investments) against liabilities (demand and time deposits, borrowed funds, and capital).[3] In general, banks with deposits nearing and exceeding $500 million were barely fringe players in this process. Smaller banks either left their bigger correspondent banks to such matters as investing their excess cash or managed them in ad hoc fashion through their president's office.

INCREASING LEGISLATION

The combination of disintermediation, regulation, and inflation brought forth the trained-rat survival skills of bankers. Commercial and investment bankers figured out ways to manage and exploit the maze of regulation and competition. Efforts of corporate CFOs to ensure that their organizations had enough cash (or credit) to meet cash-flow cycles and capital-expenditure needs reinforced pressure on the banks. The Federal Reserve Bank and the U.S. Comptroller of the Currency—consistent and concerned observers of the changing strategies of the larger banks—didn't hesitate to modify regulations or seek legislation to limit and/or to protect banks and their depositors. After little or no change in banking laws since 1935, the 1950s and 1960s were marked by a spate of regulatory milestones:

FDIC Act (1950)—Doubles the insurance for Federal Deposit Insurance Corporation coverage to $10,000 per depositor. Provides further autonomy for the FDIC and increases its funding sources.

Bank Holding Company Act (1956)—Gives the Federal Reserve authority over bank holding companies; grandfathers the existence and geographical status of the then functioning holding companies; and provides that a bank holding company cannot acquire a bank in a state where it did not already operate without permission from the new state.

Bank Merger Acts (1960 and 1966)—Prohibits mergers between an insured bank and a noninsured (nonbank) institution without FDIC approval. Specifies that any mergers will be scrutinized for monopoly or anti-trust characteristics.

Amendment to Bank Holding Company Act (1966)—More narrowly defines the role of a bank as an acceptor of demand deposits and applies the same anti-trust screens as the Bank Merger Acts.

Financial Institutions Supervisory Act (1966)—Grants preemptory enforcement authority to the Office of the Comptroller of the Currency, the FDIC, and the Federal Reserve Bank in the case of perceived necessity; raises FDIC deposit insurance levels to $15,000 per depositor.[4]

Through most of the 1960s, banks attempted to maintain the balance sheet of yore, balancing time deposits against home mortgages and using demand deposits, both commercial and consumer, as the traditional pool of funds for commercial loan commitments.

Generally speaking, the American corporation in those days was as unsophisticated as its bank in terms of financial alternatives, and was also underinformed as to the collected size and location of its cash balances. Furthermore, most corporations were substantially committed to maintaining "compensating balances" at their friendly bank as a standby fee for a line of credit that might never be used. The local banker had a full menu of services and charges for the corporate client, which that fortunate client could offset by maintaining a balance of "frozen" (inactive) funds, with a calculated earnings rate that more than covered the total charges. One of these early services was the use of the bank's wire network, essentially Teletypes, which allowed a bank to discover where the client's collected funds actually were at the end of a busy workday. Such information permitted the client to wire the money somewhere else the next morning to meet corporate liabilities.

A REGIONAL RESPONSE

As the large money-center banks began to experiment in attracting alternative

Double-digit inflation and the increasing regulations of the U.S. Federal Reserve made it challenging for First Bank Stock and Banco to compete against nonbanking institutions for customers.

A graceful catenary arch and a terraced sculpture plaza defined the new Minneapolis Federal Reserve Bank in 1973. Beset by leaks and asbestos problems, it was replaced in 1997 by a new structure on the Mississippi River—the area where the city's first banks were built.

sources of funds, the regional banks looked on in awe, envy, and confusion. Those New York City banks with offshore (European or West Indies) offices were able to manage deposits in ways that Minnesota banks were not, and a series of Federal Reserve Bank advisory bulletins warned about abuses that it saw in those practices. At last the Fed issued a definitive bulletin that said, in effect, "We know what you New York banks are doing and we don't like it. We can keep issuing these bulletins as you continue to sidestep the regulations, but why don't you just stop right now?" John Moorhead,

CEO of Northwestern National Bank of Minneapolis at the time, dutifully responded to Hugh Galusha, president of the Ninth Federal Reserve District Bank, saying (in effect), "We promise we won't do any of these terrible things. By the way, would you please explain exactly what the New York banks *are* doing?" Galusha replied that he appreciated Moorhead's support and his sense of humor. He failed, however, to enlighten him as to the New York banks' activities.

In similar fashion, midwestern bankers were learning the ABCs of Eurodollars. In

June 1968, when I was charged by Northwestern Bank in Minneapolis with learning about alternative funding, I called on the London offices of Morgan-Grenfell, an affiliate of the Morgan Guaranty Bank in New York (later J. P. Morgan). I asked Dennis Weatherstone, then an officer of Morgan-Grenfell, if he could explain in simple terms what a Eurodollar was. "Easy," he said. "Just give me a dollar." With my dollar bill in his hand, he grinned and said, "This is now a Eurodollar—a U.S. dollar in the hands of a foreigner"— and he pocketed the money.[5] (Weatherstone ended his career as CEO of J. P. Morgan.)

Of necessity, a bank has to balance its books every working day and ensure that enough funds are available to meet all outstanding commitments. While few bank transactions, essentially local, occur without going through the Federal Reserve's wire system (increasingly electronic as technology improved), the bulk of activity flows through a reserve cash account at the regional Fed bank. Toward the daily close of business, it's easy to see if anything is left in the bank's till at the Fed. Bank managers then buy or borrow funds in anticipation of outgoes exceeding inflows, so that there will be a positive balance left at the end of the day. The Fed and the banking system have some tolerance, however, so the balance doesn't have to be positive *every* day. The real day of reckoning was Wednesday, when, as a result of the need to balance in the black for the whole week, so-called Fed funds (unencumbered moneys available on a

one-day basis) could skyrocket in cost as closing grew near—or, in the event of excess liquidity in the system, the earning rate of these funds could drop to near zero. To prevent the occasional last-minute transfer of funds by a client that could cause a catastrophic imbalance, the reserve account is now calculated retroactively for the previous Wednesday.

In Minneapolis, Northwestern National Bank and the First National Bank cultivated a substantial network of smaller correspondent banks in the Ninth Federal Reserve District and beyond. Those smaller banks frequently kept their Fed funds balances as deposits with their Minneapolis correspondents, who, in turn, considered those dollars as part of *their* funds pool. As interest rates continued to ratchet upward, these interbank balances became increasingly valuable. A Fed funds market became a part of each midsize bank's funding strategy in buying the necessary dollars to meet loan commitments or in selling excess liquidity in an overnight or extended transaction. The country correspondent banks quickly realized the value of their balances. Treating the funds as overnight transactions, the larger bank paid the smaller bank an interest rate that was an eighth or a quarter percent less than the market rate, which gave the Minneapolis bank a good service to offer clients and at a slight discount. On the other hand, these funds were not volatile since the rate paid was comparatively high; thus, a country correspondent could let his Fed funds pool become disproportionately large.

The large and comparatively stable pool of funds became increasingly valuable to the big regional banks, prompting them to reinforce relationships with their regional correspondents. The correspondent bank groups at First National Bank of Minneapolis and Northwestern National had substantial latitude with their expense accounts to ensure that a visiting correspondent banker would have a *very* good time when visiting Minneapolis, or a bankers' convention, whether in Minot, Boca Raton, or Honolulu. At such events, First/Minneapolis and Northwestern each would host a lavish reception (on different evenings) featuring an extensive buffet, an open bar, and music. The country banker and spouse would arrive early, both sporting a golfing sunburn, stoke up a good supply of food and drink, and spend the evening relaxing with friends. Minneapolis bankers didn't always put two and two together to appreciate that New York and Chicago banks were doing the same thing with their midwestern correspondents.

DISCOUNT-WINDOW MYSTIQUE

One reason the Federal Reserve System was created was to make a discount window accessible for emergency overnight funds to banks in a highly loaned-up position. There was a lot of mystique, fostered in part by the Fed itself, about the discount window, which gave banks the opportunity to borrow against previously deposited and qualified collateral (such as highly rated securities or approved loans) to meet further loan demand or a run on deposits. The mystique, of course, resembled that of the homeowner's insurance policy. It was essential that one would have access to the window (or the coverage of insurance) in time of need, but one did not want to use the window (or submit minor insurance claims) too often lest the banker (homeowner) be turned away in time of need. There were no clear definitions of how much use is too much—thus mystique. Certainly, a banker did not want to be seen—metaphysically speaking, of course—hanging around the window, looking as though he needed to borrow. That could be hazardous to a bank's good name. While the Fed was willing to lend money against quality collateral, it had the propensity to ask kindly but embarrassing questions like, "How long will you need this accommodation?" and "What are you doing with this money? Nothing speculative, of course?" and, worst of all, "You certainly wouldn't be doing this for arbitrage, would you?"[6]

During the most difficult periods of inflation in the early 1970s, when Fed funds and the prime rate fluctuated at and over 20 percent, many larger banks were hurting themselves in terms of earnings and capital reserves by honoring loan commitments to critical clients at a lower interest rate than that at which the banks could acquire funds. The Fed sympathized with their dilemma, and gradually accommodated the larger banks so they could borrow (on a secured basis, of course) for extended periods of time if they were able to *not* borrow (to be paid out) for similar time periods.

THE CASH MANAGEMENT ACCOUNT

Around 1971, Merrill Lynch introduced a package concept for retail brokerage account relationships called the cash management account. The CMA was built on the platform of a typical brokerage account with a securities portfolio, but it was wrapped in what looked like a demand checking account. Merrill Lynch would sweep the cash balance in the client's account into a money-market fund every day so that the cash would earn daily interest and yet be fully accessible to the customer. Drawing a check against the account would cash in enough of the money-market fund to cover the check; should that fund be insufficient, the check would then automatically create a margin borrowing against the value of the portfolio. It was widely promulgated that the CMA was not, absolutely *not,* a checking account and that it should not be used for routine household bill-paying. Unfortunately for banks, the CMA looked like a checking account, acted like a checking account, and had enough attractive options to have an instant and major impact on the demand deposit balances of the commercial banks' more sophisticated accounts. The worst part of the CMA, in the banks' view, was that there was no charge for the account, and Merrill Lynch never balked if clients wrote CMA checks to go to the movies.[7]

A new nod to consumer access was the debut of drive-through banking, such as at First State Bank of St. Paul in 1958.

In Minnesota, the introduction of the CMA was delayed by a year due to a legal challenge, but by the time of its ultimate arrival, the operative bugs had been worked out and the account impact was still dramatic. Bankers needed better, more creative moves to play the numbers game more effectively against Merrill Lynch and other nontraditional competitors. For long-term profitability, bankers realized, they would require a long-term strategy.

A SCRIPT for the FUTURE

FOR UPPER MIDWEST BANKERS at least, strategic long-range planning was an alien concept. Asked to predict loans or deposits, bank managers drew straight lines. Very few country bankers dealt with "change" as a working concept. In the early 1970s, the specters of change were just beginning to loom, "disintermediation" was not yet a real word, and a scenario indicating generally higher interest rates (like rumors of global warming) was probably temporary, or so bankers thought, and in any case could be managed. American Bankers Association seminars on the topic for medium and smaller banks were a wakeup call, but were not well attended. The first part of the message was that just because a bank had no long-term plans didn't mean that nothing would happen to it. The second part of the message was that the president/CEO was the default planner for his bank and that he should get on with it. Essentially, managers operated their bank like a medieval fortress, with moats and battlements represented by excess deposits and reserves. They were prepared to cope with the routine exigencies of seasonal lending and annual repayments and with secular changes in home mortgages and auto loans. In worst-case scenarios, which were never specifically

defined in advance, they could expect reasonable help from their upstream correspondent and/or the Federal Reserve. Merrill Lynch's cash management account was an entirely unexpected phenomenon that breached the castle walls like a battering ram headed straight for the treasure chamber of demand deposits.

FIRST A MAP, THEN A COMPASS

For decades, bankers met annual budget planning needs by analyzing the trends of their most recent experience to forecast balance sheets one, two, and five years into the future. By extrapolating the costs of liabilities against the earnings on assets, they could derive a net interest-income total. The projected spread would cover salaries (with a 2.5 percent annual increase) and other expenses and permit a fairly precise guess at net profits. Loan officers were expected to know what their clients' borrowing needs would be; the use of a professional economist or a planning manager in any part of this "planning" process would have been perceived as a foppish luxury, certainly not needed by "real" bankers.

The bond department at Northwestern National Bank of Minneapolis did, in fact, hire a master's degreed economist in 1970 to assist in anticipating the bond market and to communicate with correspondent bank clients. The bank president approved the hire, but cautioned that he "had better be able to sell a lot of bonds." Rudy Blythe, the young economist, was a willing but not terribly effective salesman and eventually left to pursue a banking career that ended with his owning a small bank in Ruthton, Minnesota. A rural financial crisis added a tragic footnote to this anecdote: Blythe was ambushed and killed in 1983 by a despairing foreclosed customer and his son.[8]

As competitors became more numerous, more diversified, and more competent, midwestern bankers were increasingly unable to deal with the incursions on their home turf and to maintain their traditional approach to the financial services business. Oddly, neither Banco nor First Bank Stock feared competition from the other; they respected each other as similarly challenged but "Minnesota Nice" opponents who would observe Roberts' Rules of Order. Each group enjoyed winning their periodic skirmishes, but never went for the kill, particularly since they knew that their clients could change banks overnight while staying in the same community.

THOUGHTS OF DIVERSIFICATION
Banco and First Bank Stock were blessed by some balance in their enterprises. Each had strong city banks and agricultural relationships, which provided a measure of stability in the case of a regional business

downturn. But both operated within and were limited by the economic geography of the Upper Midwest. Both were serious in seeking further "diversification," the increasingly socially acceptable management strategy of the 1960s and 1970s. People like Charles Thornton at Litton Industries and Harold Geneen at ITT were demonstrating opportunism on a grand scale in blending disparate industrial and service businesses into large conglomerates (yet another new word in the banking lexicon). The Federal Reserve anxiously watched this mania, almost paranoid that banks would mindlessly join the parade toward diversification, and thus lose track of their primary responsibility: the absolute security of the depositors.

As banks tested the waters of diversification, the Fed—assisted by Congress—was ever more narrowly defining banks and their functions, clarifying the limitations on holding companies, and restricting off-shore and other international offices. At the same time, these rulemakers were allowing credit and thrift unions and the savings and loans to use NOW drafts in their competition for bank checking accounts. A NOW (negotiable orders of withdrawal) draft directed payment from a customer's savings account to a named payee. Like Merrill Lynch's cash management account, the NOW draft looked like a check, smelled like a check, and acted like a check. Banks could only resent the issuance of these drafts in the increasingly intense competition for demand deposits.

TRADITION VERSUS THE LAW

The implicit relationship between Banco and First Bank Stock had become so cozy by the 1960s that in 1963 the Eighth U.S. District Court issued an indictment of twenty Minnesota banks—almost all of which were affiliates of the holding companies—on charges of illegal price fixing.[9] There were substantial overlaps in the indictments: Seventeen commercial banks in the Twin Cities and Duluth were charged with setting common fees for correspondent bank services; seven banks in St. Paul (and First Bank Stock itself) were charged separately with illegal fixing of service charges; and four Duluth banks, plus the Duluth clearinghouse, were charged with fixing rates on loans, deposits, and services.[10]

At first, the banks all pleaded innocent, claiming that they were exempt from antitrust action and, in any case, that these practices were their traditional way of doing business. Legal counsel advised them that recent legislation and legal interpretations appeared to have brought the banks under antitrust review, and that since times had changed so should their banking practices. The twenty defendants switched their pleas to nolo contendere, and in February 1964 paid fines totaling $253,000. While this was little more than a slap on the wrist from Judge Edward Devitt (the rumor was mongered that Minnesota's U.S. Senator Hubert H. Humphrey had intervened), it was clear to all parties that future price-setting, if any, would be completed at arm's length.

During his lengthy tenure on the U.S. District Court, Judge Edward Devitt became one of the most respected and influential district court judges in the nation. His decisions were seldom reversed on appeal, and he repeatedly turned down opportunities for promotion to appellate courts or to other positions removed from trial law.

A legacy of this particular case was the understanding by First Bank Stock managers that they could not, within the scope of the decision, force cooperation between the First National Banks of Minneapolis and St. Paul. It was not for more than a decade that Dorsey and Whitney, First Bank Stock's general counsel, would accept a common-law interpretation that the legitimate owner of two properties could, in fact, manage them together. In the interim, a recalcitrant bank manager could always take refuge from certain types of corporate directives behind the consent decree. (Banco had similar problems, but the stakes were consistently lower.)

FBS DEBUTS

After forty years of intense but gentlemanly competition, the twin bank holding companies were amazingly close in comparable statistics. At the end of 1970 First Bank Stock was slightly larger, with assets of $4.4 billion compared to Banco's $4.3 billion. Banco had more capital accounts but First Bank Stock was more profitable, with net income that year of $45.7 million compared to $34.3 million for Banco. This difference dated back to the founding of the two enterprises: First Bank Stock had two large and highly profitable banks, while Banco had one large unit. The marketplace thought the companies were worth about the same, with First Bank Stock having a market capitalization of $389 million while Banco had $368 million.

In 1971, Don Grangaard was in his second year as chair and CEO of First Bank Stock—or, more accurately, First Bank System—after a forty-year career with the enterprise. The change in the corporate name was one of the last moves by Granger Costikyan, Grangaard's predecessor. While the change from First Bank Stock Corporation to FBS was more or less semantic, the intent was to mark a shift from the "family of banks" syndrome

to the concept of an integrated system, with synergism building upon the combined assets and skills of the whole group.

BUYING DIVERSITY

Both holding companies moved cautiously to expand into areas permitted by legislation and regulation. The Bank Holding Company Act of 1956, as amended in 1966, allowed expansion of "bank related activity," although neither interstate acquisition of banks nor branch banking were authorized. In 1969, Banco purchased Iowa Securities, a midsized mortgage banking firm, and established a precedent of acquiring skills and experience (and a recognized trade name) rather than trying to create what was needed from scratch. The 1968 creation of Northwest Computer Services had been more an extension of internal skills. NCS served as a landmark within Banco, as it consolidated at the corporate level the multifaceted data-processing systems that had sprung up spontaneously among several Banco affiliates.

For the first time since the Depression, banks were realizing that their bond departments might become profit centers. For years the banks had bought and sold U.S. Treasury bonds, bills, and notes, as well as federal agency bonds and notes and general obligation tax-exempt bonds. Profits in such transactions were fairly small, but as banks began to underwrite some of these issues the margins grew wider. In 1970 Northwestern National Bank of Minneapolis creatively pursued the profit-center goal by sponsoring a joint venture with larger Banco affiliates as a subaccount of its bond trading inventory. This "corporate phantom" leased office space on an upper floor of Chicago's new First National Bank Tower, opened a clearing account with Northern Trust, and became a small national player in the underwriting and sale of legal securities. The structure got even weirder when the phantom (which had secured an Illinois employer identification number) opened a subsidiary office in Massachusetts. The joint venture, named BancNorthwest after an earlier Northwestern National Bank investment banking subsidiary, became a bookkeeping partnership with investment participation and profit-sharing with the Iowa–Des Moines National Bank, U.S. National Bank in Omaha, and Northwestern National Bank in St. Paul. (These entities comprised Banco's second tier of affiliates.) The politics of the joint venture were an early move toward unifying corporate activity across state lines.

The First National Bank of St. Paul had an aggressive and generally profitable bond department that worked closely with the St. Paul Port Authority. Neither of these sales efforts, however, approached the aggressiveness of certain banks in Memphis and other cities in the southeastern states, which earned the sobriquet of "orange crate offices"—essentially boiler rooms promoting high-yield but marginal-quality tax-exempt bonds to backwoods bankers. The salesmen, paid on commission, put their telephones and heads inside wooden crates to dampen the office din and improve the acoustics of their conversations. Paying bond salesmen a commission was new thinking for bankers in those days of change. Fred Uhde, lead salesman for BancNorthwest, earned more in one year than John Moorhead, Northwestern Bank's CEO. Fortunately, Moorhead understood that this was good business and left well enough alone.

Henry Rutledge had been president and CEO of Banco since 1963; in 1971 he moved up to chair and CEO of Banco as Richard Vaughan, previously executive vice president of Northwestern National Bank, joined Banco as president. Vaughan's initial assignment was to begin a strategic-planning process for the corporation.

STANFORD RESEARCH LOOKS AHEAD

In 1967, the Stanford Research Institute, a newly organized California think tank, published a prescient study of the outlook for commercial banking in the United States. The executive summary contained five bulleted items:

• Commercial banks would roughly double their assets in 1970s; to finance this growth, banks would have to make greater use of higher cost sources of funds. Time and savings deposits would become 50 percent of bank assets by 1980, up from 39 percent in 1965; conversely, demand deposits would decline from 49 percent to 36 percent.

• The rising costs of funds would challenge bankers to compensate by much more aggressive management of other internal costs. Banks would look for fee-based products and would gradually institute charges for services that had historically been gratis.

• Banks and bankers would have to acquire new skills and techniques in marketing, management science, understanding of internal costs, and the creation of management databases. New types of professional expertise would have to be added to traditional bank staffing models.

• In the next decade, electronic fund transfer systems would become widely used in commercial banking business; the systems, which would eliminate much use of cash and checks, would begin penetration of the home market by the later 1970s. There would be economic, social, and legal barriers to surmount in this transformation, and consumer acceptance had yet to be tested.

• Increased competition by commercial banks for time deposits would have the greatest impact on savings and loan associations and, to a lesser extent, on mutual savings banks and credit unions.[11]

With the exception of the prognosis on the decline in usage of cash and checks—both of which have proved to be stubborn in their grip on customer usage—it was not until the early 2000s that plastic and electronic transactions passed paper checks in banking activity. The Stanford Research Institute forecasts were accurate in direction but conservative in scope. Nonetheless, the changes predictably affected the twin bank holding companies along with the rest of the banking industry.

For the first time in their respective histories, the ebb and flow of loan demand at Banco and FBS was driving balance-sheet change. During the groups' first forty years, the challenge had been the profitable employment of deposits sitting on their books. Now, as the region expanded commercially and agriculturally, there was not enough money available in the Ninth

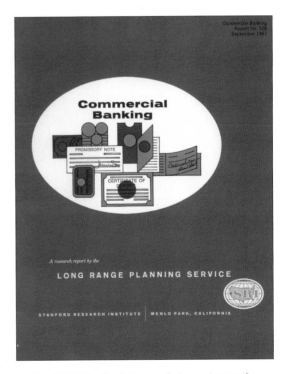

The 1967 Stanford Research Report gave the banking industry a strategic glimpse of the future. (SRI, Menlo Park, California, cover by Douglas A Hurd.)

Federal Reserve District to meet the demand for loans. Until that time, banks had acquired their assets and liabilities the old-fashioned way: they had worked for them. It was a novel experience for balance-sheet managers or those charged with funding a loan portfolio not only to be able to call a broker to buy/sell loans or deposits, but to be *required* to do so by the exigency of a deposit shortfall. (It wasn't that the deposits were no longer in the territory; they just weren't in the banks. The brokers, often using excess funds from non-bank depositors, would help the bankers buy back what had historically been on their books.)

The dimensions of growth and change suggested by the Stanford study were substantially exceeded by the holding companies. First Bank Stock assets tripled from 1960 to 1970; Banco assets grew 3.3 times. The changes in the mix of time and demand deposits were equally dramatic: First Bank Stock added $5 billion in time deposits during the decade and Banco added $6.3 billion. Demand deposits, however, declined in both companies. At Banco, 1970 demand deposits had dropped to 41 percent of total assets compared to 65 percent in 1960; the percentage decline would continue, and by 1980 demand deposits made up only 24 percent of total assets. At First Bank Stock/FBS, demand deposits were 63 percent of total assets in 1960, 42 percent in 1970, and by 1980 had declined to 21 percent.

Remembering that a bank's liabilities are client assets (demand and time deposits plus bought or borrowed funds), while bank assets are loans to business and individuals plus securities, it's understandable that banks now had the opportunity to manage their liabilities on duration and rate. The intent was threefold: to have enough liabilities available to cover assets, to maximize income, and to minimize risk. In its liability acquisition strategy, FBS chose to use relatively more in borrowed funds to balance its loan portfolio than did Banco. Doing so presaged the potential of a narrower interest-rate gap against the likelihood of higher volatility in costs and the periodic short supply of such borrowings. Meeting regional loan demand was driving the large Twin Cities banks to buy deposits and borrow funds in national and international markets. These latter sources always had funds available, but often at rates that could become painfully expensive. FBS had two large banks trolling the financial marketplace to locate lower-cost funding alternatives. Banco, with just the one bank big enough to participate in national funding transactions, used Northwestern as the primary funding conduit for affiliate relations and its correspondent bank network. In New York and Chicago, money-market dealers like Salomon Brothers, Merrill Lynch, and First Boston—all leaders of large, aggressive, imaginative packs of sales reps—found expanding markets of buyers and/or sellers for these types of funding needs dealing in assets and liabilities.

The investment bankers on Wall Street and in Chicago were inventing financial instruments as fast as they could to meet the burgeoning banking need. These new quasi-securities might generate time money through negotiable certificates of deposit or borrowings. The repurchase agreement (repo), originally an overnight borrowing secured by government securities, had morphed into a longer-term contract that could use lesser securities. As usual, the reward of higher earnings rates was offset by higher risk. On the asset side of the balance sheet, these same intermediaries stood ready to buy and resell commercial loans, retail loans in packages, home mortgages, and auto installment contracts. It was generally agreed that the Salomon Brothers crew could sell anything that carried a fixed maturity date and some rate of return, although zero-coupon debt issues became a temporary and diverting rage. A tranche is a slice across a portfolio of securities with varied maturities. A zero-coupon bond (like U.S. Treasury savings bonds) pays no regular interest; it is originally sold at a discount ($900) against its face value at a stated maturity ($1,000). The accrual of the discount would be taxable at capital gain rates rather than normal income. As the dealers became even more sophisticated, they would develop markets for securities that had neither fixed rates (zeroes) nor maturity dates (tranches).

MORE SMOKE AND MIRRORS

As the money markets expanded and matured, and as a pervasive urgency drove the "money desks" of commercial banks, the phenomenon of the petro-dollar certificate of deposit appeared. Following the early OPEC scare and the ballooning of oil prices, this wraith typically manifested itself as a telephone call from a small town banker in, say, Vermillion, South Dakota, who would have just received a call or a cable from "somebody" whose second cousin was somehow connected to the royal family of Saudi Arabia. This cousin or nebulous agent was looking for a bank that wanted/needed a certificate of deposit for $50 million (or more) to help meet loan demand. The proposed interest rate would be slightly less than the market rate because of the "special relationship," and deposits would not be volatile but would stay. Unfortunately, it would prove impossible to find the principal (actual owner) of the transaction, particularly since these opportunities always seemed to arise late on Friday afternoons or on days when banks might be closed. The phenomenon was a mirage of those (and later) tight money times, and it wore many disguises. When and if such funds existed, they were likely to be in need of a "laundry."

With more of the banks' lending activity being both incremental and marginal in funding (meaning at the margin, or "going rate," and not substandard), the profit margins of corporate account relationships began to deteriorate. A commitment fee and an unencumbered compensating balance, both ensuring the future availability of a line of credit, are more profitable than a credit line in use, especially when funds for the loan are to be borrowed in the money market. For the first time, banks were examining their mission statements (when they could find or create such documents) to see just how important it was to make such marginal loans.

Northwestern National Bank took such a look in the early 1970s and concluded that it was a "regional lending bank," and that its mission was to stand ready to make the loans to which it had committed. This was not an easily understood or agreed-upon conclusion when the existing and nonfunded lines of credit generally ran about 150 percent of the *funded* loan portfolio. The board of directors concurred that the bank should make loans at the margin when it had made a sincere commitment, when the loan was important to a major regional business, and when not making the loan would be harmful to that business, all other credit criteria being sound. The board also agreed that the bank should make such loans even if the transactions might be unprofitable in the short run due to the high costs of funding the commitments. Such thinking was much more philosophical than most of the board's agendas, and thus unsettling.

Northwestern agreed that it would increase its emphasis on controlling internal operating costs and on developing opportunities for fee or service charge revenues to supplement interest income. Actually, those efforts had positive results during the decade. While corporate

assets tripled, non-interest income rose by 3.8 times and offset 41.3 percent of non-interest expense compared to 37.8 percent in 1970. Banco continued to emphasize cost control and non-interest income across the system, and in the 1980s had even more impressive results: non-interest income expanded another four-and-a-half-fold and by 1990 represented an excellent 56.9 percent of non-interest expense.

While First Bank Stock (now First Bank System) was sensitive to the same issues, its accomplishment during the same time-frame was less dramatic. From 1970 to 1980, its non-interest income grew by 2.9 times and, in the 1980s, grew another 2.5 times to represent 47.4 percent of non-interest expense. In 1972, FBS proposed a series of goals in a five-year plan, one of which was "to generate 10 percent of 1977 income from new products or services or markets."[12] In 1977, management reported that this goal had been reached as a percentage of 1972 income (the base year) but not in terms of 1977 income.[13]

The other goals among those established in 1972 by FBS would prove wishful in a world becoming increasingly unpredictable: to generate "consistent" earnings growth at a 10 to 12 percent annual rate; to raise the system return on equity to 15 percent; to limit loan losses to no more than 1½ percent of gross loans (nor an average of more than 1 percent for the five-year period); and (almost an afterthought) to improve market share.

As both banking groups gained skills in generating funds to finance loan portfolios, each became more aggressive in seeking national lending opportunities. They hoped that these market-rate transactions would carry higher earnings potential (spread over the cost of funds), albeit at the possible exposure to somewhat greater risk. Increasing loan losses during the 1970s made FBS's realization of its 1972 goals impossible.[14] With respect to the final goal—to increase market share—the five-year statistics did reflect remarkable growth for FBS, but Banco's results were even better.

THE WORLD OF MARKETING

The 1967 Stanford Research Institute report indicated that banks would need to acquire new knowledge and skills to deal with the challenges of the next decades. Both holding companies slowly added that expertise in the areas of computerization, management information systems, human resource management and development, and (not least) marketing. These new hires were not traditional bankers, but individuals technically competent in specific disciplines the banks needed for the future. These young men and women often had more formal education that those hiring them, including an increasingly desirable MBA degree, and they spoke in the lingo of their areas of expertise. Both the banks and their new employees had to be patient and careful in learning from each other.

A major challenge affecting both banking systems, and the old and new guard of employees, was marketing. Marketing was already a norm in large metropolitan banks in New York, Chicago, and Boston, but the managers of midsized banks generally considered the discipline to be "primarily a public relations function staffed by gregarious individuals who had a less than enviable record in client credit approval."[15] Historically, any marketing effort had been essentially institutional, reflecting the distinguished existence of the banks and their respective places in the community. It was considered inappropriate or undignified to advertise retail services with signs or brochures in the formal atmosphere of a "proper" banking floor, particularly since the bank was required to advertise equally to all classes of customers. This means, bluntly, that credit discrimination could look like racial discrimination, especially when referred to in TV commercials. Product lines might be listed but they were not distinguished, and copy approval in those days was generally signed off by the CEO.

While banks initially eschewed marketing, their nonbanking competition happily embraced it. Even manufacturers financed the sales of their own products. Through GMAC, for instance, General Motors was funding almost 25 percent of all U.S. automobile loans. Sears Roebuck not only had sizable brokerage and insurance subsidiaries, it had issued some sixty million credit cards. Merrill Lynch, in addition to its phenomenal success with CMAs, had built a portfolio of more than $1 billion in home equity loans during the 1970s.[16]

Once bankers recognized that to stay competitive they needed to enter the advertising/marketing arena, they began to address customer delivery needs and positioning. Their consultants pointed out that individual banks had many images—some good, some bad, but all of which needed to be given the spin that would freshen and sell those images. How, for example, could the holding companies market a bank in Minot that might be owned by a corporation that was not only out of town but also out of state? Was the bank perceived as a detached wholesale financier or as a friendly retail organization? Technically capable or convenient and understanding? Austere or welcoming? Tailored to the needs of retail customers or fitted in generically among corporate customers? Clearly, opportunities existed to promote bank products, personalities, and corporate strength.

In the final analysis, bank marketing was functional and added value when it moved beyond a limited commitment "to image or situation repair rather than preventive maintenance."[17] As Robert McMahon noted in his 1986 *Bank Marketing Handbook,* the criteria for success were:

- that senior management accept the necessity of a marketing program and visibly endorses such efforts;

- that bank products meet and satisfy customer needs;

- that there is sensitivity to the marketing environment; and

- that marketing must help deliver an incremental return on assets with margins, and that the promotions meet all limiting regulations but also push the envelope.

Some marketing ideas floated, others sank. Perhaps based on "bank night" at the movies—a Depression-era phenomenon when theaters gave away dishes—bankers decided that giving cookware premiums to customers opening new accounts would entice a large prospective market. It probably helped. On the other hand, when Northwestern National Bank tried to launch a simplified loan form for customers, the kind that says, "You borrow, but you promise to repay," legal counsel felt that prudent management required the document to carry several more cautions. All of the fine print was also deemed necessary. That bright idea slipped away.

THE NAME GAME

Both holding companies found that the proud names that their individual banks had carried—in some cases, for more than a century—were becoming barriers to group marketing. For example, the First and American National Bank in Duluth was a Banco affiliate, while the representative of FBS in the Duluth market was the Northwest Bank of Commerce. In Omaha, Banco owned the U.S. National Bank and the Stockyards Bank, both of which represented long established tradition but were not a reflection of common ownership or purpose. In fact, there were major differences in style and managerial intent between the two entities.

With persistent prodding during the early to mid-1970s by Banco presidents Henry Rutledge and Dick Vaughan, the holding company's affiliates accepted a broader

Buddy Bear and his buddy, Barney Bear, pose for this 1972 advertisement for Norwest Bank's new campaign endorsing rights for stuffed animals throughout the nation to hold interest "bearing" checking accounts. Buddy was a little reluctant to pose in the nude, so Norwest let him sport this snazzy little yellow bowtie. (See note on page 251, Illustration Credits, under Wells Fargo Bank, for page 177.)

usage of "Banco" as a common denominator and product-brand identifier in new regional marketing strategies. Television was, by its nature, a regional advertising medium and deemed essential to effective bank marketing. Banco's Twin Cities marketing committee consisted of managing officers of several area affiliates, but was directed by an executive officer of Northwestern National who represented both the majority vote and the bulk of the budget for Twin Cities advertising. The holding company's use of "Buddy, the Banco Bear" as a Christmas sales campaign premium became the subject of annual debate among these managing officers until the use of the Banco name

and logo was eliminated in the 1981 conversion to Norwest Corporation. Similar discussions on a gut level of cost/value analysis brought an early end to a promising series of TV ads reflecting courtship, love, marriage, and domestic bliss, all supported by myriad banking services. Filmed on the University of Minnesota campus, the ads featured background music by an up-and-coming country singer, who priced himself out of the job when he raised his annual fee from $12,000 to $36,000. Undaunted, the emerging recording star—John Denver—made the commercial immortal as the cut "60 Second Song for a Bank" on his RCA release *Aerie* and featuring the phrase "May we help you today?"[18]

Don Grangaard (center), ending his career as First Bank System CEO and chair, and sucessor George Dixon (left), prepare for a 1978 meeting with NYSE security analysts in 1978.

THE GUARD KEEPS MARCHING

In March 1976, George Dixon, president of the First National Bank of Minneapolis—which had almost always maintained its status as slightly larger than the First National Bank of St. Paul, if not always the more profitable—accepted the opportunity to serve as undersecretary of the U.S. Treasury. Pete Ankeny succeeded Dixon as president of the Minneapolis bank. When Dixon returned from Washington in 1977, he became president of First Bank System and was given responsibilities that included strategic planning for the parent corporation. Don Grangaard would continue as chair until 1983.

At Northwestern National Bank of Minneapolis, John Morrison—CFO at Honeywell, member of the bank's board, descendant of one of the bank's original charter members—was elected chair and CEO on the 1975 retirement of long-time managing officers John Moorhead and Phillip Harris. Morrison was the first "nonbanker" to become Northwestern's CEO, and his election came as somewhat of a surprise to the bank, the holding company, and to Morrison himself. The board of the bank had decided that the job and the times called for a broader pool of candidates for the CEO position, and determined to hire Morrison despite the qualifications of internal candidates. Their choice was ratified by the holding company, but Morrison would prove to be the last significant managing officer selection made by an affiliate board. The enterprise benefited from his detached

Henry Rutledge rose from messenger boy at Northwestern National to CEO of Banco, its parent company, without a college degree.

As Banco's new president in 1971, Richard Vaughan began planning a more strategic approach to the corporation's future. His accidental death in 1979 cut short his goals.

179

perspective, and in 1980 Morrison repeated this barrier-jumping when he became CEO of the holding company.

BRANCH BANKING

During the 1970s, under recently enacted or modified legislation, both bank groups again were able to consider the limited purchase of additional banks. The process was piecemeal as it depended upon the independent actions of the several states within a framework of gradual relaxation of criteria governing inter- and intra-state branching and acquisition. In 1972 Iowa became the first state to pass legislation allowing the acquisition of its banks by out-of-state holding companies. In 1973, Banco proposed to acquire five Iowa banks. All but one of the transactions—a bank in Dubuque—were authorized. Before the end of the 1970s, Banco executed three more transactions in Iowa, rounding out its market coverage. First Bank System received a charter for a new bank in Burnsville, Minnesota, in 1976, and in 1977 acquired the Midland Bank in Milwaukee, Wisconsin.

Minnesota legislators had not yet accepted the desirability of branch banking, but in 1977 they approved a broadening of the "detached facility" regulations. For some time, the law had allowed construction of "attached facilities," such as a drive-through kiosk. Now it would be permissible for each Minnesota bank to build two off-premise, detached facilities, although state banking regulators and independent banks would argue for years

that an ATM was the same as a freestanding branch office under the definition of "remote facilities," and thus would qualify as one of the two newly authorized outlets.[19] Nonetheless, within the year, twenty-five affiliates of the two holding companies were building remote offices. By this time, locations of such new offices were determined by the parent corporation according to an overall marketing plan rather than by an affiliate's whim. A master architectural plan covered the size and layout of such new facilities for simplicity of construction as well as consistency of function and style. Suddenly, Banco became much more of a geographic presence on the St. Paul side of the Twin Cities.

"INTERDEPENDENT AUTONOMY"

In May 1978, the three managing officers of First Bank System were invited to make a presentation to the New York Society of Security Analysts.[20] They described one of FBS's major goals as providing consistent and stable growth over longer periods of time. A point of emphasis was "interdependent operational autonomy," which allowed individual banks in the system to work toward their own goals and objectives consistent with the corporation's overall profit and growth strategies. The officers noted with some pride that banks and companies within FBS competed with each other as well as with other financial institutions. This was curious rhetoric, as the same officers were also charged with bringing uniformity and consistency to the planning and execution of FBS's corporate strategy.

The 1982 annual report for First Bank System highlighted the transfer of homegrown management, exemplified by outgoing chair and lifelong employee Don Grangaard (front row left), to East Coast financier George Dixon (center) as incoming chair. D. H. (Pete) Ankeny Jr. (right front) was elected president, while Darrell Knudson (back left) and Clarence Frame (back right) completed the brain trust.

Another anomaly, faced by both holding companies, was the continuing existence of the boards of the numerous affiliate banks. Those prehensile bodies were recognized by the holding companies as community leaders and allowed more than nominal authority in the selection and evaluation of their managing officers. Individual directors retained the historic liability for the actions of their banks, but in fact the holding companies retained absolute control of their banks and their boards, even though they didn't begin to exercise the weight of their ownership until the end of the 1970s. The affiliate directors' prerogative had already begun disappearing within Banco in the wake of John Morrison's

1975 election as head of Northwestern Bank of Minneapolis. In 1978, First Bank System reported that it deeply appreciated the ongoing efforts of its 8,718 staff members and 730 affiliate directors.[21] This, a 1:12 ratio, was not the high-water mark in numbers of directors, but it was approaching the end.

Henry Rutledge retired as chair and CEO of Northwest Bancorporation in 1977. His particular monument within the system was Northwest Computer Services, created in 1968 to integrate the diverse data-processing systems for all of Banco and its regional correspondent banks. The new NCS facility, constructed largely below ground level, opened in 1978 and years later would save the bank and holding company's operations from incineration.

On June 16, 1979, Richard Vaughan, who had succeeded Rutledge as chair and CEO of Banco two years earlier, was accidentally electrocuted after a destructive summer storm dropped power lines near his home. Chester Lind, executive vice president of Banco and former CEO of the Duluth Banco affiliate, was elected Vaughan's successor in what was clearly a temporizing move (before Lind's prospective retirement) to fill the management gap.[22] The question was long asked as to the directions Banco might have taken had Vaughan survived, but the query was moot. Vaughan had been asking the necessary questions about the future, and clearly had broad parameters of a responsive strategy in mind. He had also begun the process of strengthening the corporate office staff to become *the* managing players. Banco was well positioned for a leap forward. As its 1979 annual report predicted, "The 1980s will be an exciting decade for Banco, our shareholders, our employees, and the many communities we serve."[23] This would indeed prove true.

And so it was that the twin holding companies had survived the ever-challenging 1970s with a handful of strategies: first, to build on those things they already understood and were doing well; second, to diversify into related areas of financial services with perceived potential; third, to restructure the balance sheet to address the challenges inherent in escalating interest rates; and fourth, to develop a spirit of cooperation with affiliates *and* with traditional and newly emerging competitors.

Blessed by strategic planning, state-of-the-art computer systems, newly aggressive marketing campaigns, opportunities for expansion, and more centralized management, the banking twins continued their parallel growth throughout the 1970s. During that decade, Banco moved fractionally ahead of First Bank System in most balance-sheet categories: Banco's assets at the end of 1979 were $12.4 billion and FBS's were $12.1 billion, both groups tripling their asset base of 1970. Banco was further ahead in loans ($7.6 billion versus $6.8 billion), deposits ($9.6 billion versus $9 billion), and shareholder equity ($719 million versus $701 million). Banco's market value of $676 million was below book value at the average price of its stock in 1979. FBS's stock was also selling at less than book value, with a market capitalization of $600.3 million. Net income for Banco had tripled during the decade, and FBS had done nearly as well. The stock market, however, didn't seem impressed since both organizations' market capitalization had less than doubled during this decade. It was not particularly noticeable in the waning days of the 1970s, but this was really the end of the beginning for the twin holding companies.

THE SCORE CARD – 1980

Northwest Bancorporation		First Bank Stock Corporation
86 (8)	Number of Banks (change since 1970)	92 (4)
$11,044,000,000 ($7,561,000,000)	Total Deposits (change since 1970)	$9,768,000,000 ($6,084,000,000)
$7,813,000,000	Total Loans	$7,413,000,000
$797,000,000 ($461,000,000)	Capital & Surplus (change since 1970)	$782,000,000 ($484,200,000)
25,926,000	# Common Shares	15,091,000
30¼ – 18	Market Range High/Low	40¼ – 3¾
	Per Common Share	
$4.39	Earned	$7.42
$1.44	Dividend	$2.24
$30.73	Book Value	$51.82
6.0%	Yield*	6.1%
$625,464,750 ($257,722,875)	Market Capitalization* (change since 1970)	$550,821,500 ($161,372,300)
	Per 2000 Common Share	
$0.37 ($0.24)	Earned (change since 1970)	$0.62 (0.39)
$0.12	Dividend	$0.19
$2.01 ($0.68)	Market Price* (change since 1970)	$4.44 ($2.22)

* based on average market price

The stagecoach used in early Northwestern employee-anniversary gatherings was eerie
foreshadowing of the 1998 merger between Wells Fargo and Norwest Corporation.

Reaching Maturity
1986–1999

THE EDIFICE COMPLEX

BUILDINGS WERE BOTH a challenge and an opportunity for bank managers. By the 1980s, many Banco and First Bank System affiliates still occupied the structures they were using when the holding companies were formed. The boardrooms still smelled of long-ago cigar smoke, their opulence both out-of-date and out-of-taste. Although the buildings were gradually modernized with air-conditioning, drive-up or drive-through access, and (perhaps) ATMs, they lacked sufficient space for data-processing systems and private rooms for client conferences. Prompted by need, ego, and, in one case, fire, the building boom was predictable.

DEPRESSION-ERA BUILDING

In 1930 Northwestern National Bank had finished its new sixteen-story office building in downtown Minneapolis. For the next fifty-six years, this classical tower provided a home for the bank and its holding company, along with Faegre and Benson, Banco's law firm; Campbell-Mithun, its advertising agency; and Allison Williams, a local securities broker. In 1949, the tower was topped by the Weatherball, an illuminated globe that echoed weather forecasts by day and night via colored neon tubes: red meant warmer weather while white meant colder; green

meant no change, while blinking (any color) meant rain or snow. The color code was remembered by children and adults alike by a jolly jingle.[1] Until taller neighbors blocked its view, the Weatherball was a beloved landmark. It was turned off and dismantled some five years before fire was to destroy the building on which it had stood.[2]

After World War II, the penthouse floor of the Northwestern tower featured the Weatherball Room, a formal, reservations-only dining suite used to host significant customers, prospects, and other VIPs. The luncheon menu (which, along with the placemats, displayed the day's weather color and jingle) included such entrees as steak and lobster tail. Some officers ate lunch in the penthouse every day. But even long-time hostess Myrt Conklin couldn't produce a martini or a glass of wine for them. For that sort of banker's lunch, they had to look elsewhere.

With a few improvements, the Northwestern National Bank Building served its owners well throughout its lifetime. In the early 1960s, air conditioning was added—at a cost exceeding the original price tag for building the tower. Later in that decade, Italian painters were imported to marbleize

Clarence Chaney, a vice president at Northwestern National Bank, delighted in painting Christmas scenes for the corporate holiday card. The images reflected downtown Minneapolis in a positive wintry scene and always included the Weatherball as a spot of color. This 1957 card included the Northwestern Bank Building and (to the right) the new First National Bank tower.

**Changing marketing strategies ultimately
made the Northwestern Weatherball obsolete.
In 1983 the famous icon was removed.**

lobby pillars and other areas that had not
been originally finished in stone. Minneapolis's first skyway, the Twin Cities' revolu-
tionary contribution to the architecture
and amenities of a winter city, was in the
works. It initially was planned to cut diag-
onally across the corner of Seventh Street
and Marquette Avenue—right through the
corner office of the bank's chair, John
Moorhead. The Minneapolis Fire Department discouraged thoughts of obstructing
that critical downtown intersection, so the
skyway, which opened in 1963, crossed
instead at midblock from the new Northstar
Center to the bank.[3] As larger computer
operations became critical to bank operations, they were moved to a new, secure,
and slightly remote Northwest Operations
Center building, freeing up several floors
for new tenants and the burgeoning bank.

As part of the agreement to merge the First
National Bank and Merchants National
Bank in St. Paul, the new entity
announced that it would build a major
tower to house operations of the combined organizations. The structure blended
the existing sixteen-story headquarters of
Merchants National into a thirty-two-story
skyscraper that would dominate the St.
Paul skyline for fifty years. The building
stood 402 feet tall and was topped by an
observation platform and a 100-foot skele-
ton of steel framing that supported the
large red numeral "1st." Described by F.
Scott Fitzgerald in a short story depicting a
young man returning to St. Paul for
Christmas, the tower's sign served as a
beacon for trains, riverboats, aircraft, and

automobiles heading for downtown St. Paul. The building was completed on time, in the teeth of the Depression, at a cost of $6.3 million. Said George Prince when he paid the final bill: "It cost a lot more than I thought it would, but I knew it would."[4] The building was not Depression-proof— ten floors remained unfinished until after World War II—but its lobby was the financial crossroads of St. Paul.[5]

Like Northwestern, First National Bank of St. Paul also featured a dining room— called 2800 for its place high on the twenty-eighth floor—with views of the Mississippi River. This suite of small, individually decorated dining rooms was used to entertain clients and guests of the bank or First Trust. It was a subtle but real mark of community standing and affluence when St. Paulites could comment that they had been asked to lunch at "the bank." (The First National was so dominant in the east-metro market that its clients needed only to cite "the bank" or "the trust company" for everyone to know what they meant.[6]) Several "pragmatic" remodelings obliterated the building's classical two-story lobby and its long

Minneapolis's first skyway, which opened in 1963, initially planned to cut across the intersection of Seventh Street and Marquette Avenue. For safety reasons, the fire department proposed a midblock placement. The skyway connected Northwestern National Bank to the Northstar Center.

189

RESTLESS IN MINNEAPOLIS

The First National Bank had a peripatetic role in downtown Minneapolis real estate. At the beginning of the twentieth century, its offices were in the Phoenix Building at Fourth and Marquette. In 1907, the bank relocated to a new two-story structure at Fifth and Marquette, which was demolished in 1914 to make way for the First National–Soo Line Building.[7] The First National occupied space in that new structure in 1915. In the late 1950s, the bank purchased the east half of the block to build a twenty-seven-story main office that opened for business on February 29, 1960.[8] The new building was the first aluminum and glass-panel design to be constructed in Minneapolis, yet it lacked the architectural dominance of the facilities occupied by its peers. Thus, the bank and its holding company readily joined with the Pillsbury Company in constructing a two-tower, full-block complex just across Second Street. The bank and First Bank System occupied most of the shorter of the towers when they moved in, in 1980.

Even this would not be the last move of the century for First/Minneapolis. It next committed to being the prime tenant in the I. M. Pei–designed building just south of the Pillsbury location, then called First Bank Place (and now known as the 225 Building). But in 1990, new management

Cleared for building the new home of First National Bank of Minneapolis, the lot at Second Avenue and Sixth Street became a public skating rink with lights and music during the winter of 1956–1957.

Painters spruce up the "1st" sign of the First National Bank of St. Paul. Throughout the years, the lighted sign has been turned off only during national emergencies.

of the holding company looked for ways to break the costly lease. When that failed, the budget was trimmed and the new management moved, grumpily, across the street. Ten years later, after some of the more onerous lease conditions had expired, the bank was once again free to move. This time, the relocation would be four blocks away, as the headquarters and most corporate offices were transferred in 2001 to a new building on the Nicollet Mall that had been originally commissioned by Piper-Jaffray, the broker dealer that had, temporarily, become a part of U.S. Bancorp.

John Greenman, a long-time employee of Banco Properties, once observed that, when it came to construction, his company went about it backward: when they built a specialized building, with the bank as a sole tenant, they owned it. When they built a commercial office tower in a downtown location, they leased it. This approach gave the bank little leverage with the landlord and gave the corporation no opportunity to build market equity.

While Banco and FBS equally indulged in the edifice phenomenon, even long-term managing officers generally got to build

First National Bank of Minneapolis occupied yet another new home by 1960: the city's first aluminum and glass-panel design. The bank's earlier home (on the right) survives.

only one new bank, one monument to that particular officer's vision, energy, and ego. The career of Pete Ankeny, First Bank System CEO, supported the "one building" limitation: though he was the determining officer for two headquarter structures, he was around only for the move to the Pillsbury Center tower.

The patterns of facility construction were similar among affiliates. Long-serving managing officers seemed able to persuade their boards to recommend to the holding company that a new facility in Des Moines, Iowa, or Duluth, Minnesota, would improve the bank's image (and that of its holding company), as well as its geographic reach and its capacity for growth and efficiency. In perhaps half the locations boasting Banco affiliates, an FBS competitor was also present, meaning that if one built, the other was likely to follow—and with a building that was a little taller, a little glitzier.

ARTFUL INVESTING

As branch banking became wider spread, and as the Twin Cities banks relocated offices to reach into emerging suburbs, both holding companies took control of the architectural design and the use of space in their outlying facilities. Critical components of the new units were accessible parking, lanes for drive-through service, and (when they were legalized) ATMs accessible to vehicles and walk-in customers alike. A meeting room with outside access was an amenity the new neighborhood banks

would offer community organizations, both during and after business hours.

With all the construction of new facilities there were many blank walls to fill, prompting a momentary fad toward purchases of paintings, sculptures, and other artworks. The argument ran that there were so few opportunities for banks to acquire equity-like investments that a fling in the "furnishings and fixtures" account (the budget line where these small art collections were recorded) might be treated as insignificant, yet could make some money for the institution.

The two First National Banks acquired relatively significant art. In St. Paul, the First purchased (and sometimes commissioned) several portfolios of works from nationally recognized photographers such as Gilles Peress and Tom Arnt. These images were hung conspicuously behind teller lines and in bank corridors. In Minneapolis, the First National Bank had built an elegant but modest collection of works by artists from the basic service region, from Thomas Hart Benton in Missouri to Aldo Moroni in Minneapolis.[9] As the bank morphed into First Bank System, the corporate art collection became a more serious focus. From 1981, Lynne Sowder and Associates, an art dealer in Minneapolis, was engaged to help the company in its acquisition of a significant portfolio of two- and three-dimensional works by internationally known artists. Sowder herself was employed in 1985 to head the bank's newly created Division of Visual

Arts, to manage accessions that eventually totaled more than $4 million during the decade, and to oversee a staff of three to five. After 1985, the division reported to Dennis Evans, an enthusiastic patron, until his departure in December 1988.

U.S. Bank Place became headquarters for U.S. Bancorp when FBS acquired the Oregon holding company in 1997.

Sowder's book, *Talkback-Listen,* vividly describes the process of introducing a challenging art collection to an audience of employees and clients who were suspicious of "modern art" and uncomfortable with it looking at them in the halls and behind teller lines.[10] Sowder created a series of workshops and brown-bag lunches to explain the accessions, but those works that resisted her efforts to find acceptance were removed from public view and placed in a "Controversy Corridor" with further didactics, including the reasons they had been banished.

The collection was problematic not only because of its content—including works by George Baselitz, Francisco Clemente, Julian Schnabel, and Andres Serrano—but also because of its timing. First Bank System's earnings were threatened and jobs were on the line, yet the management was allocating scarce dollars to buy "weird" art. Andrew Leicester, himself a peripatetic artist, filed a lawsuit against FBS for misuse of his and other depositors' funds.[11] After 1987, the corporation allocated no more money to new accessions; the staff of the Division of Visual Arts raised $1.3 million by selling works of lesser interest and held at a nice profit. By 1988 Sowder was gone, as was Evans, and in 1989 it was announced that 25 percent of the portfolio—now some 3,000 works valued at $10 million—would be sold, essentially those works that failed to meet tests of "harmony and unity." There was a temporary promise that the proceeds of the sales would be reinvested in works by

Minnesota and regional artists, but in the whirl of cost-cutting and the search for shareholder value that would accompany the Jack Grundhofer regime, not only was that offer forgotten but the Division of Visual Arts and its staff vanished into the mists of nondefendable nonbanking business. Much of the remaining collection can be seen on U.S. Bancorp walls, particularly in executive office areas, with the rest carefully kept in storage.

RISING FROM THE ASHES

The Thanksgiving Day fire that badly damaged the Northwestern National Bank Building in 1982 was a disaster of major but mixed dimensions. On the negative side was the loss of irreplaceable records and properties, plus the dispersed relocation of bank and holding company staff across downtown Minneapolis at a time when new management was preoccupied with running a newly reorganized holding company—Norwest Corporation. On the positive side was the astounding ability to conduct business almost as usual on the Monday following the fire; the success of implementing a new, untested disaster plan; the good fortune that the operations center was two blocks away and thus physically unaffected; and the boost in employee morale that comes with surviving shared catastrophe. Another bright spot: there would be an opportunity to rebuild rather than remodel. The new bank would rise from the same downtown location, designed as a modern financial-services center that did away with the dated cathedral lobby and the plethora of armed guards.

Dale Chihuly's glass sculptures found their way into FBS's art collection.

The holding company's new building, finally occupied in 1988, had main-street pedestrian traffic passing through a second-floor portion of its skyway lobby, with tellers conveniently placed where the customers walked by and with officers and staff tucked out of sight. As was true of the First Bank Place tower, Norwest's new building was of the same general height but no taller than the IDS Tower, the Phillip Johnson design that had reshaped the Minneapolis skyline almost fifteen years earlier. But with the historic competition between the holding companies and the egotism of the holding companies' architects—Cesar Pelli (Norwest) and I. M. Pei (First Bank System)—one might expect that one or even both of the newer buildings *might* be a few inches taller. Who's to know? (In February 2005, a building engineer revealed that he had added two feet to the Pei building when the semi-tiara was built. This would answer the question.)

A fire set for warmth by street dwellers spread through the rubble of Donaldson's Department Store into the adjoining Northwestern National Bank building and burst into flame on Thanksgiving Day in 1982. Norwest rebuilt a new tower on the same site.

A well-designed exterior lighting scheme continues to make Norwest's stone and glass tower an attractive component of the Minneapolis skyline. A true "Minnesota Nice" story covers a special lighting of that tower. The elderly mother of Lloyd Johnson, then chair and CEO of Norwest, lived in a nearby nursing home, and her room had a view of the new building. One night, Johnson called his mother to tell her that a test run of the building's lights was scheduled for five o'clock the next morning. She was wakened to watch the illumination and so

excited by the display that Johnson determined to light the building every night instead of just on special occasions.

Vitrines displaying the corporation's collection of art deco furniture and other artifacts initially enhanced the lobby. A decade later, however—with the renewed dedication to shareholder values that accompanies a merger—this unusual collection was donated to the Minneapolis Institute of Arts as a goodwill gesture (and a tax deduction) when Norwest became Wells Fargo.

The first night the new Norwest Corporation tower in Minneapolis was illuminated, the sight so pleased the elderly mother of president Lloyd Johnson that he decided the Cesar Pelli–designed building would be lit every night.

NEW FRONTIERS in BANKING

IN MOVIE TERMS, the 1980s would turn out to be an overbudget extravaganza, but with great special effects. In financial terms, the fiercely competitive decade would set Banco and First Bank System on a strategic path toward escaping the geographical limitations of the Ninth Federal Reserve District. At the same time, the 1980s drastically reshaped the similar personalities of the twin holding companies into distinct identities. Banco would assume a new name, experience a declining net income in five of the ten years, and lose its home office (and principal banking unit) to a catastrophic fire. By the end of the 1980s, however, Banco's market capitalization would be three times what it had been at the beginning of the decade. Meanwhile, FBS faced a bond portfolio fiasco that eventually resulted in a net loss of $309.4 million and a 30 percent attrition of the corporate equity account, not to mention severe cost controls. By the end of the decade, however, a new CEO would be imported to revive FBS and its profitability.

THE NINTH FEDERAL RESERVE
Although they were sizable in terms of assets and employees, strong in regional business matters, and significant contributors to the Twin Cities' vaunted quality of life, the holding companies were, even at their best, medium-sized players on a small stage. The Ninth District had been one of the smaller Reserve Districts from the start. With its economic mix of agriculture, timber and mining, service industries, and light manufacturing, it also had grown more slowly than the rest of the other Federal Reserve Districts.

The trade area was also limiting as the number of banks in the United States steadily declined. By 1990, the national count of banks (not including branches) dropped 58 percent, from a record 31,076 in 1921 to 13,032. But those numbers dropped by 70 percent in Minnesota, 83 percent in North Dakota, and 88 percent in Montana. While the reduced totals were accelerated by acquisitions, consolidations, and conversions, the trend toward fewer units was making it ever harder for either FBS or Banco to expand by acquisition within the Ninth District. According to tests applied by the U.S. Department of Justice to measure competitive impact, the two holding companies were already at their effective limits. By 1990, the two largest banks in Minnesota (one each from the holding companies) held 44.3 percent of all banking business in the state. In South Dakota, the two

In 1997, the Ninth Federal Reserve Bank built its new $100 million headquarters on the Mississippi River, where the banking industry in Minneapolis was born.

largest held 47.3 percent, with similar numbers in other Upper Midwest states. At that time, Banco (by then Norwest) was the largest banking entity in Montana, South Dakota, and Iowa; First Bank System stood first in Minnesota and North Dakota, second in South Dakota.

Although Norwest had affiliates in Iowa and Nebraska, and FBS held banks in Wisconsin and Washington State, their primary source of demand and stable time deposits, both commercial and retail, was always the Ninth Federal Reserve. Home-area deposits have always been the lowest

cost and most predictable source of funding for bank investment and lending, and when push comes to shove—that is, at the bottom line—the more profitable banks are those with a larger percentage of home-area deposits. The combination of a slowly growing home territory, coupled with existing marketplace dominance, was both troubling and uncomfortably limiting.

Diversification continued to be the popular strategy as the holding companies' managers and investment bankers sought acquisition/merger candidates in somewhat parallel businesses that banking staff could both understand and manage. The greater message, however, was that the groups had to grow beyond the Ninth Federal Reserve District. As soon as interstate acquisitions were permitted—first on the national level, then on a state by state basis—the groups would move forward. At first, these explorations were careful and moderate, but as they gained experience and related confidence, much more dramatic.

MANAGING UNDER STRESS

In 1980 the escalating rate of inflation peaked and then backed off. The prime interest rate, which had climbed steadily to the 20 percent level, declined to 10 percent, but worked its way back to 21.5 percent by year's end. Against this backdrop, Banco and FBS each managed a modest increase in net income.

The stressful times reinforced management centralization at the corporate level. At Banco, John Morrison moved from chair/CEO of Northwestern National Bank of Minneapolis to vice chair of the holding company, clearly heir apparent to Chester Lind. Indeed, Morrison became Banco's CEO in October 1981. In moving from the senior position of the largest Banco bank to the top job at the holding company, he took with him the last vestiges of perceived autonomy (in all but parochial matters) at the affiliate level. His intention was to expedite, and perhaps finalize, the transition of management decision-making from the Banco affiliates—particularly the nearest and biggest one, literally just downstairs—to the corporate office. Having worked on both sides of the fence, Morrison knew that the future lay in a consolidated effort directed by the holding company.

As further reinforcement to this theme, Bob Krane was elected president of Banco. Krane had been president/CEO of both the Iowa–Des Moines National Bank (second largest member of the Banco family) and the U.S. National Bank of Omaha (third largest). His promotion was significant. For decades the affiliates had maintained a reputation, if not for captiousness, then for being a predictable loyal opposition. With Krane working at the corporate level, the affiliates felt that they had an ally.

At First Bank System, Clarence Frame left his position as chair and CEO of First National Bank of St. Paul in 1980 to become vice chair of the holding company and head of its newly created Metropolitan Division, which was to manage all FBS affiliates in the Twin Cities. Promoting the last of the St. Paul bank's nationally regarded lending gurus to this position addressed one of FBS's biggest continuing challenges: integration of the two principal banks.

Despite fifty years of partnership between First National Bank of St. Paul and First National Bank of Minneapolis—during which their combined earning power had generated the capital necessary to support their country affiliates and cover the parent company's dividend—the two banks had vastly different personalities. As the dominant bank in its market and community (its assets and capital accounts were roughly six times those of its nearest competitor), First/St. Paul possessed a character and culture all its own. The bank was not unlike New York's J. P. Morgan: in its day an aggressive but discriminating lender in high-yield transactions, tremendously supportive of the city's wealthy patrons. In fact, in a tradition dating back to Richard Lilly and George Prince (and Lilly's brother Leonard), First/St. Paul was nationally regarded for its niche-lending expertise, even to the extent that one grateful client recognized Clarence Frame by naming a river tugboat after him. (The boat had no doubt been financed by the bank.) The bank also had a community development office, with bank CEO Philip Nason as the principal rallying point for many downtown St. Paul initiatives, including the Radisson Hotel and the civic center.[12]

When Bob Krane became president of Banco, the former president of affiliate banks in Iowa and Nebraska solidified Banco's relationship with all of its affiliate banks.

First/Minneapolis, on the other hand, was more like the Chase Manhattan Bank of that time: broadly based, commercial- and retail-oriented, and equipped with trust and investment services as well as a major correspondent network for country bankers that covered the Ninth Federal Reserve District and beyond. The elitist First/St. Paul disdained the common denominator approach of its sibling, but was no match for First/Minneapolis as a corporate role model around which to shape a regional holding company during intensely competitive times. So Frame's promotion killed two birds with the same stone: it depersonalized the commercial management of the St. Paul bank and, at least on paper, moved the banking élan of the St. Paul loan function into the holding company.

The rivalry between First/Minneapolis and Northwestern National Bank, across-the-board competitors for more than a century, came down to numbers rather than personalities. Sometimes one was bigger, sometimes the other. The U.S. Comptroller of the Currency required that all banks publish a minimal "Statement of Condition" (balance sheet) in their local legal journal four times each year. Call statements provided the only way to compare privately held banks.[13] Often the two Minneapolis banks were close enough in size to encourage games at call dates to balloon assets or buy deposits and thereby win the local "numero uno" ranking. Neither bank would tout that it was the largest in town or the state, but it was pleasant, even if transitory, to make such a claim at the Minneapolis Club.

BANCO DIVERSIFIES

By the 1980s, Banco had already built a broad menu of financial services: Banco Mortgage, Northwest Growth Fund (an early small business investment company, aka a federally supported, equity-based development capital fund), Banco Financial (secured financing), Banco Properties, and Northwest Computer Services. One day in 1980, early in John Morrison's regime, an investment banker recommended what would prove to be the $252 million purchase of the Dial Corporation, a $1 billion Iowa-based consumer finance company—and one of the nation's ten largest and most profitable independent factors (that is, a financial company engaged in discount activities).

Philip Nason, longtime CEO of First National Bank of St. Paul and strong community leader (center) accepts a plaque from St. Paul mayor George Vavoulis (left) noting the effective stocking of fallout-shelter supplies in his bank's vaults. The emergency rations were still there thirty years later.

The St. Paul Civic Center was one of many downtown initiatives championed by the community development office of the First National Bank of St. Paul under CEO Philip Nason.

Morrison endorsed the purchase of Dial (renamed Iowa Securities) as another entree on the corporate menu and as a business that had retail offices in many more states than Banco reached through its banking offices. Controversy plagued the deal as it became public; in the social lore of banking, small-loan clients were deemed to be of a slightly lower class than, say, merchant bankers. Yet it would prove to be a watershed purchase. The strong and fairly predictable cash flow from small-loan activity supported other corporate activities in years when more traditional bank earnings were under pressure. Iowa Securities' profit margins and high return on capital gave Banco a widely envied return on equity even in the difficult years that lay ahead.

Banco also acquired the State Bank of Worthington, Minnesota, during 1981. While the corporation had added a handful of Iowa banks in the last few years, this was its first Minnesota acquisition since its founding days and brought the total portfolio to eighty-seven banking units. In addition, Northwestern National Bank of Minneapolis opened a London office through its Canadian-American Bank partnership, and established a tentative relationship with the Peoples Bank of China.

On balance, however, 1981 proved to be a disappointing year for both groups. FBS "had a soft year in 1981 as the enterprise experienced its first earnings decline in 20 years," and "high interest rates had negative leverage on long term fixed rate investments."[14] FBS enthusiastically expanded its foreign lending activity, as First/Minneapolis formed First Bank International to buy the New York and London offices of Rainier Bank (based in Washington State). Newly popular international loans funded by FBS affiliates rose to $438 million, up nearly threefold from the $145 million reported a year earlier.

Banco affiliates sold blocks of long-term, low-yield bonds from several portfolios, resulting in a loss of $25 million. The loss lowered corporate net income by $13.4 million and caused the first year-to-year decline in Banco's earnings since 1963. The specter raised by Northwestern National's determination to be a "lending bank" haunted the holding company in those years of extraordinary interest-rate gyrations. Deposit trends were flat, with continuing attrition of demand deposits (via disintermediation) offset by purchased time funds and other borrowings to meet the regional demand for credit, supplemented by growing participation in national and international credits. The loan-to-deposit ratio for Banco affiliates went from 71 percent in 1980 to 93 percent at the end of 1982—a level that, historically, would have caused bank managers and examiners to push the panic button. Along with this burgeoning demand for credit came an increasing dry rot among challenged commitments already on the books: nonperforming loans, or credits that were not meeting agreed-upon criteria, such as timely payment of interest and principal. Narrowed

interest margins and loan charge-offs were hitting both groups hard.

Meanwhile, after a half-century as Northwest Bancorporation, Banco became Norwest Corporation in 1981 and its family of affiliates became Norwest Banks, N.A.[15] While "Banco" had been a reasonable symbolic representation of a financial institution in the Ninth Federal Reserve District and beyond, it was not the right tag for a full-service financial corporation offering much more than banking services. The new corporate name and image preserved the geographical identity of the corporate entity and its nonbanking endeavors as it unified the affiliate titles. John Morrison—and Peter Gillette, chair and CEO of the newly renamed Norwest Bank of Minneapolis, N.A.—had one busy and well-publicized day using a helicopter and thousands of green and blue balloons to visit and rechristen the one-time Northwest Bancorporation banks in the greater Twin Cities area. Morrison then took the same show on the road.

BETTER IN 1982, BUT NOT GREAT
First Bank System reported a return to higher levels of earnings in 1982, but management commented warily that "restoration of acceptable credit quality is this enterprise's principal short term problem."[16] FBS's solution, which included a national banking initiative under the leadership of First/Minneapolis, intended to rejuvenate loan growth and to pursue nonbanking diversification, but only gradually. The company as a whole would continue

its emphasis on main-line banking. An office in Singapore was added to support rapidly growing international activity.

By November it was clear that loan losses would mean that 1982 would be another year of disappointing earnings for Norwest. The low point for the enterprise, however, was reached later that month, when a smoldering fire in the remains of Donaldson's Department Store, which shared the Norwest Bank Building, burst into the renowned Thanksgiving Day fire and destroyed the bank and holding company headquarters.

On the positive side, Norwest opened an Edge Act banking office in Miami—a place where transactions in non-U.S. funds could be accomplished—with another scheduled for Hong Kong. These offices enabled making offshore (international) loans with offshore funds, bypassing the books and limitations of their domestic headquarters. Managers of Norwest Mortgage believed they had discovered a no-risk approach to the residential mortgage market, using the resources of Mortgage Guaranty Insurance Company (aka MGIC, or, perhaps more appropriately, "Magic") and Salomon Brothers. With this assurance, Norwest Mortgage expanded enthusiastically to become the nation's second-largest generator of residential mortgages in 1982, with a portfolio in excess of $12 billion.

IMPROVED EARNINGS

Both banking groups reported an improved earnings picture in 1983, with nearly identical results: $129.7 million

for First Bank System and $125.2 million for Norwest, the latter figure enhanced by $9.9 million as the net result of a $64.7 million insurance settlement from the fire.

Chairs continued to be shifted at FBS as retirement closed the careers of several long-term players. George Dixon stepped up to CEO and Pete Ankeny was named president and chief operating officer of FBS as Don Grangaard retired as chair of the enterprise after fifteen years at the helm. Also retiring were Harry Holtz, the acerbic and energetic chair of the First Trust Company in St. Paul; Charles Arner, the short-term and last full-time chair and CEO of First National Bank of St. Paul; and Clarence Frame, former First/St. Paul CEO but more recently vice chair of the parent corporation. Each loss furthered the depersonalization and diminution of the St. Paul bank's profile. Dennis Evans, who made his initial reputation as an investment analyst, was appointed chair and CEO of both FBS banks in the Twin Cities.

Not only was Evans to develop the two metropolitan banks into leading consumer institutions, synonymous with high-quality products and services, he was also expected to blend their images through "distinct but coordinated marketing strategies." FBS's 1984 annual report stated that First/Minneapolis was still charged as manager of "a carefully focused national corporate banking strategy," while First/St. Paul was assigned certain "specialized high growth potential niches in the corporate market"—jabberwocky, to be sure, but a clear acknowledgment of the persisting differences in the two banks' cultures. The blending process was proving neither fast nor easy. During 1984, FBS raised $120 million by sale and lease-back of twenty-three bank buildings; fourteen First Banks in Minnesota were consolidated. For the year, net income was up, albeit less than 1 percent, as FBS continued to be plagued by loan losses, and per share results declined slightly.

Things at Norwest were even less sanguine. Norwest Mortgage, which only two years earlier believed it had fenced off risk in its aggressive business-building efforts, ran afoul of reality in the form of adjustable rate mortgages. Earlier, Salomon Brothers, an investment house that had helped design what was to be a "failsafe" hedge, had concluded that there was no practical way to hedge an ARM portfolio and withdrew from the joint effort. Management at Norwest Mortgage confidently continued to expand its mortgage portfolio, which it still believed to be secure and risk-moderated. In 1984, however, Norwest Mortgage reported a loss of $26.1 million. The parent corporation reacted swiftly to cut losses: five of six officers identified as managers of the Norwest Mortgage unit were vaporized in that year's annual report, the ARM portion of the mortgage portfolio was sold, and the ongoing scope of the unit was sharply refocused.

Under the "when it rains, it pours" phenomenon, Norwest's commercial loan portfolio also continued to be challenged,

with 12 percent of the $1 billion international loan portfolio reported as nonperforming. An ambitious plan for a full-block reconstruction of corporate headquarters was announced and subsequently abandoned. Net income fell 44.5 percent.

As the Norwest board of directors anticipated CEO John Morrison's approaching retirement, they made it clear that, given the weight of current circumstances, they wanted to consider external candidates, even though capable internal candidates existed for the job. They mounted a full-court-press national search for Morrison's successor. On March 4, 1985, Lloyd Johnson, previously vice chair of Security Pacific Bank in California, was elected president and CEO of Norwest.

A SHAKY NORWEST

The next three years were difficult and inconclusive for both holding companies. The principal challenge for both Norwest and FBS was cancerous loan portfolios. The 1985 loan loss provision taken by Norwest was $266.3 million, a 50 percent increase over 1984. Earnings perked up, but total assets, loans, and deposits were flattened for five years as loan growth was curtailed and deposits declined slightly. During 1985, Norwest sold eight smaller banks in Minnesota and eight offices in South Dakota and consolidated its affiliate banks in Nebraska. An agreement was reached in 1985 with the Gerald Hines organization to build a new Norwest office tower, designed by Cesar Pelli and located on just half of the block site of the former building.

Not surprisingly, state and national regulators were concerned about Norwest's general health, considering the dimensions of its loan portfolio problems. At year-end 1985, Norwest Bank of Minneapolis and six other affiliates were operating subject to "letters of understanding" with the U.S. Comptroller of the Currency, while thirteen more Norwest banks were operating under similar stipulations with state banking regulators. These letters reminded the banks' respective boards of their particular responsibility in the managerial oversight of their institutions. The letters further suggested courses of action for improvement, defined limits to new business activity (including mergers or acquisitions), restrained dividends, and recommended that the boards share any business concerns with bank management.

When John Morrison retired at the end of 1985, Peter Gillette and Bob Krane resigned. Both had held significant positions at Norwest, but were passed over in the search process that had selected Lloyd Johnson. In February 1986, Norwest's corporate governance evolved further as the boards of the holding company and Norwest Bank of Minneapolis were melded. Later that year, Johnson brought in Dick Kovacevich as president of the holding company. Kovacevich had put in ten years at CitiBank, overseeing the buildup of consumer banking businesses.

The darkest financial moment for Norwest was probably 1987, during which its international portfolio experienced $204 mil-

Lloyd Johnson was the first Norwest CEO to come from outside the market, although he had a prerequisite Minnesota background.

lion in loan losses (for a total loan loss charge of $375.7 million) and the corporation reported the only net loss in earnings in its history. The result would have been far worse without input from the nonbanking businesses (essentially Norwest Financial), but it was still a reported red figure of $29.8 million. The annual report called it "an important year of transition."[17]

AN EVEN SHAKIER FBS

The mid-1980s proved troubling to First Bank System as well. The future looked brighter as management pressed ahead to consolidate its banking businesses. The intention was to build those products that appeared to have above-average potential and that fit what the enterprise hoped was an emerging image as an internationally competent financial resource. George Dixon, architect of the "new" FBS structure, retired in 1985, with Pete Ankeny succeeding his mentor one more step up the ladder to become chair and CEO. John Egemeyer, who had served an earlier stint at Norwest, became CEO of First Trust Company. His new employees would now also conduct fiduciary services under contract for the trust department of the Minneapolis bank; certain First Trust officers, doing business from Minneapolis offices, would thus be officers of both First Trust *and* First Bank/Minneapolis.

Then, after a profit and loss evaluation, FBS determined to sell twenty-eight small regional banks, seventeen banking offices, and thirty-nine insurance agencies. Corporate loan charge-offs in 1985 rose to $123.5 million—a 50 percent increase over 1984, but considerably less than the damage to be inflicted in 1986, when the charge-off total multiplied more than three times to $384.5 million. A portion of the portfolio loss, as well as write-offs incurred by the reined-in (overexposed) bond marketing group in St. Paul, was offset by sales of securities in the respective banks' bond accounts. FBS reinvested the proceeds in similar, relatively long maturities that would play a significant role in the future of the holding company, whose vision was outlined in its 1986 annual report:

> During the past three years, First Bank System has gone through a series of organization changes designed to improve our ability to compete more effectively in a deregulated environment. The effect of these actions has been to change the company from a loose confederation of more than 80 individual banks to a more cohesive organization with a common vision and strategy.[18]

The strategy involved the sale of banks in 1985 but also included a single acquisition target: a small and apparently failing bank in Omak, Washington. To ask "Why Omak? And *where* is Omak?" was obvious, but the answer was less so: at the time, Omak was inexpensive opportunism, part of a checkerboard strategy that would allow FBS (as an "in-state" holding company) to later make an offer (ultimately unsuccessful) to buy the Rainier Bank holding company in Seattle.

After the fact, First Bank System identified 1987 as "one of its most challenging years" and recorded its first decline in earnings in six years, only the third since 1962. The primary cause of the decline was a $160 million charge-off of international loans, offset by a $21.6 million gain on the sale of the First Bank building in St. Paul. International loans rose during 1987 from $2.5 billion to $3.7 billion. The total included a portfolio of LDC (lesser developed countries) loans. LDC loans were a particularly challenging type of credit, even for those who understood it.

By year-end 1987, when the Minnesota legislature acted to allow a limited form of branch banking, FBS consolidated its

Twin Cities banks into First Bank Minnesota, N.A. Consolidation made this new bank the nineteenth largest in the United States, with $19 billion in assets. Norwest Bank, Minnesota, would have only $8 billion in assets after its initial consolidation.[19] FBS also entered into an "if, as, and when" agreement with Banks of Iowa to acquire that midsized holding company if changes in the law would allow such an action within the next decade. Paul Anton, FBS corporate economist, and his small staff became early victims of cost cutting, suggesting that banks really don't need an economist to rationalize difficult financial decisions. Anton's counterpart at Norwest, Sung Won Sohn, commented in the news that the budget for *his* office was covered by cost transfers from other departments, and thus his function escaped the spotlight of corporate cost control.[20] The dialogue recalled the comment about Norwest's first economist—that "he had better be able to sell a lot of bonds."

IS THAT AN ICEBERG?

The big news, however—and the tip of the iceberg that was about to rupture the First Bank System ship of state—emerged as the corporation disclosed that its investment portfolio, purchased for $7.8 billion with some anticipation of a declining rate environment, was held at a $555 million unrealized loss. Under routine accounting, if FBS had held its bond portfolio to maturity, the enormous loss would never have been taken or booked. The problem was that $555 million is too big a number

to ignore, either by the board of directors or the media.

FBS's placatory year-end statement failed to calm worrywarts who weren't sure that bond prices would rise soon enough or far enough, and who fretted about management's judgment in hedging its portfolio against further interest rate rises/price declines just before the bond market moved strongly upward. In effect, decision-makers had limited their ability to recover with the market. At the April 1988 shareholders' meeting, Dennis Evans, president of the board, suggested that FBS banks try to deemphasize their dependence on interest-related business and noted that "(our) main source of improved earnings will come from rapid growth in fee income and diligent control of operating expenses. . . . Total customer profitability is our new measurement for success."[21] Pete Ankeny suggested that the bond portfolio was a logical investment alternative while the company reduced its loan activity. The board members demonstrated *their* positive outlook by increasing the common dividend by 50 percent to $1.64 per share. Their decision reflected a strong capital position and a further part of the strategy to woo the Rainier banking group. At that time, banks were not allowed to use excess capital to repurchase stock.

Meanwhile, the Minnesota legislature was passing bills to permit interstate banking in other states whose legislatures had approved banking reciprocity. Initially, nine states would be in Minnesota's banking region, as would the four states bordering Minnesota that had been approved in 1986 via a similar bill. FBS had acquired ownership of a bank in Milwaukee as part of the earlier bill and found itself given the opportunity to "rescue" a fourteen-unit industrial bank holding company in Colorado. In return, Colorado offered a sizable carrot: purchasing rights to its banks. FBS won the negotiation by paying $8 million to the uninsured depositors. FBS immediately bought Central Bancorporation, a nineteen-bank, $2 billion Colorado holding company. FBS thus had a presence in Colorado at least two years ahead of Norwest.[22]

Outwardly, calm reigned in the upper echelons of First Bank System as the board approved signing a lease arrangement supporting FBS's joint occupancy of 650,000 square feet in a new downtown office tower complex shared by the Pillsbury Company. Inside the boardroom and in the executive suites, however, all was not well. In November, Dennis Evans resigned as president of the board; it was not a surprise. In December, the corporation grudgingly sold $4.6 billion of long-term U.S. Treasury securities and realized a loss in excess of $500 million before tax adjustments. This concluded the open-ended portfolio loss issue that had hung over the company for more than a year. Pete Ankeny met with media and security analysts to discuss the transactions, also noting that FBS would sell its equity interest in its present headquarters building. The resulting $50 million gain

would be a partial offset of the bond losses.[23] The bottom line was a net loss of $309.4 million and a 30 percent attrition of the corporate equity account.

Ankeny had been brought up according to an old-fashioned model—to work hard, to be competitive, to stay with the job. Although a handful of FBS old-timers still held that he was not a "real banker," Ankeny was respected for his energy and professionalism. He wasn't especially outgoing, but he was committed to a community where "involvement" is much more than a slogan. Like the shy people who populate Garrison Keillor's Lake Wobegon, Ankeny was "doing the things that needed to be done." By the end of 1988, he felt that the FBS board fully understood the challenges and supported the opportunities in the group's future.

THE GUILLOTINE NEEDS FEEDING

A characteristic problem with reconstructing history from annual corporate reports is that, when there's an unanticipated change in management—as was true for FBS in the fall of 1989—the reporting focus suddenly shifts from retrospective to prospective. It's as if the new officers and the communications department decide that the reader/shareholder isn't interested in the events and people behind failed strategies and cares only about what will happen under the sure hand of a new leader. Whatever positive changes the departed management might have made are buried alongside nightmarish losses and sweet dreams of gains. The future, after all, is what price/earnings ratios are built upon. At any rate, there would be little about either Ankeny or portfolio losses in FBS's 1989 annual report.

The annual shareholders' meeting in April was a good example of the ordeals of public opinion that Ankeny faced. Shareholders sat quietly through his review of the history and outcomes of the bond portfolio fiasco and his predictions of recovery. Questions focused not so much on how the massive losses happened, but on why Dennis Evans, creator of the failed portfolio strategy, had received such substantial severance and incentive payments. Naturally, there were a few concerns about FBS's remaining loan portfolio, which was still recording a significant number of nonperforming loans. Popular that year among loan-recovery specialists were LBOs, or leveraged buyouts. An LBO involved a major borrowing of funds to purchase the outstanding equity of a going concern with the expectation that new, motivated managers would run the company so well that the LBO credit would be promptly repaid. That expectation wasn't a sure bet, however, and FBS's earlier experiences with borrowings from LDCs—lesser developed countries—did not give shareholders much to be confident about.

Throughout the summer of 1989, rumors that Ankeny had resigned added to worries that there were further problems at FBS that no one was talking about. No significant speculations surfaced about a new manager until mid-September, when

a security analysts meeting regarding FBS, which had been scheduled for some time, was postponed until November. Later that week, Ankeny reportedly brought to the board a massive cost-control proposal that would have reduced a corporate staff of 10,000 by 15 to 20 percent. The resignation rumors began swirling again.

On September 22, local media reported that the axe had indeed fallen. Ankeny had resigned, and the board appointed Darrell Knudson, vice chair of the FBS board and a lifelong employee, as acting chief executive. Richard Zona, who had been recruited by Ankeny from Ernst and Young's national Financial Services Industry practice, was designated executive vice president and chief financial officer. Richard Schall, retired administrative officer of the Dayton-Hudson Corporation and a longtime FBS board member, was named acting chair. Assigned to recruit Ankeny's successor, Schall told *Star Tribune* reporters: "I have absolutely no interest whatsoever in joining the bank in a management capacity. If I get an office there, it will simply be a place to have a meeting if I need one. Darrell is the chief executive." Asked if the board were surprised about the enterprise's continuing difficulties, Schall replied, "The word surprise is bothersome. Any time management comes in with new information, it can be termed a surprise. But the board has not been asleep and it is aware that there is a good deal of high-risk, high-return ratio consideration that goes into highly leveraged transactions."[24]

With support from the board, Knudson expedited what had been Ankeny's plan for restructuring. Included were the following initiatives, announced that fall:

- that corporate assets (and the offsetting liabilities) would be reduced by $2.5 billion, or 10 percent;

- that business lines deemed not critical would be sold;

- that employment would be reduced by 16 percent—almost half from sale of business lines—and a charge of $25 to $40 million taken to cover layoff costs;

- that extensions of LBO credits would be restricted; and

- that the merchant banking and capital markets operations would be tightened.

Some progress had been made by December, with 500 positions eliminated and the corporate art program shut down. While tradition held that banks should never reduce their dividend short of going out of business, a nudge from regulators and plain common sense led the board to halve its common dividend from $1.64 to $0.82 per share—the first time that level of calamity had occurred since 1933.

According to the weekly trade paper *American Banker,* First Chicago, a major Illinois bank holding company, was hovering vulturelike over FBS with thoughts of matrimony. Although FBS had retained

First Boston as an investment banker and marriage broker, the board had rethought the merger issue. A spokesperson denied that any of those things were happening, and Knudson further indicated that the enterprise believed it could remain independent. At the depressed level of the common stock, however, it was apparent to analysts that FBS represented an attractive target for acquisition and rehabilitation. Equally clear, however, was that if the company couldn't complete a successful recovery on its own, it was a goner.

So when at last the board announced they had found a new manager to lead FBS out of the wilderness, it was a breath of fresh air. The 1990 annual report covering events of 1989 opened with a message to shareholders from John F. Grundhofer, First Bank System's new chair, president, and chief executive officer, fresh from Wells Fargo Bank headquarters in San Francisco, where he was vice chair and senior executive officer for Southern California:

Long term, our restructuring program will improve the quality and predictability of our earnings, focusing First Bank System on those businesses where we consistently can achieve superior returns by delivering superior service. Restructuring will reshape First Bank System into a company focused on consumer banking, middle-market commercial banking, trust services, and electronic banking.

In the near term, we are concentrating on reducing costs by eliminating jobs, centralizing some staff functions, downsizing certain operations, and exiting businesses that cannot deliver acceptable levels of risk-adjusted profitability. The Company is attacking credit quality head-on. We are reducing our higher risk assets and strengthening credit controls system-wide.

The level of risk exposure in our business will be lower. The bottom line will gradually improve. The composition of earnings will shift toward less volatile sources. Our fundamental goal remains the same. We want First Bank System to be a highly competitive, independent super-regional bank serving the diversified region encompassing the Upper Midwest and Pacific Northwest.[25]

A couple of incidents interrupted the grand sweep of events in early 1990. On the humorous side, in mid-February, a voice on the phone identified itself to the Minneapolis newspaper as being that of Richard Thomas, CEO of the First National Bank of Chicago.[26] The caller stated that his corporation was interested in buying First Bank System "around $22 per share," somewhat above the market value. He added that Jack Grundhofer would "turn that bank around" and that "it would definitely be more expensive at the end of the year." The call turned out to be a hoax, but the forecast was right on target. The second event, not humorous at all, was the kidnapping of Grundhofer in November. He escaped within a few hours, but due to police and media confusion, the perpetrator was never caught.

In July, the private placement of 12.6 million shares of stock to Corporate Partners investment managers and the State Board of Florida generated a much-needed $170 million in capital, and established a strong shareholder position with a long-term focus and resistance to short-term takeover opportunism. The report continued with a lengthy list of shutdown activities: closed offices in London, New York, Los Angeles, and Chicago; downsized merchant banking, capital markets, and health-care lending; exited low-margin large credits, out-of-market lending, and merchant banking. The long-outstanding call option to buy Banks of Iowa was terminated, the commercial component of FBS Mortgage sold, and the mortgage portfolio reduced by $2.9 billion with recourse.

As expected, numerous staff resigned or were released. Ankeny had suggested a reduction of 15 to 20 percent of total employment; Darrell Knudson had proposed 16 percent. The at-risk number of employees therefore should have been between 1,500 and 2,000. Although the base had been pruned from 10,000 employees to 9,004 by the end of 1988, it had surprisingly ballooned to 10,667 by the end of 1989, the end of the old administration. Grundhofer was an easy target, labeled "Jack the Ripper" and "Black Jack" for his role in these departures.

Three points might be remembered in the aftermath of what was seen by some as a bloodbath. First, the handwriting had been on the wall for most of the truncated units

Jack Grundhofer came to First Bank System from Wells Fargo with a clear challenge: to sort thetroubled pieces of the organization, cut costs, and make astute acquisitions.

before Grundhofer's arrival. Second, the total employee population at the end of 1990 was 9,475, down 1,192 or 11.2 percent from 1989's figure. Efforts to limit and outsource functions kept pressure on the total FBS employee population, but acquisitions and reallocations had *added* 5,000 employees by the end of 1991. Third, Grundhofer's "chain saw" mentality said he meant business, although the cuts were not nearly as bad as the propaganda suggested.

Also shut down were lesser matters, beneath mentioning in an annual report,

yet significant more in terms of policy than in dollars. Included were bans on coffeemakers, office plants maintenance, excess daily newspapers, interbank messenger and shuttle services, official dining rooms, and employee cafeterias. Office square footage was evaluated and reassigned. The balance of FBS Mortgage and in-house insurance operations were sold, the internal audit function substantially reduced, and internal legal staff minimized. The corporation's foundation staff, at one time a role model for local corporate charitable giving, was cut (as was giving, temporarily) and the function of lobbying was eliminated. Simplistically speaking, if an FBS business or service wasn't in the mainstream, it was sold or shut down. If a service could be outsourced at a viable cost, it was discontinued. If space wasn't needed, it was sublet. If a capital item was needed, it had to be approved in terms of shareholder value by the chair or vice chairs.

The total effect was striking: In December 1991, much to the board's relief, the U.S. Comptroller of the Currency released FBS from its "letter of agreement," which had been closely monitoring management intentions and results since 1989.

The 1980s were definitive in establishing both Banco/Norwest and First Bank System as survivors rather than victims. Neither holding company would require rescue by a white knight. In fact, during the 1990s, both would don white armor to save fair banking maidens from fates worse than—well, a lot worse than a bounced check.

THE SCORE CARD – 1990

Northwest Bancorporation		First Bank Stock Corporation
22 (-64)	Number of Banks (change since 1980)	34 (-58)
$20.124,000,000 ($9.080,000,000)	Total Deposits (change since 1980)	$14,633,000,000 ($4,865,000,000)
$17,793,000,000	Total Loans	$13,458,000,000
$1,638,000,000 ($841,000,000)	Capital & Surplus (change since 1980)	$1,295,000,000 ($513,000,000)
102,959,000	# Common Shares	77,430,600
23⅝ – 13½	Market Range High/Low	16⅞ – 9¾
Per Common Share		
$1.16	Earned	$1.53
$0.85	Dividend	$0.82
$15.91	Book Value	$16.72
4.6%	Yield*	6.2%
$1,911,176,438 ($1,285,711,688)	Market Capitalization* (change since 1980)	$1,030,833,578 ($480,012,078)
Per 2000 Common Share		
$0.29 ($0.08)	Earned (change since 1980)	$0.51 ($0.11)
$0.21	Dividend	$0.27
$4.64 ($2.63)	Market Price* (change since 1980)	$4.44 ($0.00)

* based on average market price

TWINS NO MORE

IN COVERING the proposed megamerger of Citicorp with Travelers Insurance, *The Economist* suggested numerous motivations for such actions. In listing a series of large mergers among financial services companies, the magazine indicated that merger mania appeared to have a firm grip on domestic and international players in the finance business:

> Most financial industry executives in Europe and the Americas clearly believe that (a fundamental change) to be so. They have been merging with abandon, convinced that the future belongs to the large, the diverse, the global. . . . The conviction is widespread that those who fail to act quickly today may not be around to act with more forethought tomorrow— hence the insistence on doing something, anything, whatever the price.[27]

The editorial further opined that the jury is still out on successful mergers of insurance companies and banks, and that cross-selling of financial products is not easy to accomplish:

> That was then, bankers will tell you; this is now, when economies of scope and scale matter more than ever before. When simply guarding against the Millennium Bug takes a healthy bite out of profits, and when maintaining the latest in information technology requires billions of dollars a year, there is no alternative to being very, very big. Perhaps they are right. Or perhaps, not for the first time, the world's leading financiers are mistaking size for profitability.[28]

The same motivations for merging no doubt affected the strategies of both Norwest Corporation and First Bank System. Norwest made several small- and medium-sized acquisitions during the mid-1990s and focused on building its collection of "stores" (see table below). By using a baseline of 1989, the enterprise would report a decade of progress by 1998.[29]

Number of "Stores"	1989	1998	Compound Earnings Growth
Mortgage	180	846	50% compound
Banking	207	950	27% compound
Consumer Finance	619	1,358	13% compound

When the acquisition dust settled, Norwest Corporation became Wells Fargo, with Dick Kovacevich (right) as CEO and Paul Hazen (left), Jack Grundhofer's nemesis, continuing as chair.

At FBS, meanwhile, CEO Jack Grundhofer reminded those people who were concerned about growth through merger that the corporation he had been hired to manage was far too small, in terms of investment and volume of transactions, to build and maintain a sufficiently competitive data-management system. Without such a system, the corporation would be a target only, not an acquirer. Simply put, if Grundhofer could not grow FBS in a hurry, it would be gobbled by someone else. A look at his early FBS acquisitions—several corporate trust operations from coast to coast, volumes of accounts from the Marquette Bank group, bulked-up Colorado affiliations (to market leadership in that state)—indicates that all were designed to add transaction volume (and book assets) without complex mergers or regulator-sensitive action.

As First Bank System grew larger and more profitable, its data-management capacities expanded significantly. After two or three years of controlled growth and better internal management systems at FBS, the U.S. Comptroller of the Currency lifted the letter of restraint on certain activities, thus permitting FBS to pursue more mergers and acquisitions. The process had involved no magic, just common sense: managers determined a reasonable price for a proposed acquisition based on the premise that almost all of the new entity's backroom expenses could be absorbed by the existing FBS operations group at a nominal net increase in cost. Reducing the overhead of redundant middle and upper management in the acquired facilities contributed to an industry-leading efficiency ratio. The increase in FBS's size safeguarded the holding company as it increased its capacity to look at progressively bigger targets.

By May 1992, First Bank System was feeling well enough to increase its common dividend for the first time in four years. During the same year, the corporation expanded its presence in Colorado by further acquisitions to become that state's largest banking group. Another excitement in 1992 was FBS's purchase of part of Bank Shares, a large but elusive Minnesota banking venture owned by Carl Pohlad. The dimensions of the transaction changed during the process, due in part to regulators refusing to allow FBS to buy Pohlad's Rochester, Minnesota, bank and in part by Pohlad redefining what portions of his banking activity he was really selling. In any case, Pohlad—who received approximately 10 percent of FBS's common stock—was briefly the company's largest individual shareholder.[30] In 1993, acquisition of the Boulevard Bank in Illinois gave FBS a modest entry into the Chicago market. Subsequent transactions of some size included Metropolitan Financial in Minnesota (1994/1995) and FirsTier in Nebraska (number two in that state) in 1995/1996. FBS was ready to test deeper waters.

COMPETING SUITORS

The mating dance between First Bank System and First Interstate in California was fascinating to watch. First Interstate was a $23 billion holding company with a major presence in California and other western states, and had been built on the non–Bank of America parts of A. P. Giannini's Bank of Italy/Bank of America financial empire. The dance began in 1995 when First Interstate received a surprise offer to merge with Wells Fargo, its slightly larger California peer. First Interstate quickly determined that a merger with another California group would lead to unacceptably large numbers of First Interstate layoffs due to redundant banking offices, so its managers began looking for a suitor with a substantial presence in an adjacent part of the United States who might want to enter the California market. FBS not only had the right credentials, it also had Jack Grundhofer as its CEO. Grundhofer was interested in making the deal for several reasons. First, California represented the country's largest and fastest-growing retail banking market. Second, the price—a slight premium over Wells Fargo's offer—appeared reasonable. The third and perhaps psychologically dominant reason was that Paul Hazen was the chief executive of Wells Fargo. Back when Grundhofer worked for Wells Fargo, he and Hazen had been competitive heirs-apparent in a succession contest Hazen had won. Grundhofer remembered.

FBS made a better offer for First Interstate than Wells Fargo did, but it came with two major caveats: First, if the deal fell through, First Interstate would pay FBS $200 million in heart-balm compensation. Second, FBS would not raise its bid. First

Interstate's board accepted the condition and conversations proceeded about changes in offices and staff that would result from integrating the two companies. But Hazen, not to be outdone by his Minnesota rival, made another, higher offer to First Interstate. FBS didn't counteroffer; true to its acquisition philosophy, it would pay a reasonable price and no more. With tears in its eyes—but the $200 million dowry in its pocket—FBS watched First Interstate go down the aisle with Wells Fargo.

FBS's next courtship turned into a mega-marriage: the 1997 acquisition of U.S. Bancorporation of Portland, Oregon, accompanied by a subsequent name change from FBS to U.S. Bancorp. The assets acquired in the transaction ($33.9 billion) almost doubled the size of the new corporation and positioned it to bid aggressively on even larger national opportunities: Piper-Jaffray, a 102-year-old major regional investment brokerage firm headquartered in Minneapolis, was added to U.S. Bancorp in 1997–1998, providing a new dimension and management style to the company.[31]

As anticipated by analysts, the First Interstate/Wells Fargo merger in California had gone badly. *The Economist* described the scenario, although in general terms:

> The marvel is that any mergers create value at all. Initially, many destroy it. They throw together two teams of managers who may have spent their working lives beating hell out of one another. They scare employees, who know that "economies of scale" spell redundancy. They signal to competitors that customers, suppliers and good staff are up for grabs. They wreck carefully nurtured corporate cultures.[32]

Perhaps Wells Fargo tried to recover First Interstate's $200 million dowry to FBS too quickly, but in any case, closures of redundant facilities moved ahead precipitously. Distressed customers departed in droves, and several longtime employees took advantage of golden parachute opportunities to bail out of the combined organizations. As one Colorado customer commented, "The worst banking operation in Denver took over—and closed—the best." The merger sometimes seemed more of a rape than a marriage. Wells Fargo, the survivor, was itself battered to the point that the market considered it "in play," a target for a further merger proposal. The usual chaff in financial trade papers speculated about off-stage romances, with rumormongers sure that U.S. Bancorp would meet Wells Fargo at the altar. All that was left to figure out was who would run the show, Grundhofer or Hazen.

ELOPEMENT

When news of the engagement finally broke on June 8, 1998, the surprise was not that Wells Fargo would marry again, but that its new partner was not the expected groom. The headlines were big, black, and comprehensive:

NORWEST NEAR MERGER DEAL
New Bank Would Keep Wells Fargo
Name and Location[33]

Wall Street had known that Wells Fargo was "in play" and that some significant transaction was brewing. Norwest, however, had not been the anticipated partner. As the next day's headlines stated:

NORWEST, WELLS FARGO JOIN
MARCH TO MERGE
New Entity to Take Wells Name,
Move Headquarters West[34]

Although Norwest was the corporate survivor in the deal, it was clear that a prenuptial agreement involved the groom not only taking the bride's name but also moving into her house. Meanwhile, the *Wall Street Journal* raised the issue of mismatched corporate cultures, pointing out that Norwest had a geographically diversified range of "stores" with considerable local autonomy, while Wells was historically more centralized and organized along product lines:

NORWEST, WELLS FARGO
AGREE TO A MERGER
New Banking Giant Created
by $31.4 Billion Accord;
Culture Clash Is Concern[35]

In a parallel article, the *Wall Street Journal* introduced the rejected suitor, the one that many financial analysts had assumed would win the well-shrouded negotiations:

WELLS FARGO DEAL MAY PUT
GRUNDHOFER AND U.S. BANCORP IN
A STRATEGIC BOX[36]

Jack Grundhofer had ardently courted Wells Fargo, his former employer and winner of the earlier bidding contest to buy First Interstate, before the surprise transaction with Norwest was completed. In fact, it had been U.S. Bancorp's bid that drove Wells Fargo to seek other suitors. After intensive board meetings on May 18–19 to consider the continuing impact of the First Interstate merger and the risk/opportunities offered in a definitive but "unofficial" U.S. Bancorp proposal, Wells Fargo hired Goldman Sachs to evaluate these two questions and to search the marketplace for other suitable partners. A week later Paul Hazen called Dick Kovacevich, president of Norwest. Kovacevich was in Colorado, meeting with a group of bank equity analysts from Wall Street, but he agreed to meet Hazen at the Colorado Springs airport. Hazen offered to accept a merger opportunity that would make Norwest the technical survivor, a proposal Kovacevich agreed to take back to his board. Norwest took less than two weeks to ratify the merger of Wells Fargo into Norwest, a name change to Wells Fargo, relocation of headquarters to California, and election of Kovacevich as CEO of the combined firm. Hazen would serve as equally paid chair of the board until his retirement.

Recognizing that this particular battle was lost, U.S. Bancorp already had a plan for the future. Headlines promptly announced the holding company's partial reinvestment of what had been a substantial $2.5 billion war chest:

AFTERSHOCKS OF A MERGER
U.S. Bank Planning Big
Stock Buy Back[37]

The U.S. Bank strategists had determined that the best use of its oversized war chest was selective purchase of outstanding shares, which had the simple primary effect of increasing the book value and earnings per share (but not dividends).

TRANSFORMED TWINS

The headlines and articles that reported and evaluated the denouement of the Wells Fargo merger hinted at underlying differences between the suitors and their approaches to negotiation, but missed the larger, more classic tale of rival regional bank holding companies doing battle, for the first time, in a national arena.

Since their founding in 1929, Banco and First Bank Stock had been bastions of strength for the Upper Midwest banking system. The holding companies had competed in gentlemanly fashion for decades before falling afoul of the massive evolution of the financial services industry in the 1970s and 1980s, when the short-term cost of money soared to more than 20 percent. Banks were under serious stress and the home mortgage/savings and loan banker too often saw his bank driven to insolvency or a forced merger. Congress's efforts to protect the thrift industry only led to broader speculation, further disasters, and spectacular criminal prosecutions.

Both holding companies recovered from the regulation and inflation of the 1980s, but their management styles and cultures had been transformed. Banco/Norwest had grown by mergers and acquisitions, becoming the owner of a diversified, nationwide portfolio of personal loan, mortgage, banking, and financial services companies. First Bank Stock/FBS had also grown by acquisitions, but via traditional regional banking and trust businesses in which massive economies of scale could be realized.

Diversification efforts sometimes proved troublesome for the Minnesota banking systems, and new competition hurt margins and led to operating losses. Both groups had substantially outgrown the Ninth Federal Reserve District boundaries, which had served as historic limits to previous expansion. At the same time, the two enterprises were being stretched by national competitors and simultaneously encouraged by the economies of scale offered by data-processing technology to expand into new, superregional and national markets.

Wells Fargo thus represented a plum for either group—a major entrance into the California market and national industry leadership in several lines of banking. How strange that Minnesota's twin bank holding companies would be the final suitors for Wells Fargo. How ironic that the transaction would effectively end their symbiotic relationship of seven decades.

16

THE NEXT CENTURY

IN 1996, TOTAL deposits of U.S. commercial banks were slightly higher than $2.6 trillion. New York state banks held a little more than 10 percent of that total, with $268.8 billion. The banks of six other states—California, Illinois, Texas, Florida, Pennsylvania, and Ohio—each held more than $100 billion, but in that same year, neither Norwest nor First Bank System held more than a nominal position in any of those states. For them, it was becoming clear that continuing growth could be found only outside of the Ninth Federal Reserve District.

Despite determined efforts to grow outside the district—to become national and international players—both Norwest and FBS continued to be a part of (and substantially sculpted by) the Ninth Federal Reserve District and its economic ups and downs until the end of the 1980s. After that date, realities of risk management and the drive for survival size combined to pull both holding companies back from their widest-ranging explorations to the strength of their home region—but also to grow that base by increasingly aggressive, merger-fueled expansion of defined home territory. Though the 1998 merger with Wells Fargo took Norwest's focus south and west of the old frontier, the geographical center of

U.S. Bancorp was probably still in the Ninth District.

A generally favorable economy, particularly in the Ninth Federal Reserve District, plus a strong and supportive securities market gave Norwest and FBS the opportunity to design, refine, and successfully pursue their increasingly distinct corporate missions between 1992 and 1997. Those five years were times of extraordinary growth for both companies. While massive and multiple mergers with other organizations optimistically blurred year-to-year results, the financial data in sequential annual reports clearly reflected the companies' individual goals: Norwest diversified across the spectrum of financial services until it partnered with Wells Fargo, while FBS emphasized balance-sheet management with a focus on shareholder value and controlled risk profitability.

In a financial world where Enron and Arthur Andersen invented and verified entirely new standards of bookkeeping, it has become increasingly difficult to trace cause and effect through corporate reports. Certain gross numbers are interesting for banks, like net interest income (interest earned by loans and investments less the cost of funds used to hold those portfolios) and non-interest income as a percent of pretax income and operating expenses.

The analysis that follows goes into slight detail about interesting variables used by Norwest and FBS in reporting financial results during the transitional years when both were exploding out of regionalism into the national scene. During that explosion, the holding companies were changing from the relatively simple accounting and reporting used in more naive banking journals and using the several accounting tools available to all of the new businesses that these companies encompassed. It's wise, therefore, not to take the figures too seriously. (The degree of these transitions is also why I can't, as a layperson and retiree, pretend to do such an analysis of the two companies in the early years of the twenty-first century.)

DECIPHERING THE NUMBERS

Drawing an accurate portrait of five years' worth of financial data from a corporate annual report—the banking industry's version of the political spin process—is not easy. Loans, for instance, can be increased or decreased—bought or sold, loaned or borrowed—depending on a bank's risk and balance-sheet strategies. Similarly, time deposits may be bought or sold. Thus, depending on the degree of reliance in each transaction, a financial

James J. Hill's Stone Arch Bridge is now a deluxe walkway across the Mississippi. The magic of foreshortening proves that downtown Minneapolis's tallest building is the former U.S. Bancorp tower.

institution may own or be responsible for several hundred million dollars more or less than the stated loan or deposit total. (Degree of reliance refers to the amount of liability that was sold with, for example, a loan portfolio. If the buyer of a portfolio accepts it without recourse, it cannot come back to the seller in case of loss. If the buyer has recourse, the fact that the loan is sold and is off the balance sheet, still represents liability exposure to the seller.)

Also problematic in using annual reports as a source of financial data is that such numbers are difficult to work with during times of major mergers, corporate purchases, and joint ventures. CPAs and accountants are scrupulous in assembling and reporting detailed numbers and in calculating pro forma data for a limited number of prior financial periods. But there's no way (and no practical reason) to recalculate the balance sheet and operating earnings of Wells Fargo (Norwest) and U.S. Bank (FBS) for more than a year or so. So rather than take *restated* numbers offered by the holding companies in the annual reports, which creates a tectonic plate of difference when the restated period ceases, this history uses the numbers as *actually* reported each year. This method also presents gaps, but it is, at least, a consistent approach.

One more matter about numbers related to acquisitions: As Susan Lester, then chief financial officer of U.S. Bancorp, noted at a financial analysts meeting in

Minneapolis in the spring of 1998, the unknown risks of the Y2K technology challenge were such that merger activity in the twenty-four months leading to the year 2000 was curtailed, and that consolidation of critical financials would be deferred until after the millennial event.

NORWEST/WELLS FARGO: DIVERSIFY, DIVERSIFY

As the 1997 Norwest annual report relates:

> As we have told you for many years in this report, Norwest isn't just a bank or just a finance company. We're both and much more. We're a mortgage company, an investment management company, an insurance agency, a trust company, a leasing company, an asset-based lending company, and another fifty businesses—too many to mention here. All these businesses that are part of Norwest are in one big industry—financial services. That industry is huge. . . .

> Our goal is simple—earn 100 percent of our creditworthy customers' financial services business.[38]

The shareholders letter goes on to note that, through diversification, as little as 37 percent of Norwest's 1997 earnings had come from traditional banking activities. It's not possible, with the information provided publicly, to trace the 37 percent parameter, but it is possible to note that the earnings from the Norwest banking group were just 70 percent of corporate net income in 1997, up a percentage or two due to the relatively poorer results of the Norwest financial group. Corporate assets of $62.1 billion were employed by the banking group, roughly two-thirds of total corporate assets. That number was consistent for the last three years of the twentieth century, although the percentage of revenues declined secularly.

The difficulty of tracing dependence on traditional banking functions is reinforced by accounting consolidation in shareholder reporting, through which results of the venture-capital subsidiary, trust, and investment functions and the corporate bond portfolio are channeled via "bank results." One number that *can* be extracted from annual reports is non-interest income—the dollars earned by transaction fees for services, including bond-trading profits (losses), revenues from trust and investment services, ATM charges, and closing costs for home mortgages. (The latest source of income from the ATM systems is the imposition of a second charge. The home bank charges its client for use of ATMs of unaffiliated institutions, which in turn charge the same customer a user fee for convenience.)[39]

Norwest's non-interest income figure grew absolutely and relatively in the last decade of the twentieth century and stood at 3.4 percent of assets in 1997 ($2,962.3 million)—a 50 percent increase from the 2.3 percent figure of 1990, and a fourfold increase in the $704.6 million earned in the earlier year.

For a long time, Norwest had followed a "nibble" rather than "gulp" acquisition policy. It completed eighty-eight transactions between 1993 and the end of 1997, of which sixty-three were banking organizations and the remainder fitting into its mortgage or finance groups. These mergers had added $30.9 billion in assets to Norwest as of the Wells Fargo acquisition date, or an average of $350 million, the largest being a $3.3 billion, dollar-for-dollar asset purchase from the Prudential Home Mortgage Group. The total cost of these transactions—not including Wells Fargo or six other acquisitions pending on December 31, 1997—was $5.2 billion and/or 221.1 million shares of then current common stock. In aggregate, this represented substantial assets and a major and continuing process of absorption—that is, continuing expense—but also a steady, if modest, increase in operating earnings as each acquisition was completed and absorbed.

The proposal of marriage between Norwest and Wells Fargo was cast in light of a preemptive decision by the California corporation to seek a strong and diversified partner from another region. Though the initial pairing may have been hasty, the two groups were pleased to find in each other certain strengths that could be enhanced by their merger. Wells Fargo's product-line management structure would blend with Norwest's geographic approach—a matrix model capable of strengthening client services across the board. For Norwest, the merger created an opportunity for entry into the fast-growing states of California, Washington, and Oregon, as well as reinforcement in Texas and the Southwest. Wells Fargo was a national leader in Internet banking and the nation's largest manager of supermarket branches. In addition, it was the nation's largest generator of automobile leases, largest lender in commercial real estate, and largest provider of agricultural loans. Wells Fargo also brought a world-recognized (and nongeographic) brand name and a brand: the stagecoach. Likewise, "Norwest brought Wells Fargo what it lacks—the best community banking operation in the country, the largest and best mortgage banking business in the country, the premier consumer finance business in the hemisphere, and the largest insurance agency owned by a bank. In short, [it] brought a financial services company— much more than a bank."[40]

In recent years, acquisition opportunities appear to have favored (by asset volume) banking organizations. The Wells Fargo transaction statistically submerged the diversification strategy followed for some time by Norwest, and would require equally significant acquisitions in the worlds of personal finance and mortgage banking to maintain the strategy. A logical transaction, using the Citicorp/Travelers Insurance model, would be to associate with a large and diversified insurance company. In any case, Norwest/Wells Fargo appeared willing to continue the nibble approach to acquisition while melding the two organizations. To make the transition as seamless as possible for clients, management indicated that it would take the necessary time to make sure that computer systems were compatible, employees had reasonable job security, and long-term shareholder values were protected.[41]

FBS/U.S. BANCORP: PERFORMANCE AND PRODUCTIVITY

First Bank System/U.S. Bancorp CEO Jack Grundhofer had made the point again and again: "While size is important to some aspects of our corporation, high performance is what differentiates (us) in the marketplace. Our strategy is to manage capital for the benefit of shareholders now and over the longer term."[42] He added: "Our relentless effort to improve productivity also reached an important milestone in 1996 when, for the first time, our ratio of expenses to revenues (efficiency ratio) dropped below 50 percent."[43] The efficiency ratio was an extraordinary yardstick of performance for the Grundhofer management team. When they took control in 1990, the ratio stood at 68.2 percent; by 1991 they had reduced it to 63.4 percent. Driving toward 60 percent was thought to be difficult, although one or two role-model banking entities stood at that level. Nonetheless, that target was hit and hit again. Mergers with less effective organizations gave FBS/USB room for improving the ratio, but the transactions also slowed efforts in attaining a new overall efficiency record. As a result, the company presented two efficiency numbers for 1998: 49.8 percent overall, but by eliminating non-recurring items, as well as investment

Loan Category	As of 12/31/77 (millions)	% Total Assets	As of 12/31/97 (millions)	% Total Assets
FBS/U.S. Bancorp Loan Portfolio Highlights **1977 & 1997 Reported Data**[44]				
Commercial	$2,835.0	30.7%	$23,399.0	32.8%
Real Estate	$1,486.0	16.1%	$20,430.0	28.7%
Consumer	$1,015.0	11.0%	$10,879.0	15.3%
Total	$5,336.0	57.8%	$54,708.0	76.8%

banking and brokerage, a banking efficiency ratio of 43.2 percent—improved from 46.5 percent. Both numbers reflected remarkable internal control.

Other components of the FBS/USB strategy had the same sort of intrinsic challenge. Sorting and winnowing assets by profitability, and eliminating "at the margin" activity, was a continuing process. On the one hand, it increased profitability of the asset class; on the other, it reduced the volume of those assets. Application of this strategy was reflected in the early 1990s as FBS shrank in virtually all dimensions— assets, loans, and deposits. As assets were acquired or purchased, they could be tested for profitability and either added to the portfolio or eliminated (sold). While the enterprise carried an appropriate investment portfolio and took care to watch maturity horizons and interest-rate exposure, the loan portfolio increasingly generated corporate profits. USB's loan/deposit ratio, at 116 percent on December 31, 1998, surely would have given the old-time banker an anxiety attack, but that particular test seems obsolete in light of

the corporation's ability to acquire a range of funds from time deposits as well as money market and capital borrowings.

At the end of 1998, commercial lending was still the largest component of USB's loan portfolio, although real estate loans had become much more important during the decade and consumer loans were also higher. Some of the latter activity was clearly a function of USB's leading role as a credit-card issuer and funder. In addition to contributing a large portfolio of earning assets, credit-card activity also contributed to the measurable increase in non-interest income—that catchall descriptor of fees and charges for a menu of financial services. (The ironic side of great success in the credit-card field is a growing portfolio of *non*productive funds: balances that clients pay in timely fashion each month without incurring interest charges.)

As a percentage of assets, FBS's non-interest income showed a steady rise from 2.58 percent in 1988 to better than 4 percent before the merger with U.S. Bank and First Star in February 2001.

Assets per employee, a minor measure of efficiency, rose from $2 million in 1989 to $2.8 million in 1996; the figure in 1989 was a sharp drop from the earlier year, reflecting the huge sales of portfolio securities in the earlier period.

Despite the shortcomings of annual reports, a look at the published data for FBS/USB's loan portfolio over a twenty-year interval shows how changes in strategy and opportunity are reflected in the reported numbers.

Clearly, FBS/U.S. Bancorp was more "loaned up" in 1997 than twenty years earlier and had made a strategic shift from the investment portfolio into loans. On a percentage basis, commercial loans were roughly the same as total assets; increases in the loan portfolios had occurred primarily in real estate, secondarily in the consumer category. Approximately half of the $20.4 billion of real estate loans at year-end 1997 were retail or consumer mortgages, meaning that consumer-managed borrowings represented almost 40 percent of the total loans outstanding compared to less than 30 percent in 1977.

The $10.9 billion in consumer loans held by FBS/U.S. Bancorp at the end of 1997 were further identified as $4.2 billion in credit cards, $3.2 billion in auto loans, $0.7 billion in student loans, and $1.6 billion in other installment debt. Real estate and auto loans—nearly half (42 percent) of the loans on the books—were collateralized by the property they financed.

Virtually all contemporary loans of this type are made in categories that can be packaged and sold to a third party, generally at face value or better, depending on the level of guarantee the seller is willing to offer. There's no way of telling from the balance-sheet figures what volume of home mortgages or automobile loans FBS originated each year because the total recorded in the annual report is a net position after selling or buying such loans as balance-sheet management may dictate.

The main point of this particular analysis is that U.S. Bancorp's "on balance sheet" loan portfolio—the net figure reported publicly—is both highly secured and substantially salable in secondary markets. Historically, a loan-to-deposit ratio approaching 90 percent was considered scary, particularly when most deposits were "on demand" and therefore volatile in times of a banking panic. Today's deposits are more likely to be "on time," and thus redeemable only in accord with a stated maturity schedule. The actual figure calculated for U.S. Bancorp at year-end 1997 was 121 percent, but that number is not comparable with historical levels for concern. It does indicate, however, that management has the ability and capacity to move large chunks of its several portfolios to other owners.

It is worth noting that U.S. Bancorp's non-interest income almost doubled as a percentage of total assets in the two decades studied above—from 2.07 percent of assets to 3.94 percent. It's also worth noting that at least one New York bank, J. P. Morgan, raised the prospect of becoming merely a facilitator of loan transactions, making and reselling such commitments, realizing the fees but not retaining the paper.[45] Not only would this eliminate the low-margin paper from interest-rate disintermediation, but also the 8 percent reserve that federal regulators require for such assets. As J. P. Morgan has moved into megabanking and away from specialized, tailored transactions, this line of thought has also gone away, for the time being.

A REAL DIFFERENCE

The difference between Wells Fargo and U.S. Bancorp was still clear as they planned into the new millennium. Wells Fargo was committed to a broad menu of financial services distributed through its 10,000 "stores." USB, meanwhile, pursued a narrower focus on "those business lines (that) make sense for (the banks) and for their shareholders," namely commercial and business banking and private financial services, retail banking, payment systems, and corporate trust and institutional financial services.[46] Within its broadened trade area, USB had several strongly positioned niche businesses, including leasing, credit cards, merchant processing, online banking, ATMs, cash management, and corporate trust services.

With the exception of commercial and business banking and private financial services (activities requiring highly skilled personnel, that is, high touch/high

return), U.S. Bancorp's core focuses represented huge volumes of transactions. Competition on a national basis required a vast integrated but regionally distributed network of processing centers with staff skilled in adding incremental business without increasing overhead:

> In many ways, U.S. Bancorp is at a new stage in its evolution as a leader in the financial services industry. In the early 1990s, we standardized our products, centralized our operations and automated our processes to achieve the efficiencies that made us a leader in a rapidly consolidating industry. These advantages are important core competencies that will help us succeed as we enter a new era that is more dependent on internal revenue growth than growth by acquisitions.[47]

It's easy to understand the USB mission to maximize shareholder results through a disciplined focus on its core business strengths. But it's a challenge to management to identify and acquire (on a reasonable basis) incremental volumes of earning assets that can produce the desired growth in earnings. In pursuit of this initiative, USB described the 1998 purchase of a $900 million portfolio of high-LTV (loan to value) second-mortgage loans with servicing rights. Such loans carry a higher return and higher credit costs than a portfolio of typical home-equity loans.[48]

U.S. Bancorp has thrived on its management skills in reducing and controlling costs and in accomplishing similar results with small, medium, and large acquisitions. Such actions don't necessarily increase gross revenues. To have a significant impact on the bottom line, acquisitions will have to be relatively large and carry a component of growth. The stock market seems to be watching with a high level of cynicism for such opportunities to appear and be realized. Because of its focus on banking and technologically related activities, and its relatively small size (among larger peers), USB remains an acquisition target for a diversified, perhaps foreign, financial service empire in the early years of the twenty-first century.

HIGH TECH V. HIGH TOUCH

When in 2000 the First National Bank in Chicago proposed a transaction charge for the use of a "live" teller, a clear message was sent to the client: use the ATM, use the telephone, use the Internet—in other words, don't use our staff. As it turned out, the change in habit was already established. Many people already preferred to avoid visits to the bank, with its hassles of driving and parking, and instead were substituting direct or ATM deposit of paychecks, machine withdrawals at the neighborhood store, and small loan activity either arranged or automatically managed over the telephone and fax. Aggressive promotion of burgeoning ATM networks continues to dramatically change client behavior patterns for all banks.

In the wake of their mergers, Wells Fargo and U.S. Bancorp pursued these industry goals of transaction automation as it

addressed issues of size and diversity. According to materials prepared for security analysts, USB fielded more than 91 million telephone calls at regional service centers in 1997; 77 percent of those calls were handled by interactive/automated voice-response units. Both Wells Fargo and USB promoted further automation by encouraging customers to use noncheck, electronic-fund transfers to speed transactions. The banks endorsed credit cards as a means of automating various retail financial transactions.[49] More recently, banks have promoted the debit card, which subtracts payment from a checking account at the time of a purchase transaction instead of creating a deferred payment to be made later via the credit card. Bank customers are comfortable with the concept of float and seem to prefer the leisurely but timely use of their own funds as opposed to the instant payment. A similar attitude has affected their use of other banking services, such as automatic bill payments from checking accounts and proposed electronic payment systems.

The computer systems of contemporary banks make possible many other automated services, including checking account closings. It's always been a hassle to close an account; few people know their current balance or the balance of their overdraft coverage loan, or can recall all of the automatic debits and credits that flow through their account. With such numbers now managed in microseconds at a cost of micropennies, and with errors so infrequent (despite popular opinion to the contrary), service managers have wide discretion in agreeing with the client's account balance rather than instigate an audit review.

There's no doubt that the automated world of banking has its advantages, both for the bank and the customer. But complaints of certain retail banking customers are legion and not unreasonable: "Every time I go in the bank, there's a new face I have to tell my story to." "I used to know the president or a vice president of the bank. If I needed a loan, he or she took care of me." "All I get now is a recorded message with directions that don't really get to my problem. How do I connect to a real person?" "My account is just a small chip in a big poker game. They don't care about a little guy like me."

Bank holding companies *do* care about the individual account, but they care collectively, not singularly. Each account, if it behaves itself and can be routinely managed with technology, effortlessly adds to the massive base that generates profitable earnings and dividends for the corporation. The boundaries affecting management of a typical account are broad. Should you overdraw your checking account, for example, it can be covered by a previously arranged automatic loan, or, if you're a customer in good standing, the bank will honor your check with a small service charge. Should you need a loan, a quick visit to the local branch can result in a credit decision of moderate size made on the spot by the office manager. Should you need access

to other financial services, from savings to investing, a single representative will handle each request. More skilled professionals can address even the most complex questions of corporate finance, estate taxes, and mortgage refunding. Yet both Wells Fargo and U.S. Bancorp continue to focus on cost limitation and risk avoidance. In other words, if doing business with you requires more than a defined amount of personnel time, or if the credit challenge you present delivers less than the reasonably expected return, your account is less than desirable.

While it takes a great deal to aggravate a customer enough to change banks, a meaningful percentage of clients misses and wants a less high-tech, more high-touch relationship and will shift to a smaller, more personal institution to regain the closer association. The Independent Bankers of Minnesota, a trade association of nonholding company banks (whose membership does include small bank holding companies), recognized long ago that big bank holding companies were a periodic and regular source of new customers. By the end of the twentieth century, midsize independent retail banks—generally part of a holding company composed of two to five banks and probably one in which the owners are active decision-makers—were thriving in the shadows cast by their big corporate brethren. A midsized bank allows customers to deal with the same teller, talk business or personal financial matters with a floor officer, even share a weather observation with the guard. The combination of on-site management and family ownership, plus a far slimmer advertising budget and lower overhead than a downtown office tower, means that these midsize enterprises can earn a decent profit from a personalized customer relationship. And should these independent banks need more sophisticated advice or wish to share a large credit line, they can turn to the very bank their new client may have left for complex, counselor-assisted financing.

Randy Segal is representative of that group of customers. Segal, of Segal Wholesale, tobacco wholesalers in Minneapolis, switched from a U.S. Bancorp office to Northeast Bank, a fifty-year-old local family bank:

> "For us, it's just been going back to the way business used to be conducted—on a personal level. We know the owners. We liked that it's a family-owned bank. You get more of a personal touch there and more attention. We may be a big fish at that bank but we may just be a pimple at First Bank." Shane Segal, Randy's brother, added his perspective: "At Northeast, they have more of a handle on our business. When you talk to the president of the bank, you may be able to get things done the same day."[50]

Wells Fargo and U.S. Bancorp would argue that the Segals *can* get the same attention and service with their organizations; they simply prefer the personal touch and the continuity. As Randy Segal summarized, "You don't want to feel like you are just another pickle in the barrel." For the individual whose biggest banking transaction is a car loan or a home mortgage, an ongoing relationship with a credit union will provide more than adequate banking on the most local level.

THE FUTURE ACCORDING TO THE FED

Gary Stern has been president of the Ninth Federal Reserve District Bank, the smallest of the twelve districts, since 1985. As such, he has a perspective on the banking industry that's considered politically neutral and thus of value. His concern is with the "fairness of the playing field," a field that Stern says favors the industry in two substantial ways: First, banks and banking systems have become so large that if any were to fail, the government would almost certainly have to intervene to prevent a national economic disaster with probable domino effects. Second, the prevalence of FDIC insurance has permitted bank managers to focus less on traditional matters of depositor safety and more on pragmatic goals such as shareholder returns.

Historically, the Federal Reserve has been driven by a mission statement that gives it (by way of Congress) final responsibility for the security of the nation's banking system; this has been true even though the Fed's regional check-clearing and cash-storage functions also offer valued services. Likewise, Federal Reserve District reporting, whether financial information is published or orally presented at Open Market Committee meetings in Washington, has helped form a "national" monetary policy. Although such numbers are becoming increasingly meaningless as national bank mergers cross and recross district lines, there continues to be a national value in regional representation and reporting. As Stern has said, "We gather a lot of real-world, first-hand information . . . that's more timely than the published statistics. The regional presence is a real strength."[51]

Op-ed essays such as "Give Us a Fair Chance to Compete," submitted by the

Gary Stern, president of the Ninth Federal Reserve District Bank since 1985.

During the past two decades, there has been a steady decline in the (paper) transactions and in the number of banks in the Federal Reserve's Ninth District. The Ninth's newest headquarters suggest that the reserve system will continue and stay technologically current.

chairs and CEOs of Metropolitan Life Insurance, Merrill Lynch, and BancOne in March 1998, give Stern skeptical pause. Such editorials pursue a theme that's been pressed on Congress ever since the Glass-Steagall Act was passed, although more intensively in the last two decades:

Two decades ago, the banking, insurance and securities industries were bitter rivals, each jealously guarding its legally defined turf. Now the three of us—corporate leaders in these sectors—have united with others in urging Congress to overhaul the laws that govern American financial services.

. . . We believe that if our lawmakers do not respond to these changes quickly, American companies may not be able to hold onto their position as leaders in the international financial markets.

. . . The laws were put in place because Congress believed that consumer deposits needed to be protected from the more "risky" investment banking activities. Today, these laws are unnecessary. Almost all economists agree that "risky" securities activity didn't cause the bank failures during the Depression.

. . . Only Congress can properly create a comprehensive legal framework for our industry. Yet it has tried and failed four times over the last decade to modernize the system. Every time, factional conflicts among the various industries prevented reform. Each industry protested any flexi-

bility or possible advantage given to another industry. Today, such turf wars are self-defeating. Consumers want integrated insurance, banking and securities products.

. . . Yet our antiquated laws limit the ability of American companies to grow. They also cost consumers an extra $15 billion a year in fees and transaction costs, according to the Treasury Department. Fortunately, Congress has recognized these problems. Last week a compromise bill was introduced in the House. . . .

But we are certain about one thing: this bill is the last, best chance to reform the American financial services sector and prepare it for the 21st century.[52]

The *New York Times* ran a followup on May 13:

Far-reaching banking legislation squeaked past the House tonight by one vote, amid intensive lobbying by competing groups that have fought for nearly two decades over the possible elimination of Depression-era restrictions on financial service industries.

The House approved the measure by a vote of 214 to 213, as the Republican leadership pushed hard, with Speaker Newt Gingrich working the floor and keeping party votes in line. The Senate is expected to take it up this year, but its chances for passage (in the Senate) remain unclear, and it could face a Presidential veto.

The measure allows for the merging of banks, security firms and insurance companies into huge financial conglomerates able to operate globally with far fewer restrictions than they now face.

The very close House vote paralleled the conflicting forces that stymied the legislation in previous years, with lobbyists for banks, big and small, Wall Street, and consumer groups along with federal regulators fighting over various portions of the legislation.

With the exception of the limitation on board size, remnants of the Glass-Steagall constraints were repealed by the National Bank Reform Act of 1999. The industry sighed in relief. For decades, it had argued that the Glass-Steagall Act gave advantage to their competitors—particularly insurance companies and securities broker/dealers—who enjoyed their encroachments into short-term lending, savings alternatives, even checking accounts.

In the late 1980s, economist Arthur Burns wrote about midcentury changes in the American banking system and addressed the specter that loomed in his mind as the ultimate challenge: the size and complexity of the industry.[53] The op-ed opinions above would have fueled his anxiety that components of the system would get so large, so dispersed, and so complex that they would transcend the monitoring of the Federal Reserve, and that a massive failure could bring the nation to a standstill and/or economic collapse. The executives who wrote the *Times* op-ed would suggest that Burns was seeing ghosts.

When push has come to shove in the financial arena, Congress has never really allowed its original intentions to prevail when dealing with the hometown voter and the local bank. In politics, the consumer/voter has always outweighed the "friendly banker," no matter how good the latter might be. Depression-era legislation that established the Federal Home Loan Banking System gave depositors in thrift institutions an extra quarter-percent in interest on their savings as compensation for the extra risk they assumed in using such a depository. The risk, as defined, was that depositors in a failed savings and loan would stand in line with other creditors and recover their deposits only if sufficient assets were left at the end of liquidation. In contrast, insured depositors in the Federal Reserve System could make a claim against their account as soon as an institution was closed. The Congressional bailout of the savings and loan industry during the 1980s protected those depositors fully with no memory of the historic assumption of extra risk and no penalty.

Economist Robert J. Samuelson counterargues that banks have lost so much dominance of the financial services market to so many competitive alternatives that the prospect of a large bank failure is no longer the monster it might have been. Auto companies provide car loans; nonbank credit cards provide consumer credit; stockbrokers provide checking accounts;

insurance companies and merchant bankers provide commercial credit. Samuelson further proposes that three forces will continue to drive the merger wave leading to the ever more giant complexes. The first force is the ongoing dismantling of government restrictions intended to check bank power. Since 1994, Congress has permitted interstate branching, transcending more restrictive and archaic state laws. In the fifteen years between 1984 and 1999, consolidations within and among states have reduced the number of banks from 14,483 to 9,166. The example of the holding companies suggests that most of these former banks continue as branch offices of the survivors.[54] The second force is the prospect of profit and savings through consolidation. Samuelson proposes that the jury is still out as to the overall effectiveness of consolidation, although Jack Grundhofer and his successors would support this factor. Samuelson's third force, which ultimately propels these mergers, is "a change in perceptions":

> No one knows how customers want their (financial service) choices presented and delivered: whether by one or many sellers; whether from behind a desk or over the Internet. But if banks can't freely compete to see what works best, they will wither. . . .

> This does not mean that these mergers will succeed or that the new world of finance will be problem-free. It won't. But it does signal that banks no longer wield the influence or incite the fear they once did. . . .

The upheaval is social and political as much as economic.[55]

An unanticipated casualty of bank consolidations was the regular reporting of banking data by the Federal Reserve Districts. All of the one-time offices of U.S. Bank, FBS, and the First Bank Company that still offer banking services in Minnesota have been merged and reclassified as branches of the U.S. Bank of Cincinnati, Ohio. (There is not a U.S. Bank in Minnesota.) Ohio banks are a part of the Fourth Federal Reserve District. Reporting this data through the Federal Reserve's Cleveland offices warps the reports of the Ninth and Fourth Districts, so the following "Special Notice" was a logical footnote to history:

> Effective (immediately), the Federal Reserve is discontinuing the publication of District-specific balance sheet data of large, domestically chartered banks. . . . The reason for the change is that . . . a number of large bank holding companies have converted banks located across several Federal Reserve Districts into branches of a single bank . . . further weakening the connection between banking data reported by the Federal Reserve District and actual banking activities.[56]

On the eve of the twenty-first century, the question was whether the national wave of mergers would drive the Federal Reserve reporting system to eliminate the anomalies of cross-state branching and consolidation. The answer was "not yet."

THE SCORE CARD – 2000

Northwest Bancorporation		First Bank Stock Corporation
5400 stores (nc)	Number of Banks (change since 1990)	2,239 banking offices (nc)
$156,710,000,000 ($136,586,000,000)	Total Deposits (change since 1990)	$109,535,000,000 ($94,902,000,000)
$161,124,000,000	Total Loans	$122,365,000,000
$26,488,000,000 ($24,850,000,000)	Capital & Surplus (change since 1990)	$15,168,000,000 ($13,873,000,000)
1,718,400,000	# Common Shares	1,902,100,000
56.38 – 31	Market Range High/Low	28 – 15.38
	Per Common Share	
$2.36	Earned	$1.51
$0.90	Dividend	$0.65
$15.29	Book Value	$7.97
2.1%	Yield*	3.0%
$75,076,900,000 ($73,165,724,000)	Market Capitalization* (change since 1990)	$41,256,549,000 ($40,225,715,000)
	Per 2000 Common Share	
$2.36 ($2.07)	Earned (change since 1990)	$1.51 ($1.44)
$0.90	Dividend	$0.65
$43.69 ($38.95)	Market Price* (change since 1990)	$21.69 ($17.25)

* based on average market price

SWEEPING UP

THE INSTITUTIONS THAT are still known as banks have evolved drastically since 1929, the year that Minnesota's twin holding companies were born. Banks are no longer simple repositories of idle funds—institutions of the past where people kept substantial balances in their checking accounts because no alternatives existed that provided earnings on those balances. Modern banking institutions are managers of high-volume, high-velocity transactions with only nominal collected balances. The automatic deposit of a client's corporate payroll into the checking accounts of employees triggers myriad electronic transfers to other consumer banking accounts: a mortgage payment, a savings program, a Roth IRA, credit card and utility bill payments, even the United Way. The corporate client wire-transferred the funds to cover the payroll and other scheduled payments from its commercial loan investment account at a securities dealer rather than hold the funds in the local bank. What would have been a float of six to eight days twenty years ago—back when funds transferred from one bank to another weren't available until the check was delivered by mail—now appears overnight.

A contemporary bank's consumer level loan activity is concentrated in first and second mortgages on residential property (where the interest charged is a federal tax deduction) and in credit cards.[57] Larger institutions issue their own credit cards and fund the resulting portfolios; smaller banks act in the role of agent for one or another issuer of Visa or MasterCard. Retail clients rarely need to visit their personal banking facility other than to use an ATM, whose presence is ubiquitous (and accessible) on a twenty-four-hour basis around the world. The Greek temple bank lobby has vanished in new construction and remodeled older buildings. The desks abandoned by officers and staff no longer needed for "lobby duty" customer contact have been replaced by other businesses in space sublet by cost-sensitive building managers. Banking service windows are an incremental part of supermarkets, provide limited retail banking functions seven days a week. Concern about Y2K resulted in a thorough review and refreshment of financial systems and unearthed no major weaknesses.

Tomorrow's newspaper may well report that Wells Fargo or U.S. Bancorp is announcing acquisition of one or more financial service companies, whether banks, insurance companies, international factors, even auto-rental outlets, as they expand and reinforce present market territories and—

with bigger prospects on the horizon—position themselves nationally and/or internationally. One or both of the twin holding companies will probably vanish even more into a giant corporate entity, and it's not likely that U.S. Bancorp (or whatever its name might be then) will be headquartered in Minneapolis in 2010. Ironically, the changes in the holding company's name have permitted the incorporation of new generations of First National Banks in the Twin Cities' expanding suburbs and the reinvigorated small towns of Minnesota and the Ninth Federal Reserve District.

It's important to remember that this tale of two regional bank holding companies is not a singular narration, but one that was played out across the United States. Strong city banks, which provided financial and practical leadership to their respective market areas, were aggregated—rolled up, as it were—into larger, more effective regional groups. The individual banks joined these new unions for diverse reasons: sometimes as leaders, sometimes as sheep. Real reasons do not matter as much of this aggregation was foreordained and inescapable. The new regional groups continue to meld into national and international competitors; a revisit to Chapter 1's 1949 roster of the large U.S. banks reminds us of the extent to which these changes have already occurred. Since this national rollup has been so pervasive, only a handful of the 1949 banks have survived as unitary entities: Mellon and PNC in Pennsylvania, Northern Trust in Chicago, and the Whitney Bank in New Orleans.

In the twilight of his life, Arthur Burns was much concerned about the complexities of

	USB	WELLS FARGO
Cost of 100 shares		
1929 average	$4,975	$7,518
All-time low	550	300
Percent loss	88.9%	96.0%
Number of shares held today	4,800	14,400
Value of holding	$36.47	$35.69
1998 average/shares		
TOTAL	$175,056	$513,936
Appreciation from		
1929 average	3519%	6835%
All-time low	31,828%	171,312%

How would you have fared if you had invested in our companies back at the beginning? Pretty well, in either case.

size in the banking industry, anxious about the challenge of an institution being too large to allow to fail. Ninth Federal Reserve Bank president Gary Stern wonders how the public sector ought to react should a holding company with banking dominance in many states fall into serious financial difficulty: Should the public sector pay only the FDIC insurance and let the troubled organization fail, or is there a greater responsibility to preserve the institution? That question raised another for Burns: What if the failing banking corporation is so big and so pervasive in the American scene that no tools are capable of performing the rescue? We're not likely to know the answer to that one until after the fact.

The irrefutable fact is that the missions set forth by the creators of the two Minnesota bank holding companies were accomplished. Not only did they save the banking system in the Ninth Federal Reserve District during the Depression, when the Fed had neither the resources nor the will to do so, they provided honest, competitive banking services to the area over seven decades. In accepting the contemporary drive for more effective and efficient banking, measured by transaction volume and economies of scale, the respective boards of the companies have acted carefully, recognizing the limits inherent in the Ninth Federal Reserve District as well as encouraging their organizations to expand geographical and product-line capacities.

Shareholder value is an important measuring tool for testing a corporate mission.

Value measured by short-term stock market return, however, can be tricky, particularly in a world where a massive write-off of obsolete products or employees is tolerated—even cheered—by the stock market, while a $0.02 per share shortfall from a consensus earnings per share calculation can wipe out 25 to 50 percent of an enterprise's equity value in the blink of an Internet trade. Clever managers are unfortunately able to "store up" earnings in reserves or off-balance sheet transactions. This is all very well for the normal course of business, but the time has come when even the deepest reserve pockets may prove insufficient and the future credibility of a company may be at risk. The current stock market is much like the child's game of Flinch: when you feel your opponent's hand begin to move, you quickly remove yours to avoid being slapped. You lose if you flinch too much.

The stock market is fully aware that it passed through unprecedented high grounds into an uncertain present, but investors are still afflicted with the ancient demons of fear and greed: fear that equities may plunge on little notice, so that investors will want out, and greed for a market that still has an upward bias, so that investors want in. In such an environment, U.S. Bancorp stock seems to be more on the fear side, with something yet to prove, while Wells Fargo seems to be more on the greed side, with more optimistic shareholders. Across the country, other bank holding company stocks can be rated in similar fashion.

The twin holding companies of Northwest Bancorporation and First Bank Stock Corporation are no more, each having been renamed over their seventy years of existence. In their present incarnations as Wells Fargo and U..S. Bancorp, they dominate the Minneapolis skyline.

In truth, this story ended almost ten years ago as both enterprises left the regional arena for the larger world. The financial data in the appendices could be brought more up to date and provide more information. It would tell you that recent years have not added wealth to U.S. Bancorp shareholders—although you would hold more shares, the total market value would be almost the same as in 1998. Wells Fargo, on the other hand, is more than $20 per share ahead, adding another $300,000 to the indicated total. For this there is no credit or blame due to this tale's leading characters; the two companies did spring from similar root causes but grew in different ways.

So as the action ends, with certain members of the cast having departed, others are anxiously reading the script to determine the cues for the next scene. The entire scenario has been Einsteinian: the story of Northwest Bancorporation and the First Bank Stock Investment Corporation has had fourth-dimension characteristics, played out on a stage that was itself part of a larger drama, with road-show companies across the country acting out similar dramas. And one thing is certain: the latest acts—those that reshaped the players and their enterprises in massive and fundamental ways—are not the final acts.

241

APPENDIX A
US Bancorp Operating Statistics (000,000)

As of 12/31	Assets	Loans	Deposits	Net Inc	Per common share Earned	Per common share Dividend	# Common Shares (000)	Mean Market Cap	100 shares in 1930 adj.	Mean Value
As U S BANCORP										
2000	$164,921	$122,365	$109,535	$2,875.6	$1.50	$0.86	11,902,100	$43,424.9	6,072	138,623.76
1999	81,530	62,885	51,530	1,506.5	2.11	0.78	754,368.7	21,054.4	4,800	133,968.00
1998	76,438	58,121	50,034	1,327.0	1.96	0.70	725,800.0	26,467.6	4,800	175,040.62
1997	71,295	54,708	49,027	838.5	5.09	1.86	246,644.3	22,706.7	1,600	147,300.06
As FIRST BANK SYSTEM										
1996	36,489	27,128	24,379	739.8	5.34	1.65	141,747.7	8,504.9	1,600	96,000.43
1995	33,874	26,400	22,514	568.1	4.19	1.45	133,936.0	5,784.4	1,600	69,100.47
1994	26,219	19,281	18,791	419.8	3.57	1.16	116,300.1	3,976.0	1,600	54,699.87
1993	26,385	18,779	21,031	298.0	2.39	1.00	114,793.5	3,444.4	1,600	48,008.29
1992	23,527	15,442	18,543	276.0	2.87	0.88	93,982.5	2,420.5	1,600	41,207.67
1991	18,301	13,152	14,479	190.4	2.13	0.82	78,659.2	1,480.0	1,600	30,104.55
1990	19,001	13,458	14,633	130.6	1.53	0.82	77,430.6	1,030.8	1,600	21,300.11
1989	20,820	15,714	15,753	2.4	-0.27	1.44	63,486.0	1,345.1	1,600	33,899.76
1988	24,248	16,131	17,204	-309.4	-5.25	1.64	63,486.0	1,400.7	1,600	35,301.01
1987	26,850	13,315	15,799	49.6	0.73	1.50	59,439.9	1,630.9	1,600	43,900.48
1986	28,012	14,993	16,261	202.9	3.42	0.91	57,906.6	1,456.8	1,600	40,252.41
1985	25,484	14,484	16,039	166.8	5.68	1.60	27,833.8	949.8	800	27,299.18
1984	22,438	13,331	14,782	131.1	4.15	1.48	27,298.0	691.0	800	20,250.57
1983	20,871	10,985	13,430	129.7	8.46	2.80	15,364.2	745.2	400	19,400.95
1982	16,913	9,231	11,877	114.7	7.66	2.64	15,301.6	547.0	400	14,299.16
1981	14,911	7,843	11,023	96.8	6.38	2.44	15,193.9	604.0	400	15,901.12
1980	13,475	7,162	9,768	112.0	7.42	2.24	15,086.8	550.7	400	14,600.84
1979	12,118	6,786	8,982	101.7	6.80	2.04	15,005.7	602.1	400	16,049.90
1978	10,436	5,967	7,969	89.6	6.01	1.84	14,885.4	565.6	400	15,198.79
1977	9,222	5,252	7,234	71.8	4.82	1.60	14,837.5	582.4	400	15,700.76
1976	7,843	4,417	6,134	63.4	4.26	1.52	14,832.8	626.7	400	16,900.38
1975	7,173	4,037	5,650	61.9	4.16	1.49	14,832.8	611.8	400	16,498.57
1974	7,061	3,979	5,429	56.2	3.81	1.41	14,770.2	679.4	400	18,399.21
1973	6,514	3,661	4,890	51.8	3.51	1.35	14,751.0	892.4	400	24,199.04
1972	5,535	3,089	4,490	50.2	3.42	1.25	14,702.0	777.4	400	21,150.86
1971	5,073	2,564	4,197	45.7	3.13	1.20	14,649.8	537.5	400	14,675.97
1970	4,407	2,297	3,684	45.7	5.58	2.20	7,313.6	389.4	200	10,648.65
1969	3,867	2,177	3,068	34.2	4.68	2.00	7,292.6	397.4	200	10,898.72
1968	3,851	2,025	3,345	28.0	3.85	1.80	7,292.6	371.0	200	10,174.70
As FIRST BANK STOCK CORPORATION										
1967	3,247	1,732	2,869	26.2	3.71	1.60	7,063.6	298.4	200	8,448.95
1966	2,833	1,560	2,495	20.0	2.83	1.40	7,063.6	242.8	200	6,874.68
1965	2,694	1,446	2,359	21.7	3.07	1.25	7,063.6	270.6	200	7,661.82
1964	2,496	1,248	2,204	18.0	2.57	1.13	7,063.6	268.9	200	7,613.68
1963	2,341	1,149	2,069	15.8	4.53	2.00	3,598.9	236.2	100	6,563.12
1962	2,259	1,039	2,004	15.0	4.29	2.00	3,498.9	202.5	100	5,787.53
1961	2,023	911	1,798	15.2	4.36	2.00	3,470.4	216.0	100	6,224.07
1960	1,876	899	1,655	16.3	4.70	1.95	3,470.4	172.7	100	4,976.37
1959	1,797	862	1,595	11.2	3.22	1.85	3,470.4	170.0	100	4,898.57
1958	1,777	746	1,604	18.5	5.33	1.75	3,465.0	132.1	100	3,812.41
1957	1,670	721	1,515	10.6	3.04	1.70	3,492.1	110.7	100	3,170.01
1956	1,585	695	1,440	9.3	2.60	1.70	3,479.1	122.0	100	3,506.65
1955	1,419	618	1,278	9.3	2.86	1.42	3,257.3	114.0	100	3,499.83
1954	1,426	515	1,310	8.6	3.14	1.30	2,895.4	89.6	100	3,094.56
1953	1,379	506	1,267	7.6	2.83	1.20	2,895.4	77.6	100	2,680.11
1952	1,369	464	1,213	7.1	2.64	1.20	2,831.2	71.0	100	2,507.77
1951	1,287	412	1,157	6.2	2.49	1.16	2,831.2	63.9	100	2,256.99
1950	1,267	373	1,140	5.7	2.57	1.10	2,831.2	58.7	100	2,073.33
1949	1,222	293	1,104	6.3	2.53	1.00	2,831.2	51.3	100	1,811.95
1948	1,211	293	1,113	6.9	2.45	0.80	2,831.2	46.4	100	1,638.88
1947	1,218	262	1,133	6.0	2.12	0.80	2,831.2	51.0	100	1,801.36
1946	1,127	206	1,024	6.2	2.20	0.80	2,831.2	58.7	100	2,073.33
1945	1,205	156	913	5.9	2.09	0.75	2,831.2		100	
1944	1,004	138	943	5.2	1.85	0.70	2,831.2	44.1	100	1,557.64
1943	854	126	799	4.4	1.54	0.60	2,837.6	34.1	100	1,201.72
1942	712	139	661	3.4	1.21	0.60	2,855.9	29.6	100	1,036.45
1941	524	180	475	3.4	1.18	0.60	2,885.7	32.6	100	1,129.71
1940	489	141	441	3.1	1.02	0.60	2,920.5	32.9	100	1,126.52
1939	461	123	414	2.8	0.94	0.50	2,934.1	31.4	100	1,070.17
1938	419	105	372	2.6	0.88	0.50	2,953.3	28.4	100	961.64
1937	413	112	366	1.8	0.92	0.50	2,976.2	38.9	100	1,307.04
1936	448	107	403	1.6	1.01	0.45	3,035.3	44.0	100	1,449.61
1935	430	138	384	1.8	0.90	0.25	3,071.0	35.1	100	1,142.95
1934	394	110	337	2.6	0.83	0.25	3,087.3	24.7	100	800.05
1933	353	131	296	3.9	1.23	0.38	3,092.1	30.1	100	973.45
1932	346	145	290	4.2	1.31	0.63	3,091.3	29.8	100	964.00
1931	407	184	348	5.0	1.55	1.00	3,125.7	55.7	100	1,782.00
1930	445	185	385	6.2	1.93	1.00	3,093.8	85.5	100	2,763.59

APPENDIX B
Wells Fargo Operating Statistics (000,000)

As of 12/31	Assets	Loans	Deposits	Net Inc	Per common share Earned	Dividend	# Common Shares (000)	Mean Market Cap	100 shares in 1930 adj.	Mean value
AS WELLS FARGO										
2000	$272,426	$161,124	$156,710	$4,026.0	$2.33	$0.90	1,715,000.0	74,928.4	14,400	629,136
1999	241,053	133,004	138,247	4,012.0	2.29	0.78	1,696,000.0	69,595.4	14,400	590,904
1998	202,475	107,994	136,788	1,950.0	1.17	0.70	1,661,392.0	59,285.1	14,400	513,849
AS NORWEST CORPORATION										
1997	88,540	54,777	55,457	1,351.0	1.78	0.62	769,113.0	23,504.1	14,400	440,064
1996	80,175	48,548	50,130	1,153.9	3.07	1.05	368,703.0	14,265.1	7,200	278,568
1995	72,134	46,012	42,029	956.0	2.76	0.90	358,332.0	10,280.5	7,200	206,567
1994	59,316	33,703	36,424	800.4	2.46	0.77	310,642.0	7,651.1	7,200	177,336
1993	50,782	34,837	32,573	653.6	1.90	0.64	292,175.0	7,248.9	7,200	178,633
1992	46,657	30,082	28,704	364.1	2.40	1.08	141,041.0	5,465.3	3,600	139,499
1991	38,502	20,796	25,439	398.5	2.13	0.94	139,830.0	3,889.1	3,600	100,127
1990	30,626	17,793	20,124	110.6	1.16	0.85	102,959.0	1,910.9	3,600	66,815
1989	24,335	16,705	15,206	237.0	1.34	0.76	102,599.0	2,052.0	3,600	72,001
1988	21,750	15,073	13,902	211.2	4.52	1.30	47,417.0	1,416.8	1,800	53,783
1987	20,747	13,521	13,644	-29.8	-1.31	1.80	31,611.0	1,260.6	1,200	47,854
1986	21,539	13,967	14,100	121.7	3.64	1.80	31,478.0	1,092.0	1,200	41,629
1985	21,419	14,022	14,337	107.6	3.20	1.80	30,303.0	816.4	1,200	32,329
1984	21,346	14,101	14,615	69.5	1.90	1.80	29,570.0	818.8	1,200	33,228
1983	19,854	12,735	13,552	125.2	4.05	1.80	27,972.0	870.8	1,200	37,357
1982	17,585	11,087	11,971	89.1	3.08	1.68	26,963.0	618.5	1,200	27,527
1981	15,141	8,853	11,386	100.1	3.85	1.60	26,480.0	739.9	1,200	33,530
AS NORTHWEST BANCORPORATION										
1980	14,395	7,813	11,044	113.5	4.39	1.44	25,926.0	625.6	1,200	28,956
1979	12,416	7,642	9,573	106.6	4.13	1.28	25,852.0	675.5	1,200	31,355
1978	10,906	6,502	8,462	91.6	3.56	1.10	25,729.0	641.7	1,200	29,929
1977	9,528	5,550	7,562	76.2	2.97	0.98	25,704.0	642.6	1,200	30,000
1976	8,358	4,548	6,627	65.4	5.26	1.75	12,640.0	635.2	600	30,152
1975	7,386	4,159	6,094	57.4	4.85	1.65	11,825.0	483.4	600	24,528
1974	7,056	4,173	5,626	50.4	4.26	1.60	11,815.0	525.8	600	26,702
1973	6,517	3,900	5,193	45.7	3.88	1.55	11,786.0	735.2	600	37,427
1972	5,803	3,306	4,769	42.2	3.65	1.45	11,599.0	559.6	600	28,947
1971	5,056	2,449	3,851	37.2	3.28	1.40	11,540.0	422.7	600	21,977
1970	4,342	2,237	3,393	34.3	2.94	1.30	11,537.0	367.8	600	19,128
1969	4,105	2,119	3,269	32.9	2.73	1.20	11,511.0	387.1	600	20,177
1968	4,002	1,905	3,118	27.9	4.52	2.20	5,697.0	355.3	300	18,710
1967	3,458	1,902	3,062	24.6	4.30	2.05	5,678.0	285.3	300	15,074
1966	3,061	1,697	2,702	22.2	3.64	1.85	5,603.0	238.1	300	12,749
1965	2,852	1,575	2,496	19.3	3.78	1.70	5,609.0	267.8	300	14,323
1964	2,666	1,354	2,374	17.7	3.16	1.50	5,588.0	271.0	300	14,549
1963	2,533	1,273	2,250	16.5	2.95	1.35	5,569.0	268.0	300	14,437
1962	2,429	1,153	2,167	17.3	3.17	1.30	5,425.0	236.0	300	13,051
1961	2,198	1,028	1,955	16.9	3.09	1.30	5,399.0	239.0	300	13,280
1960	2,060	997	1,828	15.8	2.90	1.20	5,321.0	187.6	300	10,577
1959	1,986	949	1,779	11.5	2.14	1.10	5,168.0	177.0	300	10,275
1958	1,998	832	1,791	17.4	10.03	3.00	1,703.0	135.4	100	7,951
1957	1,806	784	1,628	11.7	6.85	2.90	1,703.0	114.5	100	6,723
1956	1,758	750	1,592	12.8	7.51	2.85	1,703.0	121.3	100	7,123
1955	1,701	683	1,544	11.9	7.07	2.23	1,678.0		100	
1954	1,674	600	1,531	9.1	5.53	1.95	1,613.0	78.3	100	4,854
1953	1,596	553	1,463	7.5	4.73	1.80	1,548.0	62.9	100	4,063
1952	1,555	513	1,430	7.4	4.68	1.60	1,548.0	60.8	100	3,928
1951	1,480	496	1,367	5.8	3.75	1.50	1,548.0	51.3	100	3,314
1950	1,445	443	1,341	6.0	3.90	1.20	1,548.0	46.0	100	2,972
1949	1,352	335	1,256	4.9	3.15	1.20	1,548.0	38.3	100	2,474
1948	1,332	338	1,243	5.4	3.47	1.00	1,548.0	33.8	100	2,183
1947	1,348	292	1,265	4.3	2.77	1.00	1,548.0	37.0	100	2,390
1946	1,287	232	1,210	4.5	2.90	0.80	1,548.0	41.8	100	2,700
1945	1,381	187	1,310	4.8	3.08	0.70	1,548.0		100	
1944	1,193	170	1,129	3.7	2.37	0.60	1,552.0	32.8	100	2,113
1943	949	140	890	3.4	2.21	0.50	1,552.0	21.7	100	1,398
1942	805	167		2.5	1.61	0.50	1,552.0	17.3	100	1,115
1941	544	201		3.3	2.09	0.45	1,552.0	18.6	100	1,198
1940	490	161	343	2.9	1.83	0.20	1,557.0	15.4	100	989
									100	
1939	469	147	321	2.5	1.57	0.10	1,560.0	13.7	100	878
1938	429	119	385	2.0	1.26	nil	1,561.0	10.7	100	685
1937	412	118	367	1.8	1.14	nil	1,577.0	17.3	100	1,097
1936	439	123	393	1.7	1.08	nil	1,585.0	17.1	100	1,079
1935	410	113	360	2.1	1.31	nil	1,586.0	11.3	100	712
1934	423	107	359	2.4	2.71	nil	1,592.0	7.6	100	477
1933	357	118	290	4.5	1.97	0.15	1,612.0	13.8	100	856
1932				3.4	2.73	1.10	1,614.0	23.3	100	1,444
1931	427	194	342	6.0	3.43	1.80	1,672.0	48.1	100	2,877
1930	472	223	410	6.8	3.87	1.80	1,674.0	73.0	100	4,361
1929				7.5		1.35				

NOTES

SECTION I: TWINS IN THE MAKING

1 Trivia note: William G. Fargo, an 1852 founder of Wells, Fargo, and Company, is the namesake of Fargo, North Dakota.

2 Data from Federal Reserve Bank of Minneapolis, www.minneapolisfed.org.

3 Ibid.

4 A. Hingston Quiggin, *A Survey of Primitive Money*, Methuen and Company (1949).

5 Jack Weatherford, *The History of Money*, Crown Publishers (1997), p .17.

6 Ibid, p. 27.

7 *The Economist,* December 17, 1998.

8 Harry T. Gatton and Truman Jeffers, *Banking in Minnesota*, Minnesota Bankers Association (1989).

9 Weatherford, p. 64.

10 Robert S. Lopez in *The Dawn of Modern Banking*, Yale University Press (1979), p. 6.

11 Ibid, Jacques LeGoff, p. 35.

12 Ibid, Michael Prestwick, p. 78.

13 Ibid, Thomas W. Bloomquist, p. 63.

14 John Kenneth Galbraith, *Money*, Houghton Mifflin (1975), p. 10, et seq.

15 Theodore A. Andersen, *A Century of Banking in Wisconsin*, State Historical Society of Wisconsin (1954), p. 4.

16 Jonathan Raban, *Bad Land: An American Romance,* Random House (1996), p. 170.

17 Julian Baird, "The Story of a Banking Heritage," remarks presented at the First National Bank centennial dinner, St. Paul, October 1, 1953.

18 Ibid.

19 O. M. W. Sprague, *History of Crises under the National Banking System,* Government Printing Office (1910).

20 The firm was closed abruptly at 11:00 that morning. Two of Cooke's senior partners, distressed by the hemorrhaging overdrafts by the Northern Pacific Railroad, locked the doors without advising Cooke. Henrietta M. Larson, *Jay Cooke: Private Banker,* Harvard University Press (1936), p. 387.

21 *Commercial and Financial Chronicle,* September 16, 1893, cited in O. M. W. Sprague, *History of Crises under the National Banking System.*

22 Charles Sterling Popple, "Two Bank Groups in the Central Northwest, "Harvard University Press (1944), p. 49.

23 Barbara Flanagan, *Star Tribune* column, October 20, 1986.

24 Frank P. Donovan Jr. and Cushing F. Wright, *The First through a Century,* Webb Publishing (1954), p. 43, et seq.

25 Ibid, p. 43, et seq.

26 Ibid, p. 71.

27 Ibid, p. 72.

28 Ibid, p. 78.

29 Sprague, *History of Crises under the National Banking System,* p. 233.

30 Ibid, p. 256.

31 Ibid, p. 319.

32 Dave Page, "Carter Glass" in *The Region* 11 (4), publication of the Federal Reserve Bank of Minneapolis.

33 James J. Hill, "Industry, Credit, and Banking," address given October 9, 1913, to the American Bankers Association, Boston, Massachusetts.

34 Carl H. Moore, *The Federal Reserve System,* McFarland and Company (1990), p. 14.

35 In case the reader wondered about the title of this book, this is the answer.

36 Carter Glass, *An Adventure in Constructive Finance,* Doubleday and Company (1927).

37 Moore, *The Federal Reserve System,* p. 32.

38 Popple, "Two Bank Groups in the Central Northwest," p. 57.

39 Ibid.

40 Ibid, p. 61 et seq.

41 Clarence W. Nelson, *Reflections from History: First Half-Century of the Minneapolis Federal Reserve Bank,* Minneapolis Federal Reserve Bank (1964).

42 Ibid, p. 117.

43 Louis W. Hill papers, James J. Hill Library, St. Paul, Minnesota.

44 Telegram dated November 27, 1927, Louis W. Hill papers.

45 Longhand pencil tabulations in Louis W. Hill papers.

46 Letter to Cyrus P. Brown, December 12, 1928, Louis W. Hill papers.

47 L. E. Owens letter to Kalman, December 26, 1928, Louis W. Hill papers.

48 Louis W. Hill to Ralph Budd, January 2, 1929, Louis W. Hill papers.

49 Cameron Thomson is credited as being one of the creators of the American Bankers Association's broadly based educational programs for teaching fundamentals of banking to bank employees.

50 Ibid.

51 Popple, p. 212.

52 Ibid, p. 198.

53 Ibid, p. 208. Twenty percent down, $2 per share purchased per month, deducted from salary but not to exceed 20 percent of salary.

54 First Bank Stock Corporation shareholders report, 1929.

55 First Bank Stock Corporation shareholders report, 1929.

56 Popple.

SECTION II: STRUGGLES TO SURVIVE

1 *Minneapolis Journal*, July 19, 1929.

2 Madison, Wisconsin, *Capital Times,* January 2, 1930.

3 Carl H. Moore, *The Federal Reserve System*, McFarland and Company (1990), p. 67.

4 Ibid.

5 The worst day on Wall Street in recent memory was September 17, 2001, when the market reopened after the World Trade Center disaster. The Dow Jones Industrial average fell 684.81 points from 8920.70, or 7 percent.

6 Donovan and Wright, *The First through a Century*, Webb Publishing (1954), p. 104.

7 C. Sterling Popple, *Two Bank Groups in the Central Northwest*, Harvard University Press (1944), p. 266.

8 Popple, *Two Bank Groups in the Central Northwest,* p. 268.

9 Popple, p. 268.

10 Popple, p. 269.

11 Popple, p. 294.

12 Moore, *The Federal Reserve System*, p. 78.

13 Ibid, p. 79.

14 Gordon M. Malen, *FirStory,* unpublished history of the First National Bank of Minneapolis (1980), chapter 7, p. 3.

15 Donovan and Wright, *The First through a Century,* p. 103.

16 Moore, p. 82.

17 Malen, *FirStory,* chapter 7, p. 4.

18 *Star Tribune,* September 22, 1989.

19 Malen, chapter 10, page

SECTION III: GROWING PAINS

1 Gordon M. Malen, *FirStory,* unpublished history of the First National Bank of Minneapolis (1980), chapter 7, p. 7.

2 What comes after collateral, character, and capacity?

3 J. Cameron Thomson (CEO from 1934–1956), Goodrich Lowry (1956–1963), Rutledge (1963–1977), and Richard Vaughan (1977–1979).

4 See contemporary Northwest Bancorporation proxy statements.

5 The bank was limited to making loans not exceeding 10 percent of capital accounts to any one customer.

6 See Honeywell, Inc. (the Minnesota corporation),

proxy statement dated March 9, 1998, pp. 3–5, et seq.

7 Scott McCartney, *ENIAC: The Triumphs and Tragedies of the World's First Computer,* New York Walker (1999).

8 Don Larson, *Land of the Giants: A History of Minnesota Business,* Dorn Press (1979).

SECTION IV: COMING OF AGE

1 The interest rate differential was designed to compensate the depositor in a home loan bank from a different redemption procedure in the event that the institution failed. Initial deposit insurance was only $2,500 per depositor, and those with accounts in regular banks would be paid that amount immediately through insurance; they would collect the balance of their accounts as loans and investments would be liquidated, which should also not have taken much time. Depositors in home loan institutions would be expected to wait while mortgages were either paid off or sold, which would have taken considerably longer and carried some risk of write-down—thus the modest interest rate premium intending to address the risk/reward ratio. Ironically, the differential was ultimately made moot by changes in regulation, public policy, and deposit insurance so that no depositor in either banks or savings and loans lost any money in deposits up to $100,000. This was only one clod of unevenness on a generally irregular playing field.

2 A "repo" transaction was one in which a client would buy a security—usually a U.S. Treasury bill or bond— from an investment banker who would promise, for a little transaction charge, to buy it back on demand. These transactions were generally good for one day to a week.

3 Be not confused. Your asset, a savings account, is a banker's liability; your car loan is his asset.

4 Synopses of regulations taken from Arthur F. Burns, *The Ongoing Revolution in American Banking*, American Enterprise Institute (1988), Table I.

5 In later years, Weatherstone became CEO of the Morgan Bank.

6 Arbitrage is the process of borrowing money, perhaps a lot of money, with the intention of reinvesting it at a higher rate with nominal risk. Borrowing at the discount window to buy Treasury bonds is a simple arbitrage, and seriously frowned upon. Arbitrageurs make a living on much more complex offsets.

7 Actually, the CMA check was technically not a check but a sight draft. This meant nothing to the Merrill

Lynch customer or to the recipient of the payment, but it meant a lot to the banks caught in the end run.

8 Andrew H. Malcolm, *Final Harvest,* Random House (1986).

9 Pat McCarty, "'No Contest Plea to Criminal Anti-Trust Indictments," *Minneapolis Tribune,* February 11, 1964. See also Larry Fitzmaurice article, *Minneapolis Star,* same date.

10 A "clearinghouse" in banking terms was essentially a downtown room in which messengers from the several banks in a community would meet daily (legitimately) to exchange checks drawn on each other.

11 Douglas A. Hurd, *Commercial Banking,* a research report from the Stanford Research Institute, Palo Alto, California (1967).

12 First Bank System annual report, 1972.

13 First Bank System annual report, 1977.

14 Loan losses reported by the First Bank System 1973–1986 (000,000):

YEAR	LOSSES
1973	$3.2
1974	6.5
1975	8.9
1976	13.0
1977	16.9
1978	12.9
1979	14.2
1980	22.3
1981	45.7
1982	50.4
1983	66.9
1984	80.9
1985	123.5
1986	384.5
	etc.

This represented a seriously disturbing pattern. First Bank System annual report, all years.

15 Robert J. McMahon, *Bank Marketing Handbook,* Bankers Publishing Company (1986), p. 13.

16 And in 2004, General Electric is, among many other things, the largest financial services company in the world.

17 Ibid, p. 38.

18 John Denver, *Aerie,* RCA. Cherry Lane Music Company, 1971.

19 Off-premise meaning more than 100 feet from the main banking office. Northwestern National Bank in St. Paul had to pursue extended litigation to put an ATM in the skyway building attached to the office tower. It was finally allowed as a "detached facility."

20 Presentation to NYSSA, May 8, 1978.

21 First Bank System annual report, 1978.

22 As an affiliate bank president, Lind had been a defender of the nonconformist name of *his* Duluth bank, the First and American National Bank. Anomalies such as this made statewide group marketing a headache.

23 Northwest Bancorporation annual report, 1979.

SECTION V: REACHING MATURITY

1 The formulae were mnemonically engrained in the minds of Twin Citians by a jolly jingle, from the tunesmiths of Campbell-Mithun. To the tune of ta-da ta-da, ta-da ta-da:

> *When the Weatherball is red,*
> *Warmer weather lies ahead.*
> *When the Weatherball is white,*
> *Colder weather is in sight.*
>
> *When the Weatherball is green,*
> *Little change can be foreseen.*
> *When it blinks in agitation,*
> *There will be precipitation.*

2 On July 6, 1998, Barbara Flanagan, long-time *Star Tribune* columnist, quoted Minneapolis City Council member Lisa Goodman as she proposed resurrection of the Weatherball for installation in front of the then-new Minneapolis Convention Center. A previous request to the newspaper as to the status of the old monument was given the following response: "On January 5, 1983, the Minnesota State Fair accepted the soon-to-be dismantled Weatherball from the Northwestern National Bank in Minneapolis. The fair agreed to store the bank's former symbol and reconstruct it on the fairgrounds contingent on obtaining necessary funds and finding a suitable location. So far, neither funds nor site is available and the Weatherball pieces remain in storage." Perhaps it is still in possession of the State Fair.

3 St. Paul had upstaged its larger twin by installing its first skyway—from the Golden Rule department store to its parking ramp—in 1956.

4 Donovan and Wright, *The First through a Century,* p. 99.

5 Employees of U.S. Bancorp (formerly First Bank) no longer occupy the building, but it retains its name and distinctive emblem. Though it's no longer lighted, the sign stands tall on the building and continues to symbolize the city.

6 The drive to control expenses led to the closing of guest dining rooms and employee cafeterias in both First National Bank buildings in Minneapolis and St. Paul. Even though Northwestern had just installed official dining rooms in its new tower—complete with classical-modernist furniture—and had opened its employee cafeteria to tenants and neighbors, those space went by the board when it come to a review of the effective use of funds.

7 Gordon Malen, *FirStory,* unpublished history of the First National Bank of Minneapolis (1980).

8 A casualty of that expansion was a Minneapolis landmark, Richard's Treat, a quaint and quirky restaurant (with creaky but doting waitresses) and a seasonal skating rink. Clarence Chaney, a vice president of the Northwestern Bank, memorialized these downtown scenes in a series of watercolors that Banco used for its official Christmas cards.

9 *Artists of the American Midwest,* catalog published by First Bank System, 1981.

10 Lynne Sowder and Nathan Braulick, *Talkback-Listen: The Visual Arts Program at First Bank System 1980–1990,* Winnipeg Art Gallery, 1990.

11 *Talkback-Listen,* ibid.

12 In the latter years of his career, as the story goes, Nason was offered the position of CEO of the holding company. He reportedly declined based on his personal commitment to his bank and his community. Thereafter, FBS managers worked around him where necessary.

13 Greater detail was available in periodic Federal Reserve reports, but those numbers were blended in categories so that it was difficult to determine a single bank's results. There was also a regular report on the status of "reserve city" banks, the first allowed to reopen after Roosevelt's weeklong bank holiday in 1933. Only three of these banks existed in the Ninth District: the First Nationals of Minneapolis and St. Paul and Northwestern National. The numbers for all three banks were consolidated, but analysts at First Bank System could easily subtract the figures for their two banks, leaving Northwestern's balance sheet exposed and untrimmed. The Banco analysis could produce only the combined balances of the two First Nationals, which were, as noted, apples and potatoes.

14 First Bank System annual report, 1981.

15 N.A. stands for National Association; banks were never "corporations" as such.

16 First Bank System annual report, 1982.

17 Norwest Corporation annual report, 1987.

18 First Bank System annual report, 1986.

19 Joe Blade, *Star Tribune,* September 11, 1987.

20 Dave Hage, "First Bank drops economics staff," *Star Tribune,* November 6, 1987.

21 Joe Blade, "FBS plans shift in strategy," *Star Tribune,* April 28, 1988.

22 Joe Blade, "First Bank wins bid," *Star Tribune,* June 21, 1988.

23 Anthony Carideo, "First Bank plans to sell $4.6 billion," *Star Tribune,* December 20, 1988.

24 *Star Tribune,* September 22, 1989.

25 By driving his executive staff into equity ownership through favorable stock option programs, Grundhofer brought the interests of management into harmony with those of the shareholders.

26 In 2004, the First National Bank of Chicago (aka Bank One) would disappear into the J. P. Morgan Chase financial empire.

27 *The Economist*, April 11, 1998.

28 *The Economist*, April 11, 1998.

29 Norwest Corporation Investment Profile, second quarter, 1998.

30 Pohlad sold most of his holding with professional haste. The largest shareholder of U.S. Bancorp today is Joshua Green III of Seattle, Washington.

31 U.S. Bancorp and Piper Jaffray came to a parting of the ways in 2003. The cultures of commercial banking (minimal risk) and security dealers (risk tolerant) are basically incompatible.

32 *The Economist,* January 9, 1999, p. 15.

33 *Star Tribune,* June 8, 1998.

34 *St. Paul Pioneer Press,* June 9, 1998.

35 *Wall Street Journal,* June 9, 1998.

36 Ibid.

37 *Star Tribune,* June 10, 1998.

38 Norwest Corporation annual report, 1997, pp. 3–4.

39 For the client who travels, even the combined fees are considered nominal in relation to the convenience. The older tourist remembers the virtual impossibility of cashing a check in a resort, or, when abroad, the risk of carrying all the cash for a trip in traveler's checks. A surprising characteristic of many "modernized" customers is the willingness to pay such fixed transaction fees on relatively small withdrawals; $2.50 or more in combined fees for a $20 withdrawal is not uncommon.

40 Remarks by Richard Kovacevich, Norwest (and Wells

Fargo) CEO at a Minnesota Meeting luncheon, September 23, 1998.

41 Ibid.

42 First Bank System annual report 1996, p. 5.

43 Ibid.

44 Information from First Bank System annual reports for the years noted.

45 "Bankless Banking," *The Economist*, April 11, 1998. p. 56.

46 Presentation to TCSSA analysts, March 1998.

47 U.S. Bancorp annual report, 1999.

48 U.S. Bancorp annual report, 1998.

49 Banks have been fascinated with the potentials for credit cards since Visa and MasterCard were born four decades ago. In fact, the First National Bank of Minneapolis and Northwestern National Bank of Minneapolis each forayed into its own label of credit cards in 1959–1960. The First Bank Charge Card hit the market first, according to Gordon Malen, historian for First Bank System. When Northwestern's card became available, then president John Moorhead ordered his officers to make calls— almost simultaneously—on downtown merchants who might be potential card users. Neither early venture reached a viable level of merchants enrolled or client use.

50 DeeDePass, *Star Tribune*, March 29–31, 1998, Business Section, p. D1 and continuations.

51 As quoted by Mike Meyers, *Star Tribune*, February 1, 1999.

52 *The New York Times*, March 20, 1998; op-ed submission by Harry P. Kamen, David H. Komansky, and John B. McCoy, p. A23.

53 Arthur F. Burns, *The Ongoing Revolution in American Banking*, American Enterprise Institute, 1988, p. 1.

54 October 2004 FDIC data records 9,057 institutions as new charters offset continuing consolidations.

55 *Washington Post*, April 29, 1998.

56 Federal Reserve Statistical Release, "Assets and Liabilities of Commercial Banks," June 27, 1997.

57 A special kind of open-ended home-equity second mortgage is commonly used as the security for ready reserve, checking account overdraft protection services.

BIBLIOGRAPHY

Andersen, Theodore A. *A Century of Banking in Wisconsin.* Madison: State Historical Society of Wisconsin, 1954.

Baird, Julian. "The Story of a Banking Heritage." Centennial dinner address, First National Bank of St. Paul, October 1, 1953.

Ballarin, Eduard. *Commercial Banks and the Financial Revolution.* Cambridge, Massachusetts: Ballinger Publishing Company, 1986.

Burns, Arthur F. *The Ongoing Revolution in American Banking.* Washington, D.C.: American Enterprise Institute, 1988.

Center for Medieval and Renaissance Studies. *The Dawn of Modern Banking.* University of California–Los Angeles. New Haven, Connecticut: Yale University Press, 1979.

Chucker, Harold. *Banco at Fifty: A History of Northwest Bancorporation, 1929–1979.* Minneapolis: Northwest Bancorporation, 1980.

Chucker, Harold. *Banco at Sixty: A History of Northwest Bancorporation, 1929–1989.* Minneapolis: Northwest Bancorporation, 1990.

Clark, Victor S. *What is Money?* Boston: Houghton Mifflin, 1934.

Donovan, Frank P. Jr. and Cushing F. Wright. *The FIRST through a Century.* Itasca, Minnesota: Itasca Press, 1954.

Eccles, George S. *The Politics of Banking.* Graduate School of Business, University of Utah, 1982.

Federal Reserve Bank of Minneapolis. "Carter Glass in Retrospect," *The Region* 2: no. 4, December 1997.

Fradkin, Philip L. and Andy Anderson. *Stagecoach*: *Wells Fargo and the American West,* vol. 1; *Wells Fargo and the Rise of the American Financial Services Industry,* vol. 2. New York: Simon and Schuster, 2002.

Friedman, Milton. *Money Mischief: Episodes in Monetary History.* Harcourt Brace and Company, 1994.

Friedman, Milton, and Anna J. Schwartz. *Monetary Statistics of the United States.* Cambridge, Massachusetts: National Bureau of Economic Research, 1970.

Galbraith, John Kenneth. *Money.* Boston: Houghton Mifflin, 1975.

Gart, Alan. *Banks, Thrifts, and Insurance Companies.* Boston: DC Heath and Company, 1985.

Gatton, T. Harry and Truman L. Jeffers. *Banking in Minnesota.* Minneapolis: Minnesota Bankers Association, 1989.
Glass, Carter. *An Adventure in Constructive Finance.* New York: Doubleday and Company, 1927.

Gramley, Lyle E. *Scale Economies in Banking.* Kansas City, Missouri: Federal Reserve Bank of Kansas City, 1962.

Haraf, William S. and Rose Marie Kushmeider, editors. *Restructuring Banking* and *Financial Services in America.* Washington, D.C.: American Enterprise Institute, 1988.

Jacobs, Donald P., Loring C. Farmer, and Edwin H. Neave. *Financial Institution.*City??????: Richard D. Irwin, 1972.

Larson, Don W. *Land of the Giants.* Minneapolis: Dorn Books, 1979.

Malen, Gordon M. *FirStory: From Wooden Bridge to Modern Skyways.* Unpublished personal memoir, 1980.

Moore, Carl H. *The Federal Reserve System.* Jefferson, North Carolina: McFarland and Company, 1990.

O'Rourke, Michael. *The Ordeal of Riley Reynolds.* St. Cloud, Minnesota: North Star Press, 2000.

Popple, Charles Sterling. *Two Bank Groups in the Central Northwest.* Master's thesis. Cambridge, Massachusetts: Harvard University Press, 1944.

Quiggin, A. Kingston. *A Survey of Primitive Money.* New York: Methuen and Company, 1949.

Raban. Jonathan. *Bad Land: An American Romance.* New York: Random House, 1996.

Schillereff, Ronald L. *Multibank Holding Company Performance.* Ann Arbor, Michigan: UMI Research Press, 1982.

Sprague, O. M. W. *History of Crises under the National Banking System.* Washington, D.C. Government Printing Office, 1910. Reprint, New York: August M. Kelley Publishers, 1968.

Wakefield, Lyman E. Jr. "A Star Shines on Minneapolis' First National Bank." *Hennepin County History:* Spring 1968.

Weatherford, Jack. *The History of Money.* New York: Crown Publishers, 1997.

Willis, Henry Parker. *The Federal Reserve System.* New York: Ronald Press Company, 1923.

Wingerd, Martha Lethert. *Claiming the City: Politics, Faith, and the Power of Place in St. Paul.* Ithaca, New York: Cornell University Press, 2001.

ILLUSTRATION CREDITS

AFTON HISTORICAL SOCIETY PRESS, Afton, Minnesota
p. 9: First National Bank of St. Paul, postcard; **p. 56:** Metropolitan National Bank, Minneapolis, postcard; **p. 81:** First National Bank of St. Paul, postcard; **p. 95:** Metropolitan National Bank, Minneapolis, postcard; **p. 145:** Ken Dayton, from *What Fun*, AHSP, 2002.

AMERICAN HERITAGE PUBLISHING COMPANY, New York, New York
p. 34: coin from *The Very Rich, A History of Wealth* by Joseph J. Thorndike Jr., 1976.

ART RESOURCE, New York, New York
p. 31: *The Moneylender and His Wife* (oil on wood, 1514) by Quentin Metsys, photo by Daniel Arnaudet, Réunion des Musées Nationaux, Louvre, Paris, France; **p. 35:** *Adoration of the Magi* (ca. 1480) by Sandro Botticelli, Uffizi, Florence, Italy, photo by Erich Lessing; **p. 36:** *The Judengasse* (oil on canvas, 1883) by Anton Burger, photo by Elke Walford, Hamburger Kunsthalle, Hamburg, Germany, photo by Bildarchiv Preussischer Kulturbesitz; **p. 37:** *The Rich* byAlbrecht Dürer, Gemaeldegalerie, Staatliche Museen zu Berlin, Berlin, Germany, photo by Erich Lessing.

CHARLES BABBAGE INSTITUTE, University of Minnesota, Minneapolis
p. 151: William Norris, November 1964.

CARGILL COMPANY, Minneapolis, Minnesota
p. 92: C. T. Jaffray.

CGSTOCK.COM
p. 194: U.S. Bank Place, photo by Chris Gregerson; **p. 222:** U.S. Bank Place (detail), photo by Chris Gregerson.

CORBIS.COM
p. 21: Chase Manhattan Bank, New York, photo by James Leynse, 1995; **p. 71:** Carter Glass et al, 1932.

STEVEN DAHLMAN PHOTOGRAPHY, Minneapolis, Minnesota
p. 4: downtown St. Paul, 2000; **p. 19:** 225 South Sixth (former U.S. Bank Place) and Wells Fargo Center, downtown Minneapolis, 2000; **p. 157:** Federal Reserve Bank, downtown Minneapolis, 2002; **p. 162:** Federal Reserve Bank, downtown Minneapolis, 2002; **p. 199:** Federal Reserve Bank, downtown Minneapolis, 2002; **p. 233:** Stone Arch Bridge, downtown Minneapolis, 2002; **p. 228:** downtown Minneapolis, 2001 (detail); **p. 241:** downtown Minneapolis, 2001.

FEDERAL RESERVE BANK, NINTH DISTRICT, Minneapolis, Minnesota
p. 158: Federal Reserve Bank (detail), Minneapolis; **p. 233:** Gary Stern and Federal Reserve Bank, Minneapolis.

JAMES J. HILL REFERENCE LIBRARY, St. Paul, Minnesota
Cover and **p. 62:** James J. Hill, 1916; **p. 72:** James J. Hill et al., 1912; **p. 80:** Louis Hill, photo by Day & Night Studio, Rochester, Minnesota; **p. 83:** Mary Hill and daughters, 1900.

iSTOCKPHOTOS.COM
p. 20: ATM machine (detail); **p. 41:** antique bank counter; **p. 103:** New York Stock Exchange; **p. 128:** Euro coin (detail); **p. 148:** old computer (detail); **p. 149:** punch card; **p. 151:** calculator and abacus; **p. 161:** U.S. Federal Reserve; **p. 198:** New York Stock Exchange eagle (detail).

ITASCA PRESS, Webb Publishing Company, Itasca, Minnesota
p. 47: Parker Paine's bank, from *The FIRST through a Century: 1853–1953* by Frank P. Donovan Jr. and Cushing F. Wright, 1954.

LIBRARY OF CONGRESS, Washington, D.C.
p. 148: Herman Hollerith.

MINNEAPOLIS INSTITUTE OF ARTS, Minneapolis, Minnesota
p. 195: *Brilliant Ruby Macchia with Green Lip Wrap* (blown glass, 2001) by Dale Chihuly.

MINNEAPOLIS PUBLIC LIBRARY, Special Collections, Minneapolis, Minnesota
p. 153: Peter Gillette, Norwest Operations Center, 1980.

MINNESOTA HISTORICAL SOCIETY, St. Paul, Minnesota
Cover: First National Bank of St. Paul, ca. 1905; **p. 2:** First National Bank of Minneapolis, postcard, ca. 1915; **p. 5:** First National Bank of St. Paul, ca. 1905; **p. 7:** National Farmers Bank of Owatonna, Minnesota, postcard, ca. 1910; **p. 8:** *Minnesota Street, 1967*, Francis R. Meisch; **p. 15:** First National Bank of Minneapolis, postcard, ca. 1915; **p. 18:** Savings Department, First National Bank of St. Paul, ca. 1912; **p. 24:** First National Bank of St. Paul, photo by Walter N. Trenerry, 1952; **p. 24:** Northwestern National Bank of Minneapolis, photo by *Minneapolis Star-Journal-Tribune*, December 11, 1953; **p. 25:** First National Bank of Minneapolis, photo by Norton & Peel, June 24, 1946; **p. 38:** Bank of Brainerd, Minnesota, ca. 1881; **p. 39:** First National Bank of Lake Crystal, Minnesota, postcard, ca. 1907; **p. 40:** Pope County State Bank, Glenwood, Minnesota, postcard, ca. 1920; **p. 43:** run on Farmers and Mechanics Savings Bank, Minneapolis, May 19, 1893; **p. 45:** First National Bank of Alexandria, Minnesota, 1876, photo by Newton J. Trenham; **p. 46:** Pope County State Bank, Glenwood, Minnesota, ca. 1920; **p. 48:** Parker Paine, ca. 1870; **p. 49:** First National Bank of Northfield, Minnesota, ca. 1915; **p. 50:** First National Bank of Minneapolis, 1869, photo by Jacoby; **p. 51:** Jay Cooke, ca. 1895; **p. 52:** Commercial State Bank, Two Harbors, Minnesota, ca. 1910; **p. 53:** First National Bank of Chisholm, Minnesota, 1908;

p. 54: first-prize float in St. Paul parade honoring completion of Great Northern Railroad, June 7, 1893; **p. 55:** bank building, Wabasso, Minnesota, ca. 1905; **p. 57:** Stone Arch Bridge, Minneapolis, postcard, ca. 1940; **p. 58:** North Western National Bank, Minneapolis, ca. 1875, photo by William Illingworth; **p. 60:** Farmers and Mechanics Bank, Minneapolis, August 21, 1939, photo by Norton and Peel;

p. 61: *St. Paul, Sixth and Jackson Streets* (graphite, 1926) by John M. Doherty; **p. 62:** Henry Pratt Upham, ca. 1875; **p. 63:** First National Bank of St. Paul, ca. 1905; **p. 65:** Everett H. Bailey in First National Bank of St. Paul, 1905; **p. 66:** Ferdinand Willius in National German-American Bank, St. Paul, ca. 1907; **p. 67:** Merchants National Bank, St. Paul, ca. 1906–1912; **p. 68:** Capital National Bank, St. Paul, photo by Charles P. Gibson, ca. 1925; **p. 73:** Federal Reserve Bank, Minneapolis, 1924, photo by Charles J. Hibbard; **p. 75:** Winona National and Savings Bank, Minnesota, postcard, ca. 1930; **p. 77:** Liberty Loan Department, First National Bank of Minneapolis, photo by Charles J. Hibbard, 1917–1918; **p. 79:** Security Bank and Trust Company, postcard, ca. 1925, and National Farmers Bank, both of Owatonna, Minnesota, postcard, ca. 1910; **p. 80:** First National Bank of Duluth, Minnesota, photo by Charles P. Gibson, ca. 1915; **p. 85:** Edward W. Decker, ca. 1908; **p. 88:** Stock Yards National Bank, South St. Paul, postcard, ca. 1914, and Fergus Falls National Bank, Minnesota, ca. 1910; **p. 90:** First National Bank of Duluth, Minnesota, photo by Charles P. Gibson, ca. 1915; **p. 91:** George H. Prince, ca. 1880; **p. 92:** Frank M. Prince, photo by Sweet, ca. 1900; **p. 97:** construction of First National Bank of St. Paul, ca. 1931; **p. 100:** war bonds sale, Powers Department Store, Minneapolis, photo by Norton and Peel, July 17, 1942; **p. 101:** First National Bank of Duluth, Minnesota, photo by Charles P. Gibson, ca. 1915; **p. 102:** Federal Reserve Bank, Minneapolis, postcard, ca. 1928; **p. 105:** crowd, First National Bank of St. Paul, 1933; **p. 107:** guide, Northwestern National Bank of Minneapolis, ca. 1925; **p. 109:** vaults, National Exchange Bank, St. Paul, ca. 1930, photo by *St. Paul Daily News*; **p. 115:** Floyd Olson, ca. 1930, photo by *St. Paul Dispatch*; **p. 116:** Ed Decker and C. T. Jaffray, 1955; **p. 118:** F&M Bank (detail); **p. 119:** *Downtown Minneapolis* (1940) by Edwin Nooleen; **p. 120:** Farmers and Mechanics Bank, Minneapolis, postcard, ca. 1950; **p. 121:** Twenty-Year Club, February 19, 1936, photo by Norton and Peel; **p. 122:** basketball team, First National Bank of Minneapolis, 1928, photo by Mike Liebing; **p. 123:** Aquatennial marching unit, Farmers and Mechanics, Minneapolis, July 24, 1940, photo by Norton and Peel; **p. 124:** Minnesota state treasurer Julius Schmahl, July 14, 1949, New York; **p. 126:** Federal Reserve Bank, Minneapolis, ca. 1940, photo by *Minneapolis Star-Journal*; **p. 127:** First National Bank of Minneapolis, 1915, photo by Norton and Peel; **p. 129:** *Flame Room,* Minneapolis, by Syd Fossum, 1949; **p. 130:** Charlie's Café Exceptionale, postcard, ca. 1942; **p. 135:** bowler, First National Bank of St. Paul, 1936, photo by *St. Paul Daily News*; **p. 136:** Joseph Chapman, ca. 1915; **p. 140:** *Downtown Minneapolis* (1940, detail) by Edwin Nooleen;

p. 152: IBM employee, Rochester, Minnesota, September 1958; **p. 156:** construction of Federal Reserve Bank, Minneapolis, ca. 1970; **p. 158:** Home Loan Department, First National Bank of Minneapolis, ca. 1948; **p. 159:** Christmas Savings Club crowd, Third Northwestern National Bank of Minneapolis, 1933; **p. 165:** drive-through window, First State Bank of St. Paul, 1958; **p. 168:** Judge Edward Devitt, ca. 1980; **p. 186:** clock (detail), 1937, photo by *Minneapolis Star-Journal;* **p. 188:** weatherball, 1983, photo by Art Hager; **p. 189:** Minneapolis skyway, 1962, photo by Norton and Peel; **p. 190:** skating rink, ca. 1956, photo by Don Berg; **p. 191:** "1st" sign, First National Bank of St. Paul, Nov. 13, 1952, photo by *St. Paul Dispatch-Pioneer Press;* **p. 192:** First National Bank of Minneapolis, postcard, ca. 1959; **p. 202:** Philip Nason and fallout shelter, July 16, 1975, photo by Steve Plattner; **p. 203:** St. Paul Civic Center, 1975, photo by Steve Plattner; **p. 256:** peony show, First National Bank of St. Paul, 1921.

PRIVATE COLLECTION
p. 64: *Hill Family* (1886) by J. Chelminski.

RAMSEY COUNTY HISTORICAL SOCIETY,
St. Paul, Minnesota
p. 111: R. C. Lilly, *Ramsey County Historical Society Magazine* 33 (no. 3), Fall 1998.

GEORGE R. SLADE, Minneapolis, Minnesota
p. 10: Old Goats ski group; **p. 131:** cover of Norwest Corporation's annual report 1983; **p. 132:** cover of Northwestern National Bank of St. Paul's annual report 1975; **p. 133:** cover, Northwestern National Bank of St. Paul's annual report 1975; **p. 139:** John Moorhead; **p. 141 and 142:** First Trust Company; **p. 166 and p. 171:** cover of SRI Report, 1967; **p. 178:** Don Grangaard; **p. 179:** Henry Rutledge; **p. 181:** Don Grangaard et al.

STAR TRIBUNE/Minneapolis–St. Paul, Minnesota
p. 196: Northwestern National Bank building fire, 1982. © 2004 Star Tribune/Minneapolis–St. Paul.

MARY VAUGHAN
p. 179: Richard Vaughan.

WELLS FARGO BANK, N.A., Minneapolis, Minnesota
p. 6 and p. 12: Northwestern National Bank of Minneapolis, 1957 Christmas card by Clarence Chaney; **p. 177:** Buddy Bears (caption courtesy of designer Mary Sue Oleson, who was working too late one night. Author Dick Slade liked it, so it stayed); **p. 184:** stagecoach; **p. 185:** Wells Fargo Building; **p. 187:** Northwestern National Bank of Minneapolis, 1957 Christmas card by Clarence Chaney; **p. 197:** Wells Fargo Building; **p. 201:** Bob Krane; **p. 207:** Lloyd Johnson; **p. 214:** Jack Grundhofer; **p. 216:** stagecoach (detail); **p. 219:** Paul Hazen and Dick Kovacevich.

INDEX

Peony show at the First National Bank of St. Paul, June 16–17, 1921.

This book was designed by

MARY SUSAN OLESON

Nashville, Tennessee

fonts used:

Optima

Edwardian Script

AFTON PRESS is located in the
former Citizens State Bank building
in Afton, Minnesota.